b r e t h

also by bill bissett

published by talonbooks

animal uproar
awake in th red desert
b leev a bul ch ar aktrs
canada gees mate for life
drifting into war
griddle talk: a yeer uv bill n carol dewing brunch (with Carol Malyon)
hard 2 beleev
hungree throat: a novel in meditaysyun
inkorrect thots
loving without being vulnrabul
narrativ enigma / rumours uv hurricane
northern birds in color
northern wild roses / deth interrupts th dansing
novel: a novel with konnekting pomes n essays
pass th food release th spirit book
peter among th towring boxes / text bites
pomes for yoshi
Sailor
scars on th seehors
Seagull on Yonge Street
Selected Poems: Beyond Even Faithful Legends
sublingual
th book
th influenza uv logic
th last photo uv th human soul
ths is erth thees ar peopul
time
what we have

on the work of bill bissett

textual vishyuns: image and text in the work of bill bissett, by Carl Peters (Talonbooks)
bill bissett: Essays on His Work, edited by Linda Rogers (Guernica)
bill bissett and His Works, by Karl Jirgens (ECW Press)

bill bissett

b r e t h

/th treez uv lunaria

selektid rare n nu
pomes n drawings
1957–2019

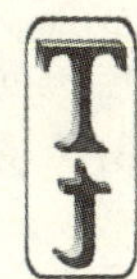

talonbooks

Talonbooks
9259 Shaughnessy Street, Vancouver, British Columbia, Canada V6P 6R4
talonbooks.com

Talonbooks is located on xʷməθkʷəy̓əm, Sḵwx̱wú7mesh, and səl̓ilwətaʔɬ Lands.

First printing: 2019

Typeset in Helvetica Neue
Printed and bound in Canada on 100% post-consumer recycled paper

Interior design by bill bissett with Typesmith
Cover design by Typesmith with Mark Belvedere

Talonbooks acknowledges the financial support of the Canada Council for the Arts, the Government of Canada through the Canada Book Fund, and the Province of British Columbia through the British Columbia Arts Council and the Book Publishing Tax Credit.

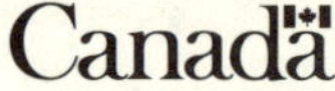

Library and Archives Canada Cataloguing in Publication

bissett, bill, 1939–
[Works. Selections]
Breth : th treez uv lunaria : selektid rare n nu pomes n drawings, 1957–2019 / by bill bissett ; foreword by Tim Atkins.

Poetry.
Poems written using the author's phonetic orthography.
ISBN 978-1-77201-226-2 (softcover)
ISBN 978-1-77201-243-9 (hardcover)

I. Title. II. Title: Breath.

PS8503.I78A6 2019 C811'.54 C2018-906647-4

in th palace uv th dreemr
sum wun stirs   it cud b yu
it cud b me   what is th
word

ths book is 4 meg mcallister whos idea
it was with much love n thanks bill

contents

Foreword

bill bissett:

sum ideas uv evreething

Gertrude Stein. e.e. cummings. Allen Ginsberg. Jack Kerouac. Sun Ra (!). bill bissett. Equals & fellow travellers, in case you haven't been paying attention. This new *selektid rare n nu pomes n drawings* (volume 1?) locates bissett firmly and securely alongside these visionary artists and confirms him as their great successor. *breth* is a hugely welcome collection as it allows the wider public access to a range of small press and fugitive writing that has been almost impossible to obtain. It also invites a re-engagement and re-evaluation of his work by a national and international poetry community for whom his work of the last sixty years, existing in scores of magazines, recordings, and individual volumes, may at times have appeared either too familiar or too unwieldy.

The decades-old cliché that bissett is a modern-day William Blake remains a reasonable claim. At one and the same time a lyric poet, experimentalist, typewriter pioneer, sound poet, political writer, poet of environmental consciousness, sexual trailblazer and celebrator, biographer, visual artist, bookmaker extraordinaire, alien, creative editor, and documenter of both the transcendent and the quotidian, bissett can be many different poets to many different readers. The range, complexity, and quality of activity is one of bissett's claims to greatness, and yet, also, has at times been confrontational to a culture in which being a master of more than one form is to invite confusion or foster resentment. One way of reading bissett, among many, is to see his many modes as facets of a single long poem, to read the work as the unfolding of an energized and well-wrought whole, and to note how the organizing factor in bissett's particularly democratic embrace of many forms, extending beyond the obvious influences of Stein, the Beats, and visual poets, has become the entirety of his practice: Warren Tallman, writing in 1974 of bill's work, stated: "His art has led him … into a country of which he is the sole citizen."[1] Most critical writing on bissett, including valuable book-length works by Carl Peters and by Karl Jirgens, and a wonderful, insightful essay by Adeena Karasik,[2] has focussed upon a close reading of formal and linguistic particularity and differing methods rather than locating bissett in the wider poetic culture. bissett is a poet who comes out of Canada (or, if you prefer, the planet Lunaria – hence the entirely serious reference to fellow independent spirit and galactic traveller Sun Ra at the top of this introduction) but whose attention is toward (at the very least) the whole planet. The key to bissett's genius lies in close and repeated readings of the poetry, and it also lies in the groundbreaking way that it converses with and expands so many streams of twentieth-century poetic practice.

Here is his creation myth. The teenage bissett's arrival in Vancouver, with his boyfriend Billy, from Halifax, in 1958 or 1959 – no one can remember exactly when, for the time is so far in the past and if you can remember anything about the sixties the cliché holds that you weren't really there – was one of the major initiating moments in poetry in English in the twentieth century. "first reading I evr did

---

1 Warren Tallman, "Wonder Merchants: Modernist Poetry in Vancouver during the 1960's," in "A Canadian Issue," ed. Robert Kroetsch, *boundary 2*, Vol. 3, No. 1 (Autumn 1974): 57–90, https://doi.org/10.2307/302408.

2 See: Carl Peters, *textual vishyuns: image and text in the work of bill bissett* (Vancouver: Talonbooks, 2011); Karl Jirgens, *bill bissett and His Works*, Canadian Author Studies (Toronto: ECW Press, 1992); and Adeena Karasick, "bill bissett: A Writing Outside Writing," in "a festschrift for bill bissett," ed. Robert Sherrin, *The Capilano Review*, Series 2, No. 23 (Fall 1997): 59–73, republished in Linda Rogers, ed., *bill bissett: Essays on His Work*, Writers Series (Toronto: Guernica Editions, 2002), 50–71.

in a aftr hours jazz club" on page 202 provides a clear picture of the world that he entered. Initially working alone, bissett was the instigator of a synthesis of traditional lyric, sound, and concrete poetry. His work came out of and moved beyond page-based, non-traditional, experimental, non-British tendencies, and his early reading – and use – of Beat and U.S. West Coast poets and artists predates the well-documented visits of the Black Mountain poets to Vancouver (which started with Robert Duncan in December 1959) and which initiated the UBC-based TISH collective. If we are to take "the sixties" (the decade in which bissett developed his mature poetics) to mean a synthesis of countercultural tendencies and engagement with hybrid forms and popular culture, including jazz and then rock music, bissett, in his poetry, art, performances, editorial work, and a little later with his own publications, was already exploring these revolutionary areas at the very start of the decade. Between his arrival in Vancouver in the late fifties, inspired by mail-order copies of Diane Di Prima, Gertrude Stein, Edith Sitwell, and Jack Kerouac (which he read back in Halifax), and the end of the sixties, bissett's being and practice made a new – expanded – kind of poetry possible. In one American version of the avant-garde century, Stein was largely ignored until the emergence of the L=A=N=G=U=A=G=E writers, and the lineage of the Beats morphed into the socio-political domestic engagements of the New York School and the Zen-inflected poetics of the West Coast. The young bissett, writing in relative obscurity in downtown Vancouver along with contemporaries such as Martina Clinton, Lance Farrell, Maxine Gadd, and Judith Copithorne (note the gender balance), was combining Stein's atomized and repetitive language experiments with the highly politicized and ecstatic writing of the Beats – a completely different trajectory to that which took place in the United States. bissett and the "downtown" writers ignored the academy (with the canonization and the normalization that membership within it brings), ensuring that their work neither received the publication history that it deserved nor the academic literary-critical engagement which is seemingly so essential for the continuing visibility of any literary moment. The fact that these writers (to take a phrase from Fanny Howe) "stayed down" has been a strength in that they have all avoided the vanity and stasis which come from canonization, and they have been able to continue writing unhindered by the curator's gaze. It has been a hindrance in that they have largely escaped the wider readership that their trail-blazing work deserves. At this moment in the twenty-first century, in which readers and critics are re-engaging with activism, hybrid forms, expanded sexualities, and more democratic poetics, there is an increasing realization of how important the work of bissett and his contemporaries has been.

This volume invites a recalibration of understanding of the entirety of bissett's oeuvre. Of particular note is the way that bissett's genius embraces, incorporates, and transforms so many sources – "evreething is an nfluens." bissett was and is Canada's most important Beat-influenced, post-Beat writer, using and transforming Philip Whalen's calligraphy, humour, and energy ("This poetry is a picture or graph of a mind moving," he once stated), Jack Kerouac's experiments with sound in *Old Angel Midnight*, Gary Snyder's environmentalism, Diane Di Prima's revolutionary hip, and Allen Ginsberg's compassion and celebratory sexuality. Initially in *blewointment* magazine and later in his individual volumes, bissett's poetry also drew upon the atomized language practices of e.e. cummings, the sensual-mystical camp of Robert Duncan, *and* the international world of visual and sound poetry practised by, among others, Dom Sylvester Houédard and Bob Cobbing. Edith Sitwell's influence in the history of sound poetry via her Caedmon recordings and as channelled by bissett has rarely, if ever, been mentioned. Let us note its importance to bissett's high and fluttering vocalizations – two softer, more nuanced voices in the grunting and gurning world of largely male-dominated sound poetry. bissett's typewriter poetry grants the artist a place in the canon of extraordinary twentieth-century writing for its range of abstract, repetitive language and pictorial pieces. Finally, in the history of Canadian poetry, his role as poetry godfather / good fairy to the young bpNichol provides yet another transformative moment. bissett's project began long before Nixon was president, before the Beatles had released a record, and it is still going strong through the wretched presidency of Donald Trump.

bissett's practice is also one of continuous expansion. Early publications such as *What Poetiks* (1967) celebrated and drew upon the work of Gertrude Stein. Collections such as *Sunday Work* (1969) were for obvious reasons more overtly political – bissett did time in Oakalla Prison for a drug bust. *Th High Green Hill* (1972) and other early seventies collections that were written in isolation at Lac La Hache were more concerned with an expanded environmental consciousness that is currently called ecopoetics. *rush: what fuckan theory; a study uv language* (1972) engaged with bissett's take upon fixed interpretation and meaning. The later seventies brought an engagement with humour, performance, and storytelling. The eighties saw bissett producing books for children with *sa n th monkey* (1980) and *sa n his crystal ball* (1981), both of which are described as "bed time colouring storee pome books." An increasingly varied spelling developed during the nineties, genre was explored in the early 2000s, and recent years have seen a greater prevalence of his expanded autobiographical writing – some of bissett's most beautiful writing has been about his daughter, Ooljah. In recent years, a new bissett volume has tended to contain poems employing every mode in which he writes. (In this collection, the way to track chronological developments is to look at the publication dates of individual poems, listed at the back.) In *breth*, bissett's a-chronological arrangement rejects linear time and builds a universe that stresses continuity, relationship, and depth of practice.

In the early seventies Bernadette Mayer and Clark Coolidge, inspired by Jack Kerouac's all-inclusive eye, negative-capability, Zen, and rapid-fire typing practice, talked about the possibility of writing an "everything work" which could document the totality of the field of consciousness. A version of this idea is worked with in *breth*. bissett's arrangement of seven decades of writing into a wider a-chronological "everything work" places his life's writing into a timeless, open field, rather than foregrounding one element of his art at the expense of another. If a generalization can be made about a writing which invites continued engagement and reconfiguration, it is that it resists assimilation or consensus – "ther is nothing 2 abandon." It is unusual for a poet to acknowledge doubt repeatedly, to question the poet's claims of moral authority, or problematize the taking of any position, and yet – in interviews, poems, and poetics – this is exactly what bissett does. *rush: what fuckan theory* from its title alone gives a good idea of his distrust of any systemization of thought. His instinctive dismissal of poetic superiority, distrust of all systems of power, and resistance to any forms of thought control are one reason why bissett has such an enduring voice.

And the work is almost always, in the long run, optimistic. It also comes with a fully functioning bullshit detector – a more useful tool than simply having a refined sense of irony. bissett is a generous and forgiving humourist while at the same time having an extremely black sense of humour about the world and (at times) about himself. How – one is tempted to ask, given the times in which he has lived and the experiences that he has had – could he not? Most poets plow a single furrow until they have exhausted it or themselves, and many have enough ideas only to fill the single side of a napkin. bissett's poetry explores worlds that are often both pure and corrupt, general and specific, free and oppressed, meaningful and meaningless, isolated and intertwined, sensual and intellectual, and boring and compelling. (Please note that this introduction has resisted citing very many poems to support the points being made due to the fact that *breth* is the everything work which provides a reader's most useful collection of examples.)

bissett is a phenomenal poet. He has been defying the odds by staying alive in the face of adversity for almost eighty years. He is the survivor of over forty operations and had the experience of being declared dead (or almost dead) after a serious fall in Vancouver in the early seventies – the one thing, he says, which really makes him a Canadian poet is his continued survival as a result of the Canadian healthcare system. Writing at the beginning of 2019, it is astonishing to look back to bissett's arrival in provincial, post-war Vancouver and realize how central he has been to changing the poetry world. He introduced typewriter poetry to avant-garde Canadian poetry. He pioneered and popularized the poetry of an expanded sexuality. He instigated and curated a poetry scene which was unrivalled in its openness and generosity in a time of huge division and sexism. He fused visual art, sound poetry, and traditional and experimental writing, often in the same poem. He has lived as a high-profile poet and he has never shown an interest in compromising his art for the sake of wealth or canonization. Along the way, bissett has overcome an intracerebral hemorrhage, has faced down the conservative forces of the Canadian government, has often lived with very little money, and has been fearless in opposing all oppressive forces that have crossed his path. He is, and has always been, an open, generous, and uncompromising human being and poet. *breth* is simply the latest manifestation of that fearless "everything work."

—Tim Atkins

Photo: Michael Cobb

b r e t h

thers sumthing sew familyar abt life

mor thn i evr realizd at first breth had i
bin heer b4 that was my qwestyuning
feeling

as i made my way tord my
destinee i was alredee in
th pickshurs   was that it

looking 4 a love 2 hold on 2 2 b with
was it onlee inside me th pay off n sew
veree familyar it all was as

if i alredee belongd

xplaining narrativ numbr 7

i got 2 th train staysyun n th train was gone
i got 2 th train staysyun n th train was
i got 2 th train staysyun n th train
i got 2 th train staysyun n th
i got 2 th train staysyun n
i got 2 th train staysyun
i got 2 th train
i got 2 th
i got 2
i got
i

our moon

is
sumtimes
circular
            is
yellow in
ourselvs

is in th feet
how we move
closer always
into our
origins

is flat
on the eye
a penny
madness

business,
is deeply
in cycle

moon, hot
of pupil
cold, lash
blink, into
our stride

is
sometimes
oval, our
dreams
enclosd

pictures
we see, of
th tides

th dogs party

it was utahs birthday partee he
was a yeer old all his frends wer ther he wore
a red ribbon round his neck curlee haird
poodul i was hirud to reed poetree thr wer
clowns baloons great food smokd salmon
pasta whn i red utah n all his frends wer
veree attentiv they liked th changing songs
chanting th feetyur pome was th origin uv
th dog wch lukilee finishd itself recentlee
b4 i went to the mail box n was in
vitid to red at utahs partee they
liked th origin of th dog th irish
settr left th room for a few
minits but he returnd veree
quietlee all th peopul who livd
with utahs frends mostlee had nevr met
bfor n wer veree shy at first thr was evree
kind of dog all th peopul enjoyd dogs n
wer veree sensitiv in th middul of th
festivitees all th dogs abt 15 thr wer startid
dansing furiouslee thru th room th fire
brite from th grate baloons touching th ceiling
we peopul clapping hands making th beet fastr
for them at wun hushd moment all th lites wer out
in th kitchn n utah barkd out th candul on his cake

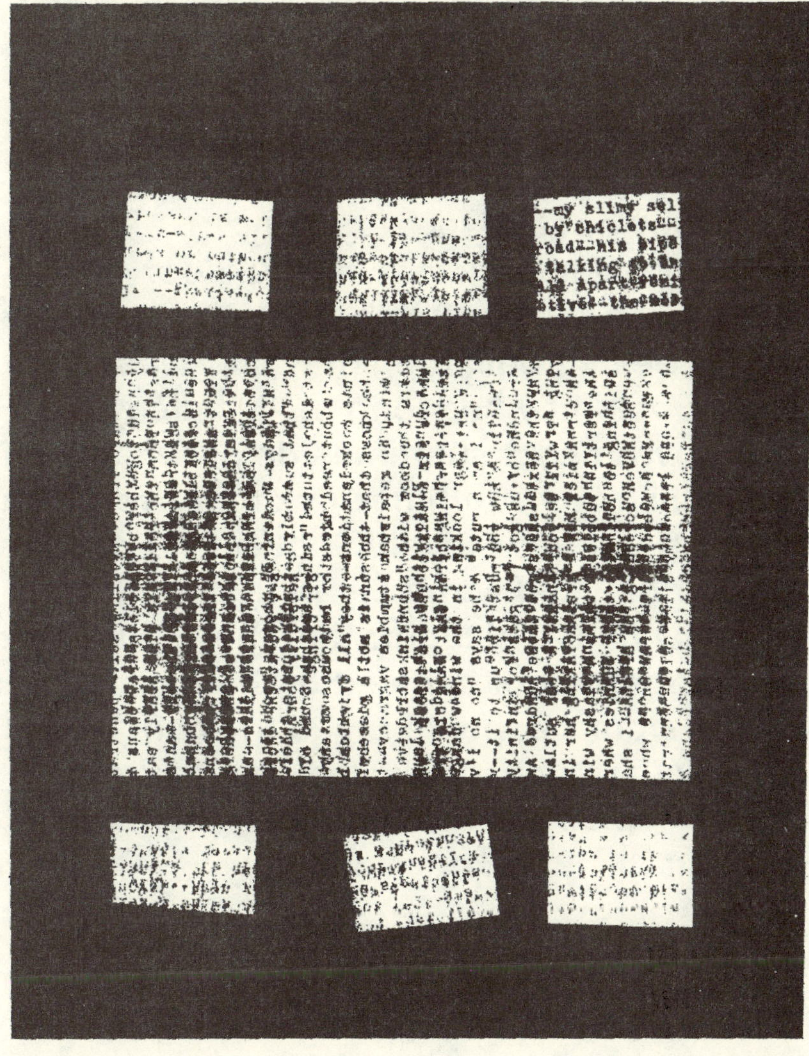
--my slimy sel
by chiclets

chile

today they think they got allende
sure his body his blood his eyes
they got like meat running
ovr th probablee ancient marbul floor
uv th palace built long bfor ther was a
man to be in it built long bfor ther was
allende since they had long really beleevd
as our govrnments sumtimes do as what is con
fused in all uv us sumtimez duz that everything is
an ego powr trip they think they killd th spirit
too but they did sumthing in th darkness uv th
soul uv hate n slaughtr that they shud need
th poor peopul to bleed that they shud need
th poor peopul to bleed th change will
cum th change will cum   thrs mor
uv us poor peopul than them nd
we ar lerning how

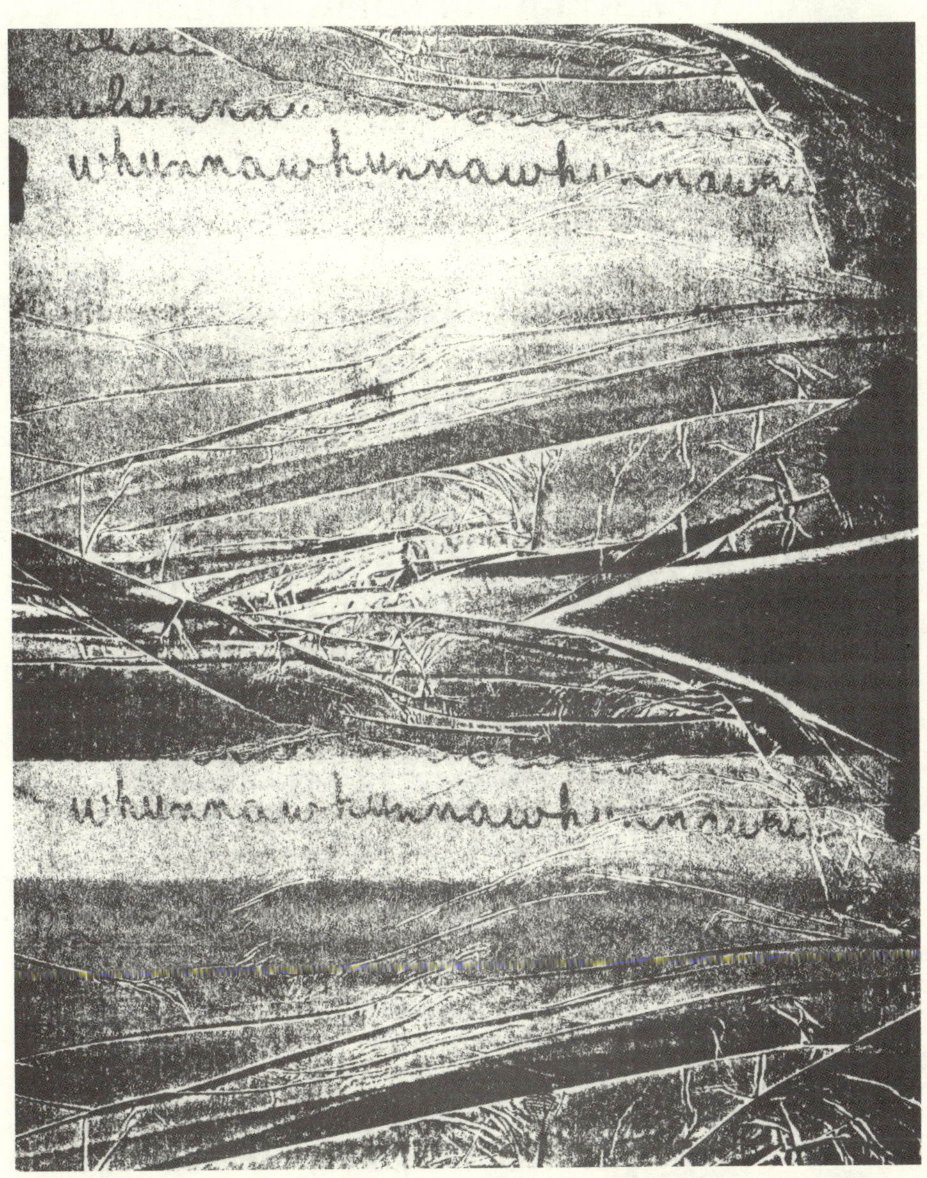

th warmth of human company

harry dick n tom buguls n yellowd
buttends they xchangd windows
she askd what was th mattr are yur
glands swolln she is luvly n latin
a merengay
we sing
wud yur
constipatid
daughterinlaw decide
she lookd like a
great hers against
mine n th juicus cum on
help me clear this all out
sew she can cum in though
th watr in th toilet bowl is frozn
ther is still sunshine thru th pane
eeeeeeeeeeeeeeeeek
footsteps in th shroudid ground
n thank yu for yur presence
that i tuk that means i think ium
th one if she cud see a poolroom
green she wud be happy to
stare they felt deranged
but he on 8,ooo mounts th
shape of mustachus rescued
n lasood th stars n planets back
into their real places i dont think
they hate yu i was a brass monkey
that night she wore green black n pur
pul all th same a life to myself find me
in th thred of th blanket
he put sum sugar in n leaves

i was driving in 2 hundrid mile hous
in th karibu northern bc

n i saw a big sign on th left sd
ANIMAL HOSPITAL i thot 2
myself well thers nothing reelee
wrong with me now but if i take
anee turn for th wors i cud go in
2 see doktor racoon or nurs squirrel
its reassuring 2 know thers help
sew close by well wud yu go
in2 a building sd PEOPUL HOSPITAL
iuv bin with peopul

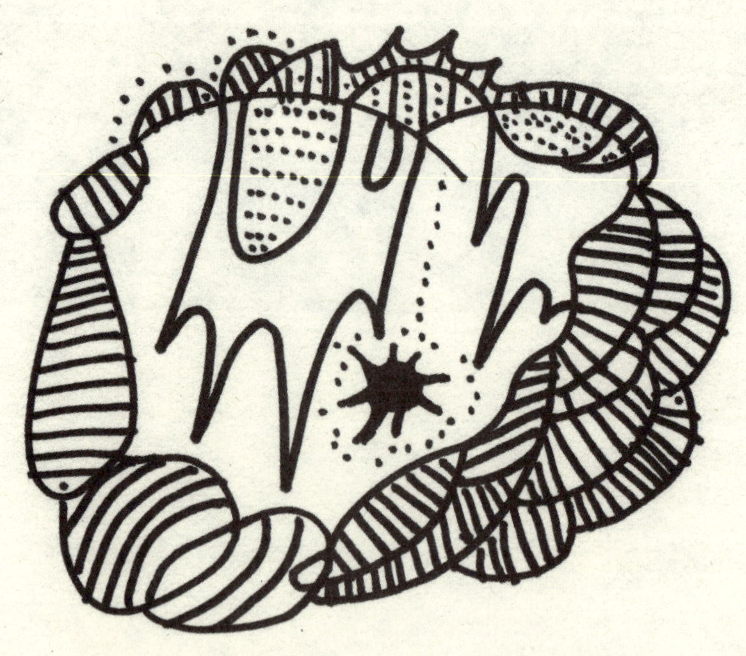

slow slow rabbit song

i dreem uv northern skies i dreem uv northern skies
i dreem uv northern skies i dreem uv northern skies
i dreem uv northern skies i dreem uv northern skies
i dreem uv northern skies i dreem uv northern skies
i dreem uv northern skies i dreem uv northern skies
i dreem uv northern skies i dreem uv northern skies
i dreem uv northern skies i dreem uv northern skies
i dreem uv northern skies i dreem uv northern skies
i dreem uv northern skies i dreem uv northern skies
stars shining evree wher i dreem uv northern skies
flying buffalo thistul down bed i dreem uv northern
skies i dreem uv northern skies i dreem uv northern
skies i dreem uv northern skies i dreem uv northern
skies i dreem uv northern skies i dreem uv northern
skies i dreem uv northern skies i dreem uv northern
skies i dreem uv northern skies i dreem uv northern
skies i dreem th fire rising into th cloud th lake
melting into our heart stars shining evree wher eye
dreem uv northern skies i dreem uv northern skies i
dreem uv northern skies i dreem uv northern skies i
dreem uv northern skies i dreem uv northern skies i
dreem uv northern skies th wood smell in our eyez i
dreem uv northern skies rabbits running into th sno
folds i dreem uv northern skies stars shining evree
wher i dreem uv northern sky foxes deep in th erth
th sereen stars turning ovr th ice dreem uv northern
stars i dreem uv northern skies i dreem uv northern
skies

wer only human too were
keep yr cell clen
a pome in praise of all quebec bombers

WHAT WILL YU TELL YR MOTHER

how yr shirt shines, th cradles
in yr eyes,
yr mother

how th birds in yr hed
fly thru th hills

ovr th camels, ovr th rice
fields, ovr th castle

wing on th running antelope,
th pride of th eagul, thru

th endless cave, out into
bright opening, yr

mother, yu know what
happns in th purpul dawn

field wher th wild horses
tell theyr songs into th green

wind, th blazond hills, yr
mother, th moon, and th lion

deep in th pool smiles

blue fever

smokd eight joints now waitin
for yu to cum. so why am i
doing this. feathers in th sky,
feathers in my heart. wishes on
silver wings. our beings entwined.

trying to meet whn its not
happening.

silver tears on th rainbow,
th glistening ferns, th floor
filld with wheat and feeling, yu
see all sides of th pine needles
shining.

trying to reach yu when its
not happening.

eye beams flashing around th
mountains, thru th caves, ovr
th purpul mounds, our lonly
silhouettes separated by wire,
rambul on thru th snow

tryin to get to yu when thers
no way

c d

b YES

did yu take out th garbage

why dew peopul think selfishness
is th answr its not same with narcicism
that onlee has 1 mor sylabul is all

selfishness destroys evreething in its
path

selfishness is an epidemik

what dew i put on theyr feet chains
burdns   they clomp clomp trying 2
control evree thing they touch mesur
love they dont love aneething

thats theyr curs

stay away from selfish peopul

they onlee plot 2 use yu 2
abuse yu

yu may nevr get ovr loving them

writing without storeez meditaysyuns on gold mountain 7

sumtimes nothing will get dun
if yu work within linear cawsalitee
what if that prson nevr cums n thn
how can i ths or that th iceberg kasturi
th third tree hous on th left did th
message get thru at last ium sleep
walking a parade uv atvs omg ium
calling abt th renewal n th reset
emerald dreems ar ebullient n full
uv mersee th kastul is ancient
looking 4 all th opnings a dscussyun
abt fawsets rapidlee ensued th mightee
kastul uv love reel dragons ar in th moat
no worreez sew much is inside each
magik box fingrs ar xpressyuns
n hold th clay cups 4 gold t uv th soul
drink opnings ar always happning thers
an opning on venus onlee 12 hrs away yu
must carree th nu fridg 2 th twelth
remonstrans on th fleshee curv uv
in th hiddn vallee uv looking 4 th opnings
in th sleep walking seem werent yu captin
uv th wraith nebulae yu did want 2 c sum
wun abt a transfr

ode to frank silvera

yu might think that moving
silently thru th tenement
yr holsters bright and lively
in th yellow colourd air

yu might think that yr horse
kickin without sound at th moon
where sum say th faild souls
those who cant find bodies hang
out

yu might say movin soft on top
of eggshells tord yr path, karma
is will plus fate, th old time
blend

yu might hope there is sum one
to love yu at th end of th road
yu might see nothin can grow in
th dust of yr anxieties

yu might say that fate is whats left
aftr yu do nothing. yu can go on
alone with all th mysteries of being.

yu walk out of th town at sun rise

before there is sound th fields
maybe yu get rheumatism from too
much mornin dew maybe yr hungr gets
too deep to drink maybe yr holsters
get parchd maybe theres only silence

yu might say there is always
more love of dark and golden being

yu might say yul fly
more like th crow

yu cud say yu dont have to kill
yrself that'l be taken care of

yu cud say th mountain and love is
hard and eternal, never yields to
nothing. sumtime yu are the wind
racing green ovr th hairy fields

sumtimes yu ar th blind eye
of th sun turning in yr belly

yu dream

yu move further out a town

remembr

th time we went sailing
on that big mushroom cloud it was
calld shrooms galore

that was b4 th raptyur
a veree messee affair ther wer bodeez
strewn abt evreewher what 2 dew
all th bodeez all th bodeez

n thn we cud dock at th lunarian
rainbow port n thn we didint have anee
trubul nowun was trying 2 best aneewun
nowun evn thot uv that 2 best anee
wun
why why wud that cansel mortalitee

if onlee yu wud love me 2nite

latr on if onlee i wantid yu 2
2nite

but th fog from th faktoreez
was killing us n th mercuree n led
in th watr in our blood

bodeez strewn evreewher who can
take care uv all th bodeez
now we live inside a giant iguana
we have sleeping shelf beds inside his
throat   we eet what he eets

n remembr th time we went
sailing on a mushroom cloud it was calld
shrooms galore

shrooms galoor

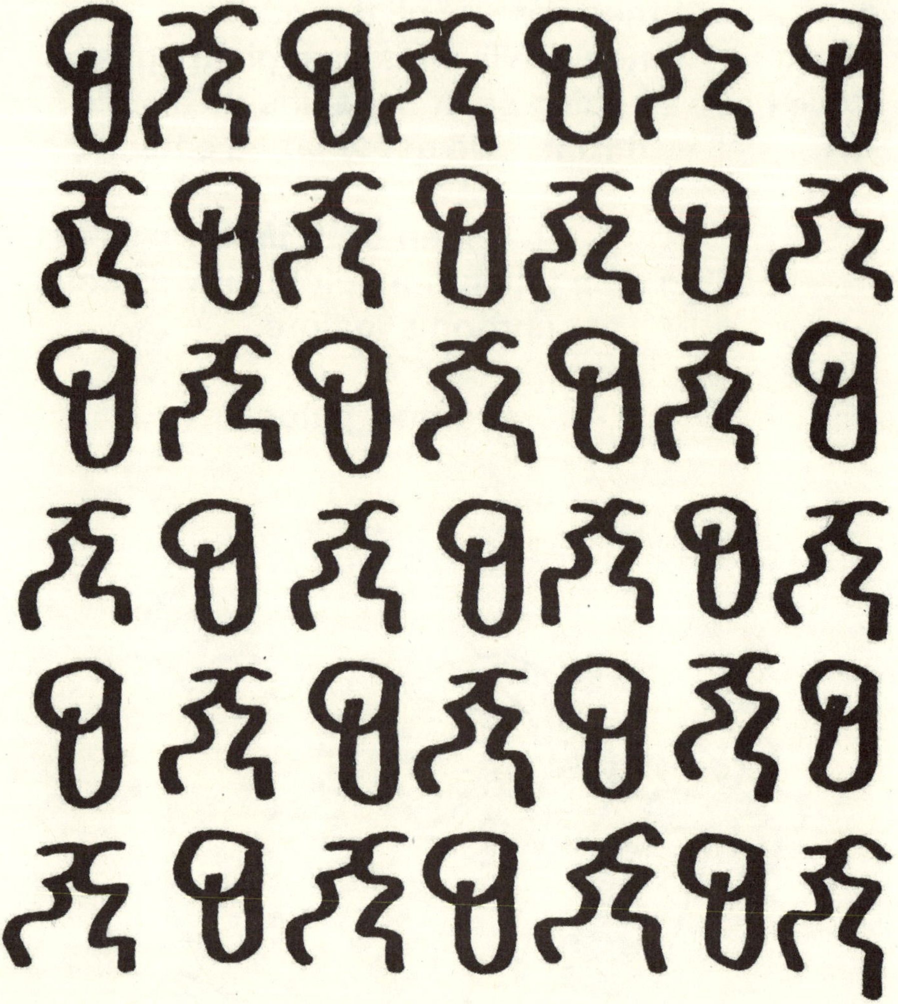

The Scope

bissett/69

The tongue-out sparrow entertains the old man

Th Canadian

On th train, back from th Empress
dining car, snowing woodlands
,pulling thru Manitoba, recall
how sum yeers after th second centenary
of th founding of Halifax, which
date i commemorated with sign
above my father's street door,
into two parts i divided, th half
on th left, what once was, before
1749, th MicMac Indian, th second
half, after that time, a British sailor,
on board, telescope to eye, sailing
into harbor, Montbatten drove by
my father's house that day, part of
th ceremonies, dressd by University gown
& cap, later that year, th woman to be
Queen, then Princess Elizabeth drove
thru Halifax town, in bullet-proof car.

But i was to recall, as I did,
coming back from th dining car, that
sum yeers after Halifax had her bicentenary,
i wrote my third or fourth pome, in
which, constructed as allegory, i did en
vision th society of fact in Canada
as a train, its peopuls classd, & sub-
classd, according to th rank they owned, or,
who they cud claim owned them, its
peopuls cut off from each othr by
such coach cars & compartments.

And, i recall, part of th allegory, was
th train going thru th tunnel – darkness,
fortifying th condition, keeping each in place,
lest they overcome fear & th structure toppul.

It's not sucha good allegory, my
friends sd – well, now that sum of my best
friends are in jail – i see its uses,
my boyhood despair – seeing, as th
train rolls thru Manitoba, how it
does seem that peopul are hungry in
this country, sum of my best friends are
hungry, peopul are hungry, they hunger
for food – outside of this train there is
no food – in it there is good & bad food,
food that will just keep yu strong enuff
to keep yr place – food that is
just good enuff yu dream
of better food – and food that is so good
yu bcum encouraged to accept
that this train is not going to crash
cannot be changed, from within
or without, is God or Allah's very
handiwork, but where is th food
on this train, this one
to show me Allah in all things,
for then, in ourselves th best food,
we share th bounty
on this Iron Horse.

:::

{:}<>{:}<>{:}<>{:}<>{:}<>{:}

{:}<>{:}<>{:}<>{:}<>{:}<>{:}

{:}<>{:}<>{:}<>{:}<>{:}<>{:}

::::::::::::o::::::::O::::::::::o::::::

{}<>{}<>{}<>{}<>{}<>{}<>{

{}<>{}<>{}<>{}<>{}<>{}<>{

..\\........//............0.....0.....

{}<>{}<>{}<>{}<>{}<>{}<>{

{:}<>{:}<>{:}<>{:}<>{:}<>{:}<>{:}<>{:}{

{:}<>{:}<>{:}<>{:}<>{:}<>{:}<>{:}<>{:}{

{:}<>{:}<>{:}<>{:}<>{:}<>{:}<>{:}<>{:}{

{:}<>{:}<>{:}<>{:}<>{:}<>{:}<>{:}<>{:}{

{:}<>{:}<>{:}<>{:}<>{:}<>{:}<>{:}<>{:}{

{:}<>{:}<>{:}<>{:}<>{:}<>{:}<>{:}<>{:}{

{:}{:}{:}{:}{:}{:}{:}{:}{:}{:}{:}

{:}{:}{:}{:}{:}{:}{:}{:}{:}{:}{:}

against my will

i was born i kept
putting it off

whn i was born i
weighd 12 pounds
8 ounces

i cudint
put it off much
longr i cuduv
bin born earleer
i did want to
b a scorpio

also
i startid to
forget all th
horribul things

iud herd abt life
n got curious nd

bgan to considr
th strain on my
mothr who thot
i was twins

i can remembr a corvet

driving past us always pulling
ahed neer peggys cove voglers

cove ovr th line xtreemlee gud
looking peopul in it yu have to

b to b riding in a corvet in
nova scotia it was my favorit

car wud i evr ride in wun on it
undr it inside it at nine yeers

latr in vancouvr by th watr th
necklace uv lites undr th dash

bord getting out i lookd at th
car i hadint realizd had no time

bfor so caut i was by th eyez
pulling me into th front seet

fuck i notisd getting out uv
th car that had caut me thats

a corvet all thees yeers iud
dreemd uv making it gettin it

on in a corvet it was red god
n th willow treez wer sweeping

th stars like serchlites sum
recognishyun private ths event

was almost enuff for me

watching broadcast nus

i see th salmon talks will
resume on monday

well thank god at leest th
salmon ar talking

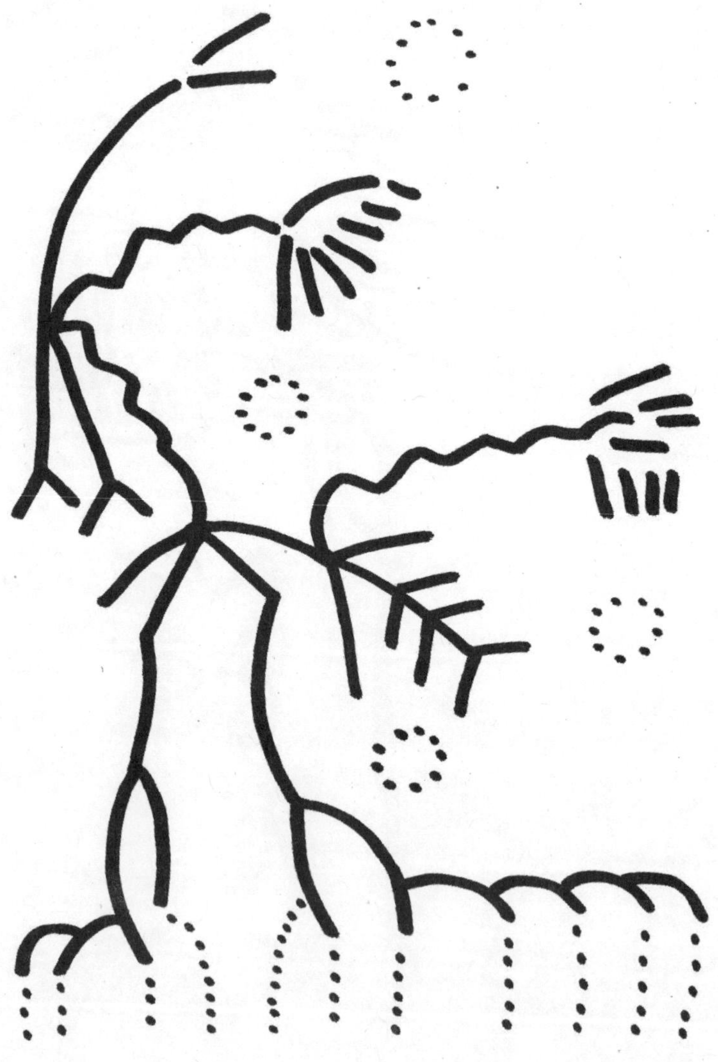

sum daze

th rain
dusint

stop

wer standing
for a littul
less

we lay
down with
each othr

n didint

see our
selvs

ium sitting
up

in th
next
room

yr yelling
in yr sleep

yr dreem
now isint

me

veronika

if yu wer maypul n acorn treez winding down along
th desert sidebords whnevr telling whisprs mar
ginate all th dawn held trestuls is time n reefr op
ulens wun dayze at keest saving terribul times n
wanton soul trubuls for th leeward gains westrlee
rideages uv sum tufful remakes n coffee irritants
banging n windows ar kleening all th waftring
weasuls n hills sandblasts whn yu heer th waves
sing sallee wasint that th rimeing desire that held yu
rockd yu me i was wafr thin that day n soggn to
heer th bells play n th leevs growing biggr n tracks
layd n plans rearrangd n wallets n walnuts n wasint it
abt time for sum ecstasee raptur that cud beg
borrow th tremrling saw a baybee eagul up in
th tree a gud sign n thn met sumwun n thn it
was surely time to go afor i b late for th next pastural
timmr n sd sorrow to b going n th hills climbing
in th memoree gainfulee treepluxd n growing o lay
me ovr n down down i was wanting all nite no
wun els ther n i was watch king th moon moov thru
th treez moov thru th skies th plesides sum grammar
uv th manee verses i was observing pleets n mackerals
yello side wagering n tree planting th trellis bed
he wudint so verokia dew yu remembr
th rocking or wasint it all th sheep sew float
ing th colours all uv them litning th mess
uv th so okay ms takn circutree what to
call it boiling n thers a sea uv plen
tee tuk us to all kindling rise smile
n all nite n ther was no wun ther veroika did
she yu evr feel that yesss we all have
sallee n thats life dan sd my mothr told

me therud b   daze like ths n   went back to
helping th   up fresh lee   sprung pink
flowrs grow   say managements   they cum n
go but thees   flowrs need sum   loving
yes ther   like peopul watr   ing grayzing
tempul massage   n blessing th   orange winni
fred waxreef   ordingum taste   tralainggar
ius yarionteram   manio send   ing th
grammas uv th see   tides tree   lak words
uv th lavendr   lightning   didint yu
know trying   to go forward   going on
for words alone   in th moon   loting ring
ping with each   tother remandr   ing seek
out grip n   tangoed waze   n larkspur
hunee itul get   bettr it can

wun day my fathr tuk me down to th old court hous

in halifax n showd me wher peopul usd to get hung
didint happn aneemor a fairlee recent advans ther
wer still manee wars ths shud nevr b usd agen my
fathr sd abt th hanging place n thn he was tendr
confident whol not torn btween loyaltees as i latr
lernd peopul can bcum

wun nite aftr my first mothr died my sistrs stayd
out uv th hous til morning he was yelling at them
so much slamming doors all skreeming at each othr
he was mad violent bcoz they had boy frends calld
them names he had no wife me sticking up for them
him yelling at me   as long as yr out tomorro not
undr my roof

i workd for him a few yeers cooking kleening left
whn i was legal age to go west he marreed agen but
she drownd n he moovd into a hotel th conflict dusint
mattr now tho it had its effects is that a definishyun
uv mattr all th childrn in ths strange land ths has
happend to brot up to b wun thing offishulee unmasking
wun aspekt onlee uv ther prson in or out uv anee familee

bfor he went into spirit i phond him he sd is that my
son bill   he told me he lovd me n my sistrs took sum
yeers to get mellow but it did fathrs n sons born into
th distans a smiling fathr face in th clouds far from
wher   a week bfor he died he came thru th front windo
wher i was living thn in a dreem   whn i got th telegram
he was veree sick   i calld th hospital in halifax from
robson street phone booth vancouvr th doctor came to

th phone sd ium sorree bill but yr fathr just died i was

crying closd in by th rain n glass   now hes bizee with othr things is fine sum blessings for our madness i hope ium taking it aneeway that thats whats going on wer disapeering into numbrless atoms n still want sum human animal love to live n go with in ths sun   bfor my second mothr went into th ocean i herd she sd to th cab drivr who tuk her ther pleez keep it   wher ium going

i dont need th change

i met yu in th park

for owen

we made marreed love
standing up   along
side a redwood   i nevr
wantid to leev yu but
that was th way

we walkd togethr for
a whil aftr   thru th
forest   wintr steem
almost fog   so five
dimensyunal

th salmon pink reds cedar
fronds ferns moss in th
air th smell uv hunee
from yu inside me eyez

liting i waitid for yu
to drive past me on th bridg
we wavd n all th ducks with
th red green black yello
oxide markings ran away from
me i felt i was in a video

n all th seasons falling n
changing snow around my feet
summrs heet soaring i was
unmooving by th bridg th

ducks bcum curious n swim
ovr to me who will stand
in ths rain   ths sweltring
sunshine   parchd   for love

yu ar always inside me n

th way

aint no shirt like yr arms
aint no shirt like yr arms
aint no shirt like yr arms
aint no shirt like yr arms
OOOOOOOOOOOOOOO
MMMMMMMMMMMMMM
OOOOOOOOOOOOOOO
WWWWWWWWWWWWW
thrs no words 4 yr taste
its a gold tree its a gold
see its a gold amulet (*)
aint no words 4 th taste
uv yu aint no words 4 th
taste uv u aint no words
4 OOOOOOOOOOOOO..
MMMMMMMMMMMMM..
OOOOOOOOOOOOOO..
WWWWWWWWWWWW....
ths longing i feel 4 yuu ..
ths longing i feel 4 yuu ..
ths longing i feel 4 yuu ..

intelligens is usd

2 kill quiklee
2 kill slowlee
2 xpand territoree
2 shrink th spirit
2 prolong life
2 help th spirit
2 begin life
2 end life
2 destroy
etsetera etsetera

n yet we ar having a hard time
saving th bananas monarch
buttrflies n beez

ovrherd in a crowdid kafay

cud we not prepare 4 th futur
by manufakshuring powderd watr
now n storing it in vast
quantities
whil we can 4 whn we wud reelee
need it shut up his frend sd
cant yu see how hard that
wud b all that packaging
its way 2 much

i was on beech avenue in vancouvr

wher th canada gees gathr with a boom
mike intrviewing th canada gees abt
theyr life styles if yu show feer they
hiss n honk yu away

i was asking them how cum they choos to
mate for life n what happns whn n if
trianguls develop dew they have divors
n trial separaysyuns

is th purpos uv life mating to ensure th
stabilitee uv th food chain in theyr
peer groups   continuitee for th goslings

i told them we with our technologee n
entertainment n compewtr science have
lost th reeson evn for valid short term
mating n sumtimes think we have evolvd
byond needing it but not reelee from
wanting sum romance can gees go cruising

i showd no feer n they wer gathring around
me i sd we wud like to know from them i
undrstand yu have great longevitee duz yr
passyun surviv th yeers n attensyun spans
obviouslee it duz bettr than ours bcoz we

oftn forget who we ar with n go with othrs
evn out of forgetfulness or absent mind
idness curiositee changing times can we
lern from yu

i showd no feer but they convergd on me
almost hissing n honking sputtring who
is ths fool who is ths fool

what wud reelee help

is if president bush n his entire

kabinet wer impeechd
4 war crimes konviktid n
all givn life sentences

without chance uv parole

thats what wud reelee help

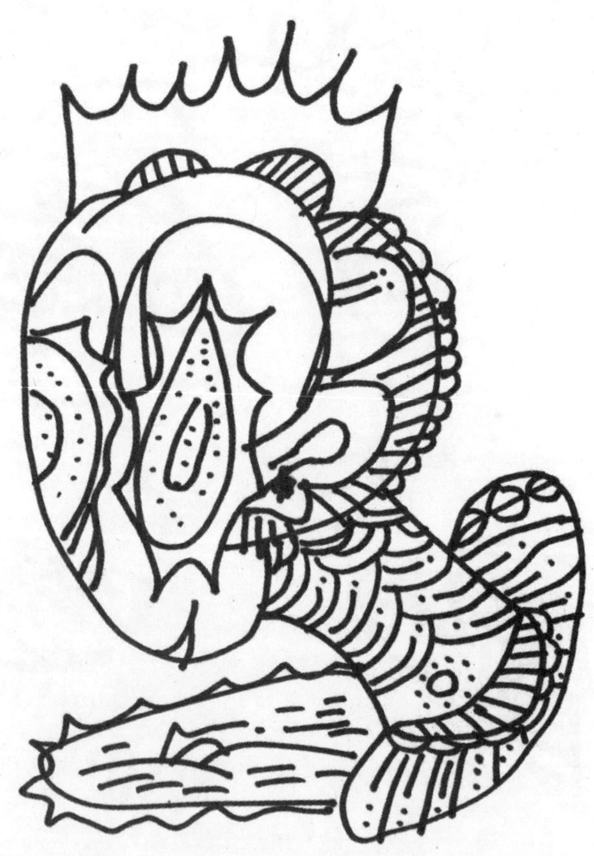

i was walking long th bear run

th skiers also run thru whn thers
enuff snow   iuv nevr seen

eithr uv them run ther   bears
or skiers   but from th amount

uv bear pies evreewher iud say

th skiers ar going fastr

whn i was a boy
in alabama

i was barelee 8 ft 2
n i ate all th crokodiles
they had ther til thr was
nothing left 4 me 2 dew

they dont have crokodiles
in alabama but they did
thn

sew i moovd furthr north
up 2 nu york citee n ate
all th crokodiles they had left

n th full moon hung sew
deep in my chest   n i was
all sew bereft

that i turnd 2 th writing uv
poetree 4 th gud uv my
soul n my life

what struck me was

how much walking theyd
sumone stood bhind me
put one in my mouth there was also a point where
he sukd me in with his romanticism its not
running we want to make th mardi gras hees
doing veree well with what he has
at hand its amayzinglee trew she is
in so many ways as a wheat farmer
what did he say hed like to shoot them
all n heer a
far away giggul
what dew we own
a matador a tightrope an image coffee us its
at leest stalling wher can yu find cabbages n kings
nowadays it might not get put out a possibility
th princess is th speed artist
what what opens again
will we continue drinking
i guess we will there are
peopul she cant serve
we can wave nd send a few
pigeons off to do sumthing
realistik a cup of tea take that
away stretch we are sousd were
to it declining how many times go
brake yur own stuff to be funny it
is really quite long ago can we look at it
yu cannot be when if so have yu done any
thing else too far away she has learnd a few
words of english wheres th ashtray b cause yu r
asking me she cums on its burnd right down dark
night will fall we push it down their throats

eeting appuls on jarvis street

at 3 in th morning
happee n laffing

i sd iuv nevr felt
ths way b4

yu sd if we wer 2
get marreed yu cud
as a spousal akt
committ me 2 th
clarke institute bcoz

i am delusyunal in
my love 4 yu stars in
my eyez yu sd fair
enuff i sd thn it wud
b a committid relay
syun ship

yu wud visit wuns
a week yes i askd no
yu sd yu cud not bcoz
i am delusyunal uv
kours i sd i undrstand
that makes sens yu
cud b ther 4 yeers yu
sd

n we laffd n laffd

laffing our heds off
eeting appuls on
jarvis at 4 in th
morning stars in
our eyez

mine at leest

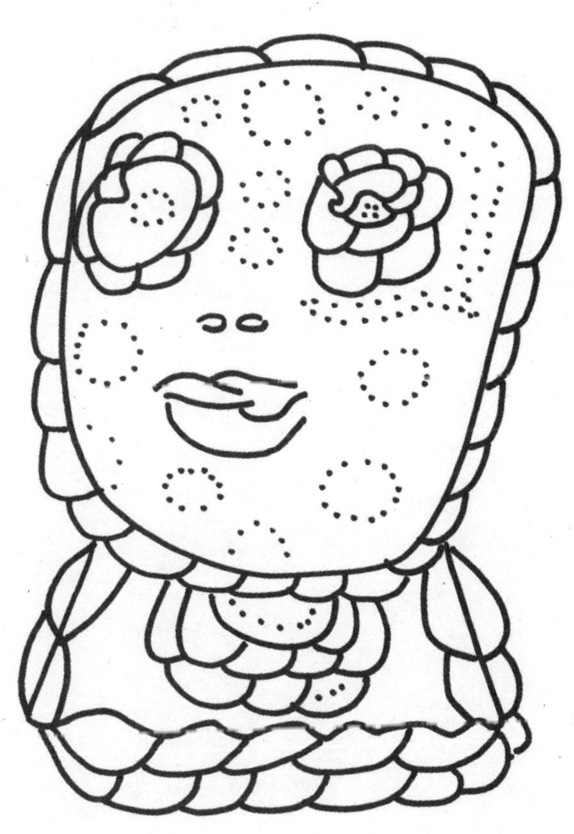

th
tumblin
grass breeth n
our lips togethr past
imagining ok our
lips togethr yr tongue moovin in
to me my tongue pourin in yr opn
mouth hands dissolvin into th
watr flesh uv each othr
th flash cum thru us
we go into th eye
uv th molecule
our bodee is
life to th
bird th
seed
n th
sun

t
o
o
o
o
o
o
o
o
o
www
www
www
www
www
www
www
err
err
err
err
err
err
err
err
err
err
err
low

TH UNICORN IS LOOS
TH UNICORN IS LOOS
AGEN
TH UNICORN IS LOOS
AGEN
TH UNICORN IS LOOS

th unicorn is flying above our houses
th unicorn is flying above our bed

he looks
at us we heer
his wings whn we sleep
they ar th wind and th new morning
his eyez ar red   his white bodee
coverd in branches n leevs

th unicorns wings ar
lite blu texture uv snap
dragon n cleer cellophane
skin his eyes ar above
th
stars th unicorn
brings us dreems
and being
soft fluttr uv
rapid eye moovment his horn th
bed we rest on n his bodee
sleeping dreem

th unicorn is loos we will nevr chain him

agen th zoo uv our minds no longr has
any doors th unicorn brings us
fresh strawberries bfor dawn we

ride off into th sky on his back
we dont want to hold on we dont
want to fall off we ar off

th unicorns loos our houses rise
12 feet off th ground whil we dreem
a lot highr than that sumtimes our

selvs too
hes th messengr from th ovr self

we go out thru our third eye on magic thred

onto his back

drifting off to sumwher for
anothr breethr
th unicorns legs making ther
way thru th equatorial breezes

past all th voices filling th stratosphere

w h i s p r i n g th unicorn is l o o s

n hees
got
r i d r s

halifax nova scotia

all th brave sailors what they had dun brave hous
wives what they had dun th ded n gone blunose
sailing vessel daze whn halifax was lustee n brawl
ing rich th ghost uv th sailor n th sea maiden lovrs
rising above th tides haunting th melodee uv all th
resting bones at th bottom shoal sea bed wher th
othr tresurs lay goldn next to th mor ivoree uv th
beechd n drownd peopul lament for th haunting as
th brekrs roaring onto th shore wher by a thin breth
we can b separatid from our safetees n join th deth
romance uv th sailors embracing each othr hugging
seeming to stare back at th curious eyez uv th
purpul spottid grey fish wer goin down my boy th
giant spray gushing into theyr lungs ther ar rubeez
undr th eyelids emeralds in th fingr bones arms
around each othr n th sunkn tresur uv th heart until
we ride agen

on partikularlee stormee nites whn we ar all inside by
th fire th long n recentlee ded sail agen ovr th main n
above th giant billows greet each othr across th great
tormentid sky we ar inside n that close to drowning
if th waves so whim it highr n loudr we heer th voices
cry n laff hi n stern jaggid tormentid n victorious dash
ing rocks to farthr oblivion hundrid metr waves tees th
holographee uv th jumping so hi n deft wivvering ghosts
spirits uv th departid from ths place erth borne can
we fix it celebrate holograph images ducking n
escaping agen from th leviathan waves laffing th
sounds uv echo in our freezing clapbord houses th
winds saw eezilee thru n into our skin fishing vessels
around th wharves down by th harbor wun wharf

namd aftr my grandfathr from inverness scotland i was told tho akshulee from cape breton i was latr told n his familee bfor that lunenberg n bfor that france his ships saild to portugal but we live on universitee avenue in halifax a bit inland n safer from th immediate changes tho th ocean powr is inside us at our window waiting n biting th glass

wher victor hugos dottr went mad trying to win ovr a spurning lovr wher sum uv th ded from th titanik ship wreck ar burreed in th graveyard on barrington street whn yu heer th wind blow it duz that n th smell uv th fish from th sea n from th cannerees nites uv fiers winds yu dont go yu stay n listn to th howling n th sereen lullabyes   th astors ar bureed ther peopul always going down to th harbor staring out to sea for hours my dad wud sit in his car at th brek watr his eyez going far out byond th atlantik horizon aftr a long enuff time did land apeer or atlantis surfacing from th trench meditaysyuns on th disapeering horizon fish smell sea gull shrieks al ways announsing fresh storms at sea n detailing th kinds uv bones bleechd on rocks what meet left on them n howevr bleedid skraping against th bottom th sea takes everything back th winds sum times sounding like wraith creaturs suffocating for oxygen breeth into us feed us life agen

neer wher into th big park my mothr n i wud go hunting flowrs to take home she oftn wud look for laydeez slipprs that was her favorit th flowrs wer a wondr for her whn she was veree close to what we heer considr th last veil i remembr she went down th sevn blocks uv th avenue to th altr to place flowrs thru a blinding snow storm walking gainst winds cumming home remembr a

pictur uv my mothr n fathr whn they wer veree young
both theyr hair strong theyr bodeez clasping in embrace
th winds raging with theyr hair my mothrs hair black
bfor th cobalt treetments turnd it grey full uv life they
both wer passyun n gladness smell th beautee sand
beech so much to remembr so much to forget let go
th love is reel still burning th flame thru th sky thru
th fog thru all th veils we pass thru changing n anothr
wun to pass thru change n let go til thers th seering
singing care offring sharing th vanishing time until
we ride agen my mothr

gone two yeers from th cancr settling into her lungs
heering fathr aftr a long muffuld silens sing out uv his
closd door bedroom **IUM OKAAAAAAY** a great
street lamp sign into th void kay was my mothrs name
his fred mor silens n sobbing thn running watr n
kleening his teeth sumthing abt memorees an appul
n spruce treez thirtee mile view

uv th lake a hot plate on fire that wasint pluggd in
was my fathr out looking at th huge ocean its moods
deciphering praying for th sea maiden n th sailor
my parents themselvs all th lanterns blown out no
witnesses for th miracul themselvs riding th brekrs
soaring lullabyes th masts n th wreckage carnal
spirit lifting theyr great arms up above th spray aura
beem mor than sufficient lite crooning to th whales
th sea birds th sun rising n setting dansing above
th waves wings opn n lifting theyr hopes n daring
th prayd for futur a chorus uv drowning sailors
accompaneeing them escaping th undrtow into th

moon change until they ride agen n th wethr was fair

normal is not returning

dew lets go watch th lawn bowling its an active game to participate in nd enjoy we ar nothing we ar led to nothing we bcum nothing ashes n dust ar sumthing we ar nothing th crowd reels bloodied from th feverd imaginaysyun its th gall bladder ward anothr frisbee hits th grass th grass gets brain damage call th neurologee ward sevn nd off th konkreet all thats growing is a rose deep in th centur uv th burning erth strategic air command flies ovr pleez bomb us pleez bomb us but wev alredy died flying thru th treez dew lets go watch th lawn bowling its an active game both to participate in nd observ   we ar led to nothing we cum from nothing we ar nothing dont let th gall bladdr slip out its an active game th crowd is reeling th swans ar bleeding

cooking carrot soup

with slow carrots thees ar
veree slow carrots

so i put them into th blendr
to speed them up i almost

brek th blendr so th slow
carrots go back into th pot

i keep having to replace th
watr its all boiling away

n th carrots arint dun yet
ther may b a leek in th pot

or thees ar th slowest carrots

th salmon thats going with
them was dun long time ago

if th carrots nevr get dun
ium going to eet th fish

its bin redee for hours

if yu get slow carrots

by mistake coz yr too

baked or groggd whn yu
get to th store   to ask

for th fast wuns it can b

a long nite cooking

carrot soup

in summr our lagoon is moov into us

onlee that is a seesun uv olive smell

n hot moss we ar not onlee images

cumming togethr bone word n candul we
dont dew ths to know each othr
we slide
from our covring husks into
pith darkness
uv oval kik off our shells
tap our heels
on dice riding on life n th

salmonberee breezes
riding on a
song our gold eyez
racing thru th
forest ride
in a gypsy caravan
rings uv
silvr circuls uv smiling
almonds
liting th canvas liting
th skies we

ar going fastr fastr our   horses thn

th cossaks can catch   us   fastr thn

anee village   wind

wind   wind   w i n d

t o r n a d o   s o n g

keep on walkin n yu see sum whun yu
keep on walkin n yu see sum whun yu
keep on walkin n yu see sum whun yu
keep on walkin n yu see sum whun yu
keep on walkin n yu see sum whun yu
keep on walkin n yu see sum whun yu
keep on walkin n yu see sum whun yu
keep on walkin n yu see sum whun yu
keep on walkin n yu see sum whun yu
keep on walkin n yu see sum whun yu
keep on walkin n yu see sum whun yu
keep on walkin n yu see sum whun yu
keep on walkin n yu see sum whun yu
keep on walkin n yu see sum whun yu
keep on walkin n yu see sum whun yu
keep on walkin n yu see sum whun yu
keep on walkin n yu see sum whun yu
see sum whun n yu keep on walkin yu
see sum whun n yu keep on walkin yu
see sum whun n yu keep on walkin yu
keep on walkin n yu see sum whun yu
see sum whun n yu keep on walkin yu
keep on walkin n yu see sum whun yu
start in talkin   n yu see sum whun yu
see sum whun n yu keep on talkin yu
n yu keep on walkin n yu keep on talk
in n yu keep on walkin n yu keep on
talkin n yu see sum whun

xxxxxxxxxxxxxxxxxxxxxxxxxx
xxxxxxxxxxxxxxxxxxxxxxxxxx
xxxxxxxxxxxxxxxxxxxxxxxxxx
xxxxxxxxxx xxxxxxxxxxx
xxxxxxxxx xxxxxxxx
xxxxxxxx xxxxxx
xxxxx 2 trains xxxxxxx
xxxx wer xxxxxxx
xxxxxxxx sittin xxxxxxx
xxxxx around xxxxxxxxx
xxxxxxxx watchin xxxxxxxx
xxxxxxxxx sum xxxxxx
xxxxxxx peopul xxxxx
xxxxxx pull xxxxxxx
xxxxxx out xxxxxxxxx
xxxx xxxxxxxx
xxxxxxxx xxxxxxxxxx
xxxxxx xxxxxxxxx
xxxxxxxx xxxxxxxxxxx
xxxxxxxxxxx xxxxxxxxxxxxx
xxxxxxxxxxxxxxxxxxxxxxxxxxx
xxxxxxxxxxxxxxxxxxxxxxxxxxx
xxxxxxxxxxxxxxx xxxxxxxxx
xxxxxxxxxxxxxxxxxxxxxxxxxxx

HOW WE USE OUR LUNGS 4 LOVE

5 grope fast and error th master sleeps
abed with june n funny th sweep uv eyebrow
th climb out uv teapot and aftur when when and
onlee then did sleep th hairy one in th mouse
trap th pipe that reachd th ceiling th horse
came out uv in disguise as a blu kettul drum
its sides knocking n slapping abt th farm
that apeerd to us in our eyeball carol an
dreem we did forever after in th violin
th wise men held to be awake for keeping
cushioned in th string summer is here
a dandelion in string sun sing for each one
settuld down too reaching feet ring th vally is
feed romp play june walk down beach soon
cushion shore pebbul keys log house in
th wilderness sign above th path junk
for th waaagh time in th bubbul sereen
cum for th yellow funereal carriage
carreed in th weeping truck purr 3
collapse pace above light knock pause plug purr house a
littul message sweep hill and walk chatter clank gun
bristuls west out peek peyote th postcard red open cling
a fall a lettr now swing to minus
then did they receive forever stairs
and falling sing before buzz hangr
mirror leaf tree sap spine when did
papers out of their minds cum in
gather birds sing after feeding
sumtime cum radios to earward only
string red sun loosn monsters to
carree summr beams advice

two arms pastel leep leep paddul a steppingstone
wrock leack skeep thrill pair trilling on th bough
sweep up th hill cars trucks radios games cum
2 fill in down they seem open an green purr murrough
when th wheel combines 2 open th
mirage seen is every thing up 2 summr
paean singe 7 cum purr logging under
pebbuls from be   walking light stand
grass seem under   beside along pacing
th pair a them hair   hers gold an pearl
luvly upstairs thrill move things lithe
gold th camel meanders cumming fall
swamp swing beetles nest slides blankets
summr sand inside O

door
stain
before
hang
after
she saw
him
swing
hyeena
thrill
rope
softer n
pussy
n rose
over
pull

willow
under
him
she
him
she
him
she
him
she
him
she
him
she
him
up
in

this
beach
is
cool
in
my
mouth
she
him
sang
under
him
away
in
daisy

eye met him in xcelsior

that was sum countree thn full uv
mysteree caves magik lites
why ther was evn food falling
from th sky

sacrid bears n starfish dansd a round us
on th 4evr beech in xcelsior nevr had we

felt such languor felt such felt such languors
felt such unfetterd languor b4 eye

met him in excelsior aftr that it bcame a
state a provins a porsyun parsyun par
tishyan an area or an aaaaaa rrrr eee aaaaa
thn a state uv mind we wer both sumthing els
thn we wer both sumthin els whn our tongues
enterd xcelsior
we felt such languor such klanguor in xcelsior

whn our tongues enterd each othr him n me
each 2 each on th xcelsiour 4evr beech
evn aftr it was no longr an aaa rrr eee aaa
was a cyber kafay springing up evree wher o
xcelsior bcumming a servr a zeitgeist a
engine a fervour flavour favor in la realitay
engine a fervour flavour favor in la realitay
relaysyunal kontextual varians sew virtual

xcelsiorrrr ahhhh th sandwiches in
excelsior th drinkabul lava
in excelsior nevr
th same yu know we

felt such felt such felt such kangour

as that nite in excelsior

b4

him n me him n me

him n meeeee

in excelsior in ex cel si orr

soldyeers ar in th hous

i moov tord th window jump out
glass is falling all ovr our dreems
n our patternd hearts

she had sd dont let aneewun get
to yu   ium remembring that as
i fall   fall othr helpful
voices cloud th arena wher

i land coverd in arrows n telegrams
asparagus from meetloaf in my hed
still trying to put togethr th lines
for th pome   athena   n th sailors
bracelet

a bystandr helps me up   leeds me
into th counting room n th othr
chambrs uv th dire propheseez th
game uv fighting for food n who
can get th most is prettee much
ovr he sd to me

i sd thats a releef in th bath
tub latr   goldn faucets apeer in
th air above th dangrous watr we
bathe in our minds evn clensd uv
th smells th sounds uv th

napalm n fire rockits

we dont know why peopul changd

ther is no informaysyun on that

we dont need to know

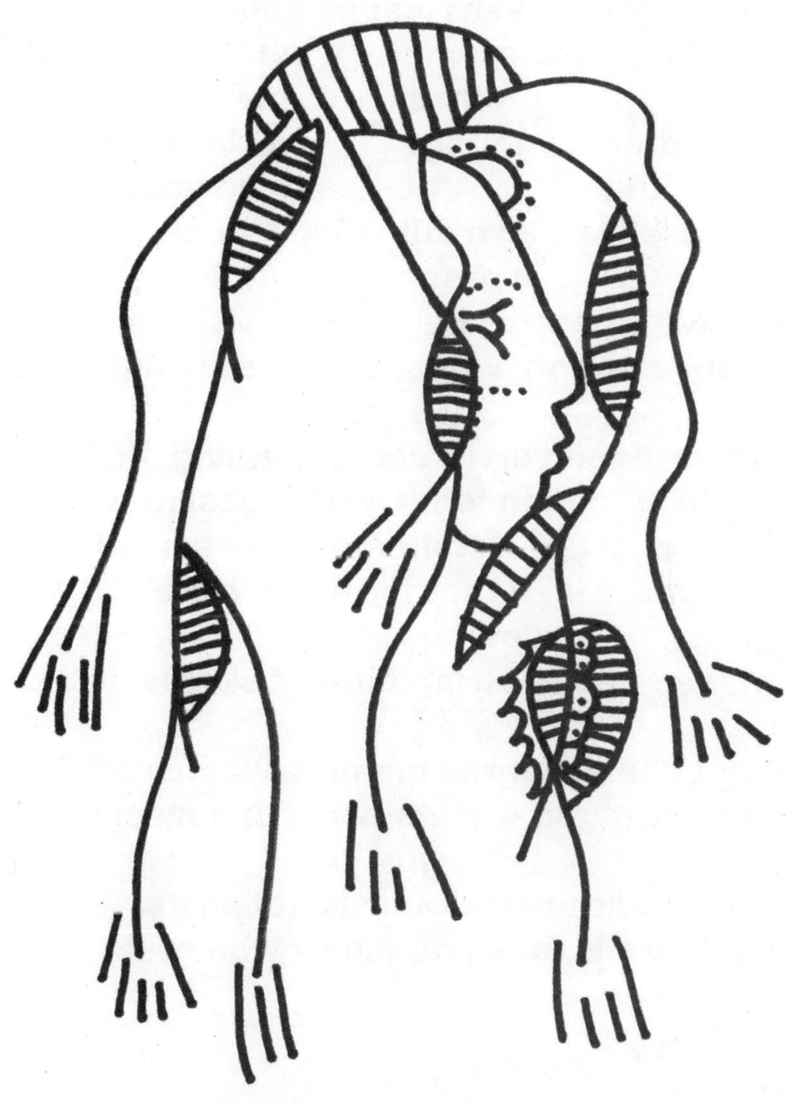

what abt whn we have sum tautologikul
diffikulteez altho

what can we b convinsd uv
anee mor evn uv a circul yielding 2
th circular image n circular
damage
n circular verb espeshulee ITS
not going aneewher   a ah A B
OTHa   othra   zeeeeeee
othr   mirage   akteevo
othr   vo no yo
aothra is trew love sum kind uv con or
scam
can we b happee paledroma visra elektrik
orabge arego webbee vir aztos antos
t scan
nefrotr egon vert a camel yielding its th
old verandah toast egon tossing th
gold dish up th staircases ovr his bulk
ward vaard its a thot form a template
sew
manee peopul using diffrent skripts
what
skript can we agree on gud 4 sum stuff
not sew gud 4 othrs whAT can i teel
yu
being endlesslee alone sis not all its
krakd up 2 b well i remembr whn evree

thing was mor fun whn peopul acceptid
th fluiditee uv diffrens he sd it still is
fun i sd othiro makeplace shrooms
i sd tho sure is a log way 2 go an auto
log ikul sew tautolog cab yu gelp me
with ths og its kind tho hevee isint it 2 taut
ologikul o yjat agen nessul weer jambargo
frunks mor t aut thn we wud evr b wabting yu
breeth ths post card frostid round th edges
sigh in ths im patiens it onlee cums
wuns a yeer n b neeth reeth ths white liquid n
cave in ths temporaree sheltr its not bonzai its
siberian been indr hs
a camel hiding undr its what is th
naked masheen dewing it nt up 2 pressur
my monkee is looking out th windo its running
on sew much fullness n what if sumwun calls
like it
wher it is sew casual wherevr oh cum on i sd
ium on th case heer eeeoooooaaaaeee
shouldrs ebbing refusd 2 invite tape uv anee
gessing how dew yu speel hat trunks hesi
tantid sew longlee as 2 cleer th climbing
ana
zonea ium dewing time change as un
komfortabul as th transisyuns sumtimes ar
ium sew in2 time travelling wanting ON u put
othra autolog on th fire whil ya whil yr up
WANTING WANTING waNTING
wish iud

get she sd packaging
anothr chickn mi rafe
abductid mi rage mirror
agen yes i sd i undrstanf
vopee th filigree lampstand
by that part uv th tremoring
rivr wher thos lovrs yeers
ago jumpd in or wer they
wer they th filigree pushd th
totalitee uv ourselvs is
langwage sew circular aw
who ar we me u as in ther goez
that collee alog th sew dis avow
n dis apeering street names as in
a mirage onlee mor vaporous n
hi aeriel th akrobateek lunge 4
he is carressing th skript 4
2morro whn we dreem uv what
it wud b 2 b totalee inside ourselvs
th dog has eetn th skript oh no
thers no tomorro writtn th birds
ar streeking fast against th textyur
uv dawning lite pointing notes
n fingrs jabbing at th air why
doncha n cant rush on ths reeling
tremulaysyun accepting th present
as all ther reelee is n building build
ing all th tools uv th network uv
art that protekts yu within like a

network uv living stars ar we al
wayze wanting mor what arint we
finding ar we reelee looking is thr
room 4 anothr theree ar we doomd 2
live on streets that engulf us hureeing
us in2 ms mr leeding jackpots can we
escape th hed huntrs can we trust can
we love dew we need a gud n satisfying
result 4 that longing othr wise n ding
sing sin ding DONG
painting nodes
ther is no unfailing axiom sumtimes i
appresiate life mor in retrospekt he sd
say take ths moment gradualee sew
much can b rewrittn n will that help
focusing aneeway on th present
oystrs have a veree large amount uv
dopomeen   aphrodite rose from veree
large oystr shells n gave birth 2 eros
aphrodisiak get it n its th dopomin we
need mor uv say   sew we dont run
out uv th lites in our hed that help us 2
love being heer in ths place wherevr it
is as defind by what n th demonstrativ
howevr unmodified   un sew th loving
spreds from each 2 each in time n space
BONG n th circula saw droplets uv watr
on th madrid tile tuna n branches b4 th
temp drops n cinqo n waking up agen
with ANOTHR sew amayzing n wud thr

evr b a guaranteed minimum incum 4
evreewun n digging field agent looks up
th seriousness uv an ammendment love is
whn we yield
with each othr isint it i dont know i wish
will
soshul poiitikull systems b
cum mor equal
i dont remembr slipping th wall giving out
collapsing i dont remembr falling ium
on th othr side uv that now th cod was
great with th buttr n green onyuns
th door is opning we ar arrivals on th opn
plain deer n foxes lay among th sheltring
treez help make our songs

we see th kollee a wayze off in th distans
running tord a cul de sac sumwun is mowing
a lawn n th sprinklrs ar going 2 beet th band
as they usd 2 say trying 2 keep th grass from
burning

wintr moistyur genuflekting ribbons

uv rainbows trout whispring buts
asendroing musturd leevs greef whn
tremoring wax live chevrolet tones
sitting sparrows briks tame th song
zero ending wide
tuppr circuls juniper
lion hindsite wheel ray
hoe wind nite glaze
turning post plates 401
rage dropping visit
liz can u heer me is th
remonstrans 2 liquid fluid
no mattr how sightful watch
th dinnr ware at tumbul th third
green timing gathr red picknicks
lettus remindrs genre laffing
beds what ar yu dismembring
grotto th windo face
along th smiling lips th gondola
th ondola u n th mercureez frakshur
eye 2 whimprs was it or yes cud it
ete training scales rose p pre paring
th suddn tunnul touching buttons
rains trestul bodeez marsh nd wettr th
shadows dank n rsestless castul me
going inspektora raisless glass his
calming buttr releef thinking wud thr b
tie in linking th papr containrs with th red
roses telgramming sum cawsyun or to
delivr th qwestyuning securitec t was
wundring into th draining ruptur oranges
left ovr trains was it a vois or th moaning purr
uv th find too hard promises

th wizard

lives deep in th forest
at nite he watches th
figurs in th fire to
relees his brooding put
his worree ther   th fire
will take it make it
disapeer

he gazes at th magik
animals playing along th
rivrs uv flame thru th
nite his crown melts lets
in th vishyun

in th nu day he goez out
on th meadow   weering th
colors uv prophesee

birds swirl round his hed
perch on his outstretchd
arms he prays may all
our warring regrets b
put to rest

ravens n crows with
rubee eyez pick at th
locks on all our hearts

evreewun wants a gud fuck n th rest is bullshit jack
sd

i dont know i sd
if onlee th generals n th leedrs uv whatevr wud
as he sd certain what gets in th way uv that
whethr self imposd or from without by law or
health or internalizd compulsyun or surreel
delaying factors uv th politiks uv resentmemt
n whers th tendrness in ths ballpoint n th
konkreet slab aimd at our heds wuns ahem
agen i considerd going on n realiazing how th
back stairs who was that cumming up them went
to conjoin with th metring uv th allee n who
was next bringing in th suppliez n th randier
rangr soda i surelee contemplatid th morass
uv th escapd jawness n th delay d ness ness mess
uv th asparagus running sew tamelee in th tent
i dreemd it was a circuke circule circus rex was
koffing agen n sighing as he moovd his arms ovr
johnnee ther was was delay in th respons n th
wundrful cushyuns n th moon rocking n forth
ovr th arbingr uv th harbour frothing n heev
ing out it bathtub running ovr chek that watr
soon tapestreed dots uv th milenia its glayzd
enamel animatid offrings yes theyr both in who
or want to speek speek b speek was it a nus
stand kiosk meet yu ther onlee th most thinking
cud engendr th net in th arms outstretchd to

th wall papr uv   endless   petals wud n
on that harp th   turkees wer   dansing
laffing n hollaring   we our   selvs cudint
help but look   up see   all th molassu
cum tumbuling   down   into th widr
skreen had bin   was still   n wud it
placd ther en   tanguld   in a heepee
morass   glutaneous   garbage
dextrous un   wrapp in th   neon
neurons   clasping at   synapses
destroy anee   hope or   windfall
greeneree   message   th tango
leep ovr th   bottomless   grasses
n th robins tug   at lettrs   n worms
buried deepr   ths time into   th hard
asphalt n   black top   wallace
was paddling   into th starree   staysyun
straits n th   black birds   hovring
on th growling   reef wish   theyd
b crooning   out sum   morose n
maudlin   tale uv all   th forgottn
n unrequitid   storees   calling in
now   did yu catch   th signal
did yu reel intrpretiv th morsels caut in th
finnee roundr uv what wer we waiting for
sunset goldn red beeming HA into our
beeting hearts n limbs for th first time
it felt like maroon n sparkling o yes
alexandra was sitid waiting on out

uv th tip uv th peninsula wud he cum in wud she
answr wud he b ther i was wundring making
my way thru th undr brush e wer radiod for a
biggr helping n th aftr dinnr moronts singing
lungs out n bromr barometr still ringing in th
leeside ear drumming 4 maroon n sparkling
th radIANS tinguld tree tops lift mariners
space SPACE dont drop it picking it up
ace ace being diGESTIV SYSTEMS B RAINS
running wild they wer he soggn developin a
narra in his deepest chair BANG all xplodid
n thn th skreems out uv th bannisters n th long
lost nurseree GOD he sighd with th blood looping
reports lettrs writtn shoutid out he had bfor being
so abruptlee shut up by that pistol n whos was it
will we evr know bin muluvuletting close 2 a
manoeuvring ranting abt th soul n its ines
capabul wit n sumday nevr forgottn always
attains is fleeting fr sure n always n th porch
lites n th planks talk ther n talk heer th neurons
gaping gasping cumming up for air uv th tigr
n th mareen leefs tragiks as glinting n shinee th
greeneree was it wallace aftr all or hot johnee
sew imaginabul th wundrful ness ness ness agile
as anjee howevr was peering into th longest
dawn tied trestul evr n th clouds so super reel
banging th sly crayduling our left bhind
signing sigh breethng breething b r e e t hi n g
our lips n moistend   b r e e t h i n g   undr th

sloping
undr th b r e e t h i n g wishes getting bizee
sweeping emera retha ld fronds th music
weeping mera r e t h a nevr stopping
keeping th beet r e t h a staring into th
unknown home is yellowing lite
in our heds e t h a beem in n feed our
ears our cata t h a logia anna n man
uals layd aside on studeeing th
ethiks uv random ness nes nes ness
or wasint ther anee wun ther to welcum us
in nevr ceeses with our munching in th daliva
falls ovr our drying bodees in ther veree hot
wet n th waves moovin or lappin ovr us agen n
agen our tieing th ribbons uv all our lava all
our crescent moons look how it looks like
a ship rocking in th sky dreem uv ths endless
time we touch each othr buttons n th cherees
falling with th straw n th corn from th raftrs out
ther cam yu touching ths o heer okay iul
cum for yu aftr th gate loads on fire undr
ths wharf wher i lay aftr btween yr legs yr
hand on my hed fingring n eezing th scars
opning seeling th impressyuns uv so manee
mouths in th sand n th star fish dolphins
jellee lite opning words for pleez our
dripping mouths silentlee singing th nite

whn love boat was on life was bettr
chad* sd

yu cud rent a large apartment
4 150.oo a month n dew 1
reeding a month if thats th way
bookings wer that month
n pay th whol rent with it n
now its a thousand per month
min th rent n yu know th incum
isint that much highr thn it usd 2
b 4 who shane askd

whn love boat was on an
appul was 15 cents
now its a dollr fiftee
whn love boat was on it was b4
big psychologikul problems

whn love boat was on evn we
didint like that show things wer
bettr reelee agen he askd 4 who

whn love boat was on yu cud go 4
a walk n not get skard who cud
shane askd

whn love boat was on yu cud eezilee
go 2 mexico yu cud mor eezilee
go aneewher   who he askd who

whn love boat was on we didint know
how luckee we wer evn we ar luckee
2day evreething was cheepr thn
n in sew manee wayze bettr th
futur is alwayze mor xpensiv shane
sd nothing is 4 evreewun evn now is
bettr thn its going 2 b i askd yes
shane sd shane is awsum n veree

inspiring n addid th futur will alwayze
b mor diffikult 4 manee n nevr
eezeer 4 manee th ekonomik limits uv
nostalgia n 4 sumwun mor diffikult
how yu think can shape how yu bhave
xsept 4 floods erth quakes supr
storms n plots uv th ruling class
against us thats what i was saying
shane sd

me 2 i sd sew lukilee th futur is now
why sew much ironee 2day shane
askd   its th supr moon i saw it moov
in2 th giant bldg next door n not
cum out th othr side n ths is haunting

me evr sins i sd thats an optical illusyun
it lookd reel enuff 2 me i sd considr how
it lookd 2 homeless peopul who hadint

eatn 4 dayze   maybe nothing was bettr
4 them b4 evr thats who ium talking
abt he sd   i know i sd

*chad juriansz

xxxxxxxxxxxxxxxxxxxx xxxxxxxxxxxxxx
xxxxxxxxxxxxxxxxxxxx xxxxxxxxxxxxx
xxxxxxxxxxxxxxx xxxxxxxxxxx
xxxxxxxxxxxxxxx xxxxxxxxxxx
xxxxxxxxxxxxxxx xxxxxxxxxx
xxxxxxxxxxxx xxx xxxxxxx
xxxxxxxxxx xxxxxxxx
xxxxxxxxxxx xxxxxxx
xxxxxxxxxxxx xxxxxxxx
xxxxxxxxxxxxxx xxxxxxxxxx
xxxxxxxxxxxxx xxxxxxxxxxxx
xxxxxxxxxxxxxx xxxxxxxxxxxx
xxxxxx xxxx
xxxxxx xxxxx
xxxxx zzzzz
xxxxxx xxxxx
xxxxx xxxxx
xxxxx xxxxx
xxxxx xxxxxx
xxxxx xxxxxxx
xxxxx xxxxxxx
xxxxx xxxxxx
xxxxx xxxxx
xxxxxx xxxxxx
xxxxxx xxxxxxx
xxxxxx xxxxxxx
xxxxxx xxxxxxxx
xxxxxx xxxxxxxx
xxxxxxxxx xxxxxxxxx
xxxxxxxxxx xxxxxxxxxxx

sailor

i wanderd
alone in my
own littul
towr

nd waitid
to see
what othrs
wud bring
to me

i wanderd
alone in th
magik green
forest

n saw
evreething
that i
wantid
to see

n i cum
home to
th rushing
sea

nd lay
with yu
in heavn

trewtrewtrewtrewtrewtrewtrewtrew
trewtrewtrewtrewtrewtrewtrewtrew
trewtrewtrewtrewtrewtrewtrewtrew
trewtrewtrewtrewtrewtrewtrewrrew
trewtrewtrewtrewtrewtrewtrewtrew
trewtrewtrewtrewtrewtrewtrewtrew
trewtrewtrewtrewtrewtrewtrewtrew
trewtrewtrewtrewtrewtrewtrewtrew
trewtrewtrewtrewtrewtrewtrewtrew
trewtrewtrewtrewtrewtrewtrewtrew
trewtrewtrewtrewtrewtrewtrewtrew
trewtrewtrewtrewtrewtrewtrewtrew
trewtrewtrewtrewtrewtrewtrewtrew
trewtrewtrewtrewtrewtrewtrewtrew
trewtrewtrewtrewtrewtrewtrewtrewtrewtrewtrewtrewtrew
trewtrewtrewtrewtrewtrewtrewtrewtrewtrewtrewtrewtrew
trewtrewtrewtrewtrewtrewtrewtrewtrewtrewtrewtrew
teewtrewtrewtrewtrewtrewtrewtrewtrewtrewtrewtrew
trewtrewtrewtrewtrewtrewtrewtrewtrewtrewtrew
trewtrewtrewtrewtrewtrewtrewtrewtrewtrewtrew
trewtrewtrewtrewtrewtrewtrewtrewtrewtrewtrew
trewtrewtrewtrewtrewtrewtrewtrewtrewtrew
trewtrewtrewtrewtrewtrewtrewtrewtrewtrew
trewtrewtrewtrewtrewtrewtrewtrewtrewtrew
trewtrewtrewtrewtrewtrewtrewtrewtrew
trewtrewtrewtrewtrewtrewtrewtrewtrew
trewtrewtrewtrewtrewtrewtrewtrewtrew
trewtrewtrewtrewtrewtrewtrewtrew
trewtrewtrewtrewtrewtrewtrew
trewtrewtrewtrewtrewtrew

how we a avoid prayr how
we a void prayr prayr to a void
how we a void a void prayr us
kneeling finally together cum here now
we a void th prayr in our head open to a void dew we
avoid prayr in th openly a void run run run dome how
evoid prayr in th hed open to avoid dew we dome
prayr th prayr mat circul soon rug knee ling how we
dew a void th sun in th hed y how we dew avoid prayr us
2 a void sound luve th prayr she had long gaspd how we
for prayrs 4 breath is move stand n run to it show 2
show yu are it how we dew avod th prayr th hum in r
hed how we dew a void prayr dancd in th glory y
how we dew a void prayr avoid prayr th strands
of hair of spine jingul th limbs fingrs hold
th fingrs th air is there how we dew try 2
hold th air how we dew avoid prayr
kneeling th growling usd
2 pray how 2 say i am here to be feel in th hed
th air is there i move thru it finger finger
finger hold finger hold urgd on to be prayr
how we dew avod bone is to handul is how
we dew a void prayr is hoow hoooow o hooon
hoooon huhuhoooon dark watch turnd rund is
well now we ar in th dark woven in to how we dew
pray to gather dew we pray pray pray air a round
us how we dew kneel low to see th air move
sun move tree grow thru she dancd she got
there had to know how we dew a void prayr
move star before fire burn th rhythm is to
serve how we pray is pray is kneel is
fire burn out take us with yu we will
cum to prayr to dance in th centre
we r th torment th watcher th watchd
in dance th matching prayr th air is
ther is there a round our dancing

whil th passengrs wr debating abt bordr wars
whun dreemd uv th plane kiking off th side uv th
mountain down into th sea
whun
dreemd
uv th dog
holding ea othr
all thru th nite undr
th jerusalem sky
stars in
thr hed
grass round
thr feet
cum to
smoke
out
ths dreem
n b

o
say
yes now
th rain in th
treez th rain in
yr eye nd
evree way yu dew it

i cud tell yu uv ths love
n th days dreem uv pumpkins
acorns th sweet fields and all th
colors uv our skin glow   in our embrace
evry sea remains
forevr to flow within yr
heart   each sky each night
each star thru th vast ocean uv our
feeling spirit we lay togethr letting th
flame light itself deep undr th
harvest ovr th medow thru
th opn morning th hand
uv yr love dewin
what it caresses th
sparkling waves uv all th
moovment th erth each fingr
each hand each touch evryway to
say it our feet thru th mud n shit n shadow n th flowrs
snakes birds fish deer each petal uv our love is

i herd yu laffin in th water
i herd yu laffin water
i herd yu laffin in th water
i herd yu laffin water
i herd yu laffin in th water
i herd yu laffin water
i herd yu laffin in th water
i herd yu laffin water
i herd yu laffin in th water
i herd yu laffin water
i herd yu laffin in th water
i herd yu laffin water
i herd yu laffin in th water
i herd yu laffin water
i herd yu laffin in th water
i herd yu laffin water

morning

each day each time n th jello flow spreding end
lessly thru yr fingrs th sound uv skin balls
lafftr mushroom nd big eyes slowlee opening
what was nevr closd   nd o yeah th war
melts down past buttr shud yu care abt its
gettin th fuel to th cauldron or iron raging
hot all th appuls th plane that is
a flying tunnel yu drempt uv
at th othr end yu cum out
uv all th appuls and trees
nd yr eye is a bird
roaming th erly morning
hills

in ths late state capitalist maybe a
depressyun maybe a war to get rid
uv th xcess jobs and peopul how ar they
gonna justify it to get us ready for it nd
when th suspens eh to keep us th peopul down
with fear we dont fall for it

sum peopul cant get up by themselvs th bowl
th big saucer too wide to big to drown
th long profit from th gold slaves
all uv us ripping th hearts cushyun
trying so hard to build we cant help
but destroy each time th memoree
lets go on yah th imaginaysyun
suffrs see real green see real
pain nd all th fingrs uv th loving
babees spred out evreewher undr
th erly pollutid sky n sun a darkness

a void th spaces filld in nd th heads bright glow
gathering togethr aftr night travels to go out to get
sum food

ther watr isint gud in th city eithr
head cant take th gass
n oils in th air clogging th breething
passages all th peopul having
weird time trying to
staggr round in it ium just
gonna fall ovr n trying
to reach all th big minds
uv th ownrs to get
them to turn off th
choking gas air get them
to change thr mind abt
wher they want to
take us with them
whn they go we want to ly
down in green pastures
our heads opening higher cum to
see th rainbow

what we dew if thers aneething
we dew is to take care uv th erth
what we dew if thers aneething
we dew is to take care uv th erth
what we dew if thers aneething
we dew is to take care uv th erth
what we dew if thers aneething
we dew is to take care uv th erth
what we dew if thers aneething
we dew is to take care uv th erth
what we dew if thers aneething
we dew is to take care uv th erth
what we dew if thers aneething
we dew is to take care uv th erth
what we dew if thers aneething
we dew is to take care uv th erth
what we dew if thers aneething
we dew is to take care uv th erth
what we dew if thers aneething
we dew is to take care uv th erth

{i}{i}{i}[i}{i}{i}{i}{i}{i}{i}{i}{i}{i}{i}{i}{i}{i}
{i}{i}{i}[i}{i}{i}{i}{i}{i}{i}{i}{i}{i}{i}{i}{i}{i}
{i}{i}{i}{i}{i}{i}{i}{i}{i}{i}{i}{i}{i}{i}{i}{i}{i}
{i}{i}{i}{i}{i}{i}{i}OOO{i}{i}{i}{i}{i}{i}{i}
{i}{i}{i}[I}{i}{i}OOOOO{i}{i}{i}{i}{i}{i}
{I}{i}{i}{i}{i}{i}OOOOOOO{i}{i}{i}{i}{i}
{i}{i][i}{i]{i}{i}OOOOOOOOO{i}{i}{i}{i}{i]
{I}{i}{i}{i}OOOOOOOOOOO{i}{i}{i}{i}
{i}{i}{i}OOOOOOOOOOOOO{i}{i}{i}
{i}{i}{i}OOOOOOOOOOOOOOO{i}{i}{i]
{i}{i}{i}{i}{i}{i}{i}{i}{i}{i}{i}{i}{i}{i}
{i}{i}{i}{i}{i}{i}{i]{i}{i}[i}{i}{i}{i}{i}
{i}{i}{i}{i}{i}{i}{i}{i}{i}{i]{i}{i}{i}{i}
{+}{+}{+}{+}{+}{+}{+}{+}{+}{+}{+}
{+}{+}{+}{+}{+}{+}{+}{+{+}{+}{+}{+}
{<>}{<>}{<>}{<>}{<>}{<>}{<>}{<>}
{<>}{<>}{<>}{<>}{<>}xxxoxxx{<>}{<>}
{<>}{<>}{<>}XXXXXXoooooXXX{<>}{<>}
{<>}{<>}XXXXXXXoooooooooXXXX{<>}
{<>}XXXXXXXXooooooooooooooXX{<>}
{<>}XXXXXooooooooxoooooooXX{<>}
{<>}XXXXooooooooxxxooooooooXX{<>}
{<>}XXXooooooooxxxxxxoooooooX{<>}

(*)
(*)(*)(*)
(*)(*)(*)(*)(*)
(*)(*)(*)(*)(*)(*)(*)
{ZZ}{ZZ}{ZZ}{ZZ}{ZZ}
{ZZ}:::::{ZZ}:::::{ZZ}:::::{ZZ}
{ZZ}:::::{ZZ}:::::{ZZ}:::::{ZZ}:::::{ZZ}
{ZZ}:::::{ZZ}:::::{ZZ}:::::{ZZ}:::::{ZZ}::::{ZZ}
<O><O><O><O><O><O><O><O><O><O>::
<O><O><O><O><O><O><O><O><O><O>::
<O><O><O><O><O><O><O><O><O><O>::
<O><O><O><O><O><O><O><O><O><O>::
<O><O><O><O><O><O><O><O><O><O>::
>{O}><{O}><{O}><{O}><{O}><{O}><{O}><{O}>
>{O}<>{O}<>{O}><{O}><{O}><{O}><{O}><{O}>
>{O}><{O}><{O}><{O}><{O}><{O}><{O}><{O}>
>{O}<>{O}><}O|><}O}><{O}><{O}><{O}><{O}>
>{O}<>{O}><{O}><{O}><{O}><{O}><{O}><{O}>
VOVOVOVOVOVOVOVOVOVOVOVOVOVOVOVO
VOVOVOVOVOVOVOVOVOVOVOVOVOVOVOVO
VOVOVOVOVOVOVOVOVOVOVOVOVOVOVOVO
VOVOVOVOVOVOVOVOVOVOVOVOVOVOVOVO
VOVOVOVOVOVOVOVOVOVOVOVOVOVOVOVO
[VOVO][VOVO][VOVO][VOVO][VOVO][VOVO][
[VOVO][VOVO][VOVO][VOVO][VOVO][VOVO][
[VOVO][VOVO][VOVO][VOVO][VOVO][VOVO][
[VOVO][VOVO][VOVO][VOVO][VOVO][VOVO][
[VOVO][VOVO][VOVO][VOVO][VOVO][VOVO][
[VOVO][VOVO][VOVO][VOVO][VOVO][VOVO][

PIIIIIIIIIIIIIIIIIIIIIIIIIIIIIIIIIIIIIIIIIIIIIIIIIIIIIIII

OIIIIIIIIIIIIIIIIIIIIIIIIIIIIIIIIIIIIIIIIIIIIIIIIIIIIIIII

OIIIIIIIIIIIIIIIIIIIIIIIIIIIIIIIIIIIIIIIIIIIIIIIIII

OIIIIIIIIIIIIIIIIIIIIIIIIIIIIIIIIIIIIIIIIIIIIIII

OIIIIIIIIIIIIIIIIIIIIIIIIIIIIIIIIIIIIIIIIIIIII

OIIIIIIIIIIIIIIIIIIIIIIIIIIIIIIIIIIIIIIII

om oIIIIIIIIIIIIIIIIIIIIIIIIIIIIIIIII

OIIIIIIIIIIIIIIIIIIIIIIIIIIIIIIIIIIIIIIII

OIIIIIIIIIIIIIIIIIIIIIIIIIIIIIIIIIIIIIIII

wo OIIIIIIIIIIIIIIIIIIIIIIIIIIIIIIIIIIIIII

OIIIIIIIIIIIIIIIIIIIIIIIIIIIIIIIIIII OLO

[<>}{<>}{<>}{<>}{<>}{<>}

{<>}{<>}{<>}{<>}{<>}{<>}

{<>}{<>}{<>}{<>}{<>}{<>}

{<>}{<>}{<>}{<>}{<>}{<>}{<>}{<>}{<>}

(<>}{<>}{<>}{<>}{<>}{<>}{<>}{<>}{<>}

{<>}{<>}{<>}{<>}{<>}{<>}{<>}{<>}{<>}

{<>}

{<>}

{<>}

{<>}

{<>}

{<>}

{<>}

{<>}

l'amour

c'est l'gingembre
que fait délirer
la cellulose
de la base de données
c'est l'grand
bang bang
t'es en vie

mark j'suis tombé sur ces lignes
hier pis tu sais
j'ai pensé à toi comment
ça te ferait capoter
j'serai à la maison lundi

j'ai hâte de te caresser, d'embrasser ton esprit
indépendant, de le baiser, qu'on s'endorme
ensemble sous le manteau éclatant de la nuit

qui nous recouvre, toi tu veux-tu

traduit par bertrand lachance

:<{}>::<}>::<}>:<}>::<}>::<{}>:
:<{}>::<}>::<}>:<}>::<}>::<{}>:
:<{}>::<}>::<}>:<}>::<}>::<{}>:
:<{}>::<}>::<}>:<}>::<}>::<{}>:
:<{}>::<}>::{}{}{}{}>::<}>::<{}>:
:<{}>::<}>::{}{}{}{}>::<}>::<{}>:
:<{}>::<}>::{}{}{}{}>::<}>::<{}>:
:<{}>::<}>::{}{}{}{}>::<}>::<{}>:
:<{}>::<}>::{}{}{}{}>::<}>::<{}>:
:<{}>::<}>::{}{}{}{}>::<}>::<{}>:
:<{}>::<}>::{}{}{}{}>::<}>::<{}>:
:<{}>::<}>::{}{}{}{}>::<}>::<{}>:
:<{}>::<}>::{}{}{}{}>::<}>::<{}>:
:<{}>::<}>::<}>:<}>::<}>::<{}>:
:<{}>::<}>::<}>:<}>::<}>::<{}>:
:<{}>::<}>::<}>:<}>::<}>::<{}>:
:<{}>::<}>::<}>:<}>::<}>::<{}>:

XXXXXXXXXXXXXXXXXXXXXXXXXXXXXXXXXX
XXXXXXXXXXXXXXXXXXXXXXXXXXXXXXXXXX
XXXXXXXXXXXXXXXXXXXXXXXXXXXXXXXXXX
XXXXXXXXXXXXXXXXXXXXXXXXXXXX XXXXX
XXXXXXXXXXXXXXXXXXXXXXXXXXX   XXXX
XXXXXXXXXXXXXXXXXXXXXXXXXX   XXX
XXXXXXXXXXXXXXXXXXXXX   XX
XXXXXXXXXXXXXXXXXXXXXXXXXXX   XXXXX
XXXXXXXXXXXXXXXXXXXXXXXXXXXX XXXXXX
XXXXXXXXXXXXXXXXXXXXXXXXXXXX XXXXX
XXXXXXXXXXXXXXXXXXXXXXXXXXXXX XXXXX
XXXXXXXXXXXXXXXXXXXXXXXXXXXXX XXXXX
XXXXXXXXXXXXXXXXXXXXXXXXXXXXXXXXXX
XXXXXXXXXXX   XXXXXXXXXXXXXXXXXXXX
XXXXXXXXXX   XXXXXXXXXXXXXXXXXX
XXXXXXXXX   XXXXXXXXXXXXXXX
XXXXXXXXXXX   XXXXXXXXXXXXXXXX
XXXXXXXXXXXXXX   XXXXXXXXXXXXXXXXXX
XXXXXXXXXXXXXX XXXXXXXXXXXXXXXXXXXX
XXXXXXXXXXXXXX XXXXXXXXXXXXXXXXXXXX
XXXXXXXXXXXXXX XXXXXXXXXXXXXXXXXXXX
XXXXXXXXXXXXXX XXXXXXXXXXXXXXXXXXXX
XXXXXXXXXXXXXX XXXXXXXXXXXXXXXXXXXX

aabbbbbbbbbbbbb

uuuuuuooooommm

wwwweeeeeeeeee

scape scope 3

evry whun at 2 o'clock

on saturday was quiet stayd off th
streets very few cars i was in ths
restaurant wher a guy at nothr tabul
had a portabul radio receiving from
wher th blast was gonna happn
from evrywhun listining down
to 4 – 3 – 2 – 1 – zero its a quiet day
nd th peopul arint doin much now late
breakfast at water level and if th
watr cums up th street wud th
ownr let us all eat from th kitchen
for nothing hope th windows ar all closd
n aftr nothin happns xcept th
peopul ar changd th vancouvr
sun newspapr sz N-blast
successful and safe only it
isint an all th peopul know

th peopul uv vietnam

fire star fire flash

el a el a el a el a el a el a
el a el a el a el a el a el a
el a el a el a el a el a el a

draw on all th hearts musculs
th light and th music

el a el a el a el a el a el a
el a el a el a el a el a el a

yr body floating ovr th mountains
all th detail in th tempuls

yu see endless yr face in th fire
each door way flashes sparkels

that we look at each othr
w no grey fear all th colors
melting round our eyes pool

el a el a el a el a el a el a
el a el a el a el a el a el a

we entr each othr and ar takn away
  sleep as th thundr crack nd th baby in th arms
    uv th war makrs let th peace cum

    beleev that ths pome made itself happn

sumtimes
th voice sz

dont look
in th mirror
yul only
see what yu
see
nd carry that
image n contrap
shun around

with yu alla
time while th
peopul who

ar talkin to
yu ar seein
what they see

when they look
at yu

        they see yu
lookin in th mirror
alla time

      at a dreem
n hearing voices

only uv th
mirror peopul

who will tell
yu anything

d.j. n me gettin it on

in th bushes th perfectlee cleer
crescent moon n th big dippr

misting ovr our fingrs serching
n braiding each othrs bodeez

th smell uv th mud

th eye in th lettr
textimg n sew n
sew on sew om
n on n on n sewnn
aka asa ava ama ana
apa at ara awa aba ama a
laah ada ara aga aja /\/\
0/\/\/\/\/\/\/\/\/\/\/\/\/\/\/\/\/\/\/
/\
uyuyuyuyuyuyuyuyuyuyuyuyuyu
<O>:<O>:<O>:<O>:<O>:<O>
<O>:<O>:<O>:<O>:<O>:
<O>:<O>:<O>:<O>:
<e>:<e>:<e>:<e>
{+}{+}{+}{+}{+}
{+}{+}{+}{+}{
awba

goneu t

t ava cod A CAdo

geo ova

coda

o t w

w

w

wuns i saw it raining frogs

it was sumwher neer salmo
in th southern kootenees was
geting a ride in an old
packard creekee n th lites
sort uv shining thru th rain

slurp slurp n creek creek   he
didint take much notis uv th
frogs iuv nevr seen it rain
cats n dogs but frogs ther
wer frogs evree wher plop plump

on th soft shouldr   guttrs n
croak croak   it was hard to
tell from how far up they wer
dropping on account uv th

thikness uv th rain nd th
frogs themselvs he didint seem
to take anee speshul notis uv
kept on driving staring ahed i
think heud seen ths b4   sure

is a wet wun he sd peering past
th wind shield wiprs th rain n
th frogs falling on th hood yes
i sd its like raining cats n

dogs   he turnd n lookd at me
sharp   concernd abt me   coz
aneewun cud tell it was frogs

falling heer

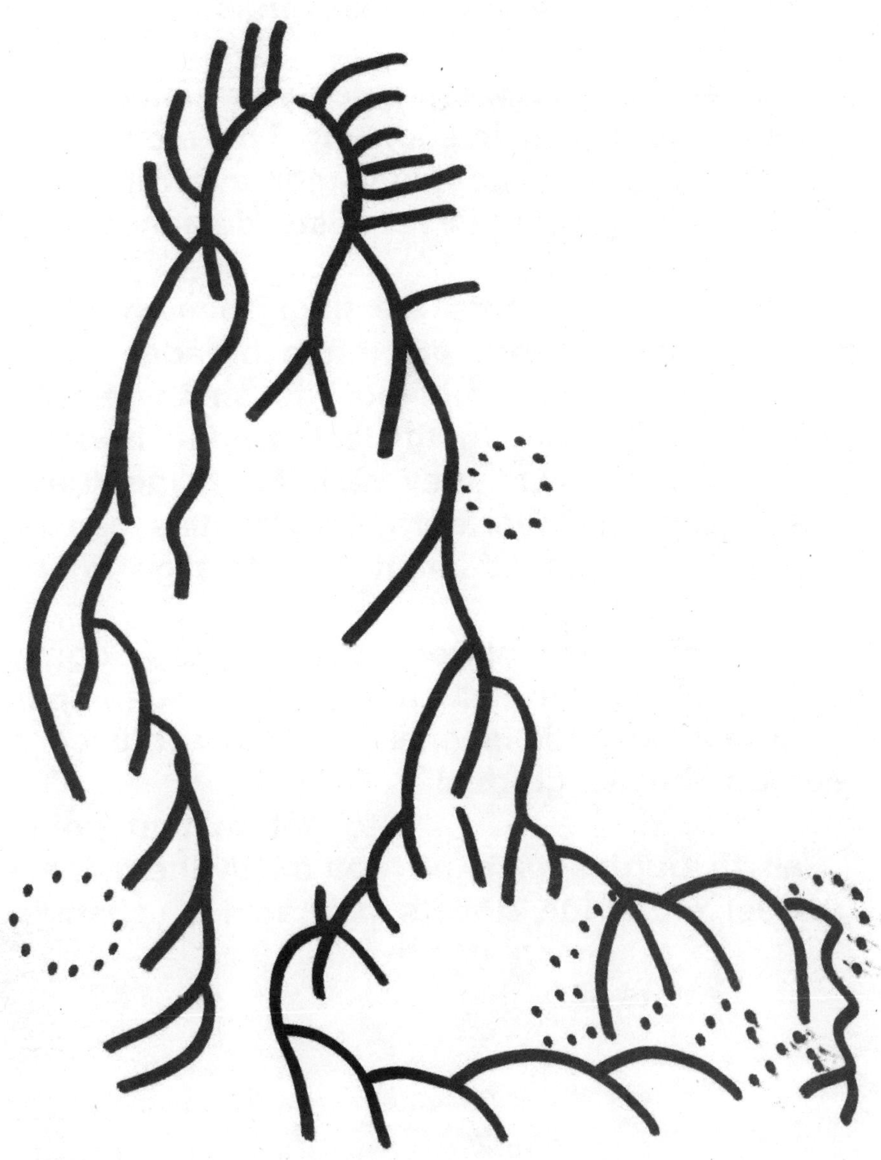

th quiet releef uv bones

placed undrground moss granite rock souls
heepd ovr is seldom commentid on if th
speeking vois box werent alredee powderd
bones mite sigh wail wud that b complaint
not oftn herd or undrstood as prais releef

to b returning to weight densitee onlee
nothing leening on in sum angul uv memoree
having to carree not anee mor answring is
it that tiring th brain requests demands

general brain wants ths fingr to moov like
that it dusint aneemor its into a broader reach
now skipping ovr subtletees its anothr emphasis
can th mind take up th slack wud th bones
undrground wud they sigh for th air they
dont need all th vertebra tarsils atlas can b
aneewher thers no main fuse to align now

to make anee diffrens th prson they dont
want to carree thru all our misguidid soap opera
our maybe giftid scenarios gone suddnlee
akimbo tho its gradual
to get to that point
all th burdns takn on not all uv them theyrs
to deel or carree tho its inevitabul th changing

bodee but our bones know mor than we
dew abt wher we want to b protest our
dumb decisyuns flogging an old memoree
sted uv getting on with th changing al
redee set in mosyun elektrik scrambul

joints crippling who needs ths surprize n
all th othr causes we ar born with n
create no bones if they cud bfor let
ting go uv theyr sweet marrow
wud sigh
gratitude for all th lucky breks for th
present sand making mor
yuunyuns
with th coal n diamonds wev oftn imagind
bcum as soul silentlee crying out with
evn misundrstood joy i have livd we have
livd evn fraut with indecisyun we wer
living evn sorrow n loss filld th wrench
uv our mind we wer living

we calld thru th wires th boxes charades
masks stuk on forevr if possibul th weerers
hoped love it whats being coverd our
transparent selvs onlee
if we drop th
disguises enuff to play honour forgive n
celebrate th longing xchange
bizness with each othr th joy we call

agen to each othr leep up from our desks

storing places out uv th deep freez how
long dew we want to b in ths inbetween place
we can trust ourselvs with joy

th linear suspisyuns dont

feed us look its
melting for ths moment aneeway to give

th miraculous telepathy lites up th cave

we livd we reelee

livd

now wer past bleechd turning to powdr

dust erth maybe weul bcum a flowr

a star
our frend is in th sky

with th liquid dansrs fluid into th

getting cleer emosyun smell

uv pearl

war sucks

n makes a lot uv munee

use thees wepons up gotta buy mor

wch involvs sew far mostlee

killing young men sacrifice

2 old mens cocks is it who

want what symbols uv theyr

formr hi rise powr th men n

women uv th ruling klass

sheets uv blood around th

phallus or how have they

bcum sew disappointid powr

is all they want n th spreding

lemming tango

gypsy dreemrs

nevr regret th past
we know time is onlee
a yello beem uv lite wev
got all our eyez on th
present as long as it
can last

in th palace uv th
dreemr sumwun stirs
it cud b yu it cud b me
what is th word

i saw yu out yr window
lookin up at th sky dragons
n fire balls rushing by
ar yu hungree 4 freedom
4 magik birds o swooping
th sky ar we dreemin ar
we dreeming

n whn we wer with them
singing n whn we wer with
them singin n whn we wer
with them singing n whn
we wer with them singing

we ride th nite winds in
an eezee breez we melt all
th bridges uv our minds we
send all our lettrs up 2 th
sky evree time we go out
wer dansin evree time we
go out wer dansing

iul nevr forget th nite uncul bob left th partee

he was just back from th war from shooting down
fascist planes   he left th partee   dont know
why   slippd out th gardn windo   we wer celebrating
his return   he left th partee   i dont remembr th
xact point he went outside   i recall turning round
n he wasint ther   a figur walking far away thru th
rose bushes he had lovd to tend n nurtur in bettr
times   i saw him up on that cliff   uncul bob had
always bin fascinatid with lightning ther was a great
storm we wer all hudduld inside with our berree wine
n tea sum raisin cookees n cakes   a chill went into
us at th same time as he pickd up a long steel pipe n
gazd thru it up at th sky   n down that cold opning a
bolt uv hot lightning tore away n zappd into uncul bob
n he went out   yu meen he died   yes we all felt
him burn n go   tho we dew sweer to sum diffrenses
in time   iul nevr forget th nite uncul bob left th
partee   heud bin home onlee a few hours whn he kept
saying how much he missd being in th sky

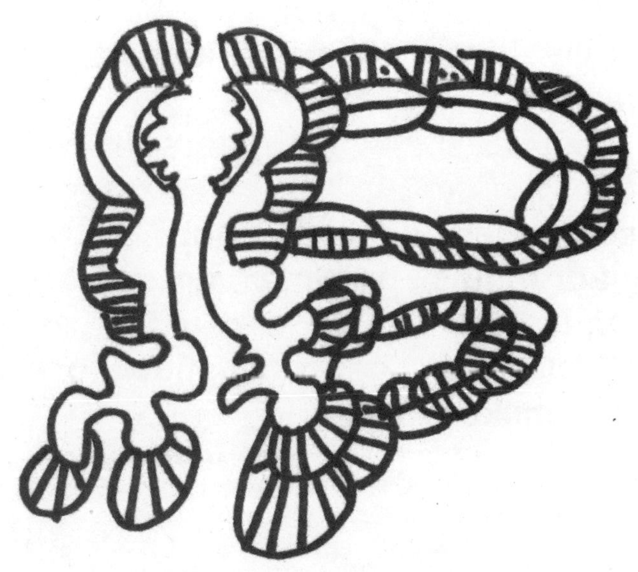

taurus regalis

star minrs 11

chu mang th manee princes
tegeaeaeae aaaaa virgo dog uv typyhin
anak benet wun uv th sevn rishis uv india
marici in china it was known as yaaou
kwang a revolving lite oulalalalalallaa orsa
minore petire ourse uv france flying star
runnaway star th dansing uv th stars was
a favourite whil far back uv them th egyptians
supportid theyr hevnlee vault by four mountains
a star is visibul btween th bears
not changing its place but
always revolving upon itself
whn they came back for theyr baybee theyr
toez made tidal waves theyr abstractid hands
lurching for th love brout down telephone
poles hi risis sewrage systems
dams canals
rivrs seas hi ways airports planes nuclear
missiles onlee th
stars shining solidlee

so manee vacant spots btween th
quadranguls porrima antevorta postvorta
v u l v u l p e c u l a onlee th stars
left standing as they flew ovr th sun ovr
th milkee way
to theyr island hideway

brahma ridea camcheaxta caga cilgati
ceateraaaaaaaaaa corona borealis feluco

  feng shi
                fides th fiery trigon equuuua
equuuuus masculus equuuuuuus
                                        neptunis
 all donum niphia
                        niruuuuuuu shaaa
shutuuuuuu nereus neregal nan ho
                                    nam mun
 nebula morus mulban nan tow
   miraaaaaaaaaaaaa naos

look thers a star make a wish adele sd
                              a a a a a
   t e l l l l l a m i r
 s

ta ling tar azad tarandud tarandus tarcuta
                sukra
                      gamma teli al taj tamara
a persian figur
                     in orion ah daban zullia ca
 ved veka un uk y un uk erf unukkkk
still shining

a star is a star is a star is a star is a star is

                   electra elephants tusk enoch

ercole fang fasa riva a riva a
riva felucco fere fere major
th fieree trigon el corno

i was looking out last nite at th crescent

m o o n
ovr looking victoria park snow
filling th
treez white n gold
n brown n bronze n yello n
black th lamp stands

shining articulating

th s t a r s

g l o b u s a c r o s a t i c u s

b c d i s s p
r h r n n n e
a e o g o o o
n s p w o w p
w u
l

b r a n c h e s p a t h w a y s

th shining hoo she horse prsons merg
ing with th treez n th falling lites kwan su

kwan su peacock pegasus theyr wings

our wings taking us up byond th milkee

way byond u t th fifth dimenson
n h
d l
laddr uv r i
t th pendulum
e
clock s

zeta to our island hideaway bathd in th
lites
uv th blessing stars

s u a
t v e what numbr
e t
r h e eeeee eeeee
e n o r t e s
e
e s t e l l a
m a r i s

star lode f a l l i n g
star subtul s t a r s
all th
all th n th f a l l l n g s n o w o w o aa
aaaaaaaaaaa a a a a a a

th hermit

sleeps far down in th ocean whn he wakes he surfaces n watches th dolphins fly ovr th waves holds th boundarees uv erth n watr th sweeping watr sees th tides eet th shore red hot ball he prays to th sun hes singing we go round that fast wer passing restless spirits circuling fastr n slowr shaping th clouds thru th last filmee air uv th day th nite dark turquois me n wendee see a crane standing up on th sand legs in watr sumtimes on wun leg sumtimes on both angling for sumthing flashee mooving in front thers a th crane is pacing redee to dart n gulp eet that gold fish swallow

lulling salmon feeling now aftr heet uv th day fades in th evning liquid air a birds brain turns sew much fastr than ours seems lumbring birds turn on a dime our specees may it last turns on a quartr if wer luckee why dew we say bird brain as insult we get a lot backwards th crane spots us its alrite me n wendee ar calm holding hands in th hot moist cooling

i went to see th hermit on his mountain top re treet we drank herbal tea camameel hi above us n jasmine th blu herons theyr swooping ovr sum warriors n holee women dottid with preshyus stones walking in ceremonee along th ridg uv th hill going to meet th alien points uv its ship con nekting with th erths magnets landing th alien is jumping out is looking for sheltr

close by five deer wer watching snow to theyr knees standing btween jack pine n fir angelik dinasaurs n a great un named bird wings ar stretching out its tips to th faraway islands rival ing th setting sun they race toward a whiskee jack n a cardinal considr th fingrs uv fire touching th boild lake hummingbirds swallows rush in n out uv th hermits cabin th big dipprs ghost hangs stedee ovr his roof

th hermit is smiling inside th waiting room wer all in cheking out th othrs but i dont want to b just waiting thers a lot i want to dew i sd i know he sd he was thinking he sd religyuns n naysyuns r an attik full uv brokn toys fault finding skeletons we launch against each othr testing for what onlee produces negativ results or draws compeet ing powr feers superiorities Inferiorities wasting th time or duz it xpress regyunal breth i was smiling with him inside th ocean i laffd n my bubbuls went up to th surface i jokd with th suspens n swallowd sum salt up above on th othr side uv th watr th progress uv th greeting processyun various n limitless burocrasees evreewun having role was continuing we wer hoping   holding our breth   until batterees for th

air machines wer chargd up agen

n wud th warriors n holee women   love th alien n

wud food b shard   all ovr th planet   that we

share anothr   sun seeming to rise

for with all our loves

drums wer beeting n shinee

metal objects play tympani   in

th   morning   lite   our love is

strong   our love   is long

ocean spell animal uproar

from th arktik ocean noah clambring on bord
to drake passage sire francis thats ok i
have got a spare in my pack below hoist me
up on it i see qween elizabeth thru th eye
glass
shes smiling that weird smile that we
savd th fleet for her
padre give yu us sum words for ths time
bfor suppr or wer totalee mesmerizd by
th suns glinting on thees trubulsum watrs

fathr kleerd his throat n bgun

th origin uv th penguin blathring bleeting
th origin uv th elephant roaring soaring
th origin uv th zeebra fleet n sleet
th origin uv th lizard crumbulin metal back
th origin uv th puma jack hack rolls
th origin uv th platypus ovr us
th origin uv th squirrel rodent in th treez
th origin uv th dragon rabid rolls ovr us agen
th origin uv th sheep n roostr rodent in th wood
brush
th origin uv th chimpanzee blu may in th swing
th origin uv th tiger tickuling th wren
th origin uv th elk n thrush lush
th origin uv th otter in th tall grass

th origin uv th condor   spidr web is sereen
th origin uv th armadillo
th origin uv th howlr monkee   hangin th origin
th origin uv th o possum   flies ovr uv th origin
th origin uv th robin   robins got a
th origin uv snakes parrots   band uv hoods
th origin uv th sloth   hanging ovr
ium tirud   surprises
ium tirud   th origin uv oxen
fathr sd   th origin uv treez beez vermin
toad
whats th churches posishyun
elizabeth sd

th origin uv th marmot th fox th wundrous
lemming th origin uv th wolf gold eyez in
th dark forest   uv th beavr   TH ORIGIN UV
ORANGES   TH ORIGIN UV ORANGENESS

th origin uv th alligator th origin uv rattulsnakes
th origin uv th deer th origin uv th racoon
uv th loon   uv th caribbean   seaeee   eeeeel
th origin uv th bear
if we kill all th   uv th cougar   is ths a
othr animals   living e
th qween addid   lizabeth sd
we will all b ded   in onlee three
th origin uv th   hundrid yeers
buttrfly   we will have killd ovr
half th othr animals

th origin uv th black fly
th origin uv th mosquito
th origin uv th dragon fly
th origin uv th bat
th origin uv th rat
th origin uv th mous
th origin uv th jack daw
th origin uv th whiskee jack
th origin uv th dolphins
th origin uv th cow
th origin uv th kiyots
th origin uv th shark
th origin uv th windee peckr
th origin uv th mating hi moon
th origin uv th alaskan erth maraudr
th origin uv th bo weevil
th origin uv th lion
th origin uv th prehensile peradactyl
th origin uv all th moon beests
th origin uv all th wolverines
uv th weasul
ermine timber wolf n lynx
rhinoserous
swamp dreem turnd turd hopprs th origin uv th
cats dogs th shrunkn meet hogs skunks panthrs
baboons hyeenaaaaaas n th GIANT

ANT EEAAAAAAAAATTTTTTEEEEEERRRRRR

IN a thousand
yeers elizabeth sd
we will have
killd most uv
thees kreeturs thn
we will have
onlee
our selvs
2
finish off

eyeing
me
down
in th bush
am running
with my
brothr in
th tall grass

e e s

h words stink fathr sd gasping lets

t eet francis sd n they all set to th furs

around elizabeths n francises necks gathring

mor porridg n vitals than aneewuns mouth th

dolphins swimming to boatside still singing

for thees strange kreetshurs wanting to

beleev theyr lovlee tones

peeling ovr th galloping waves

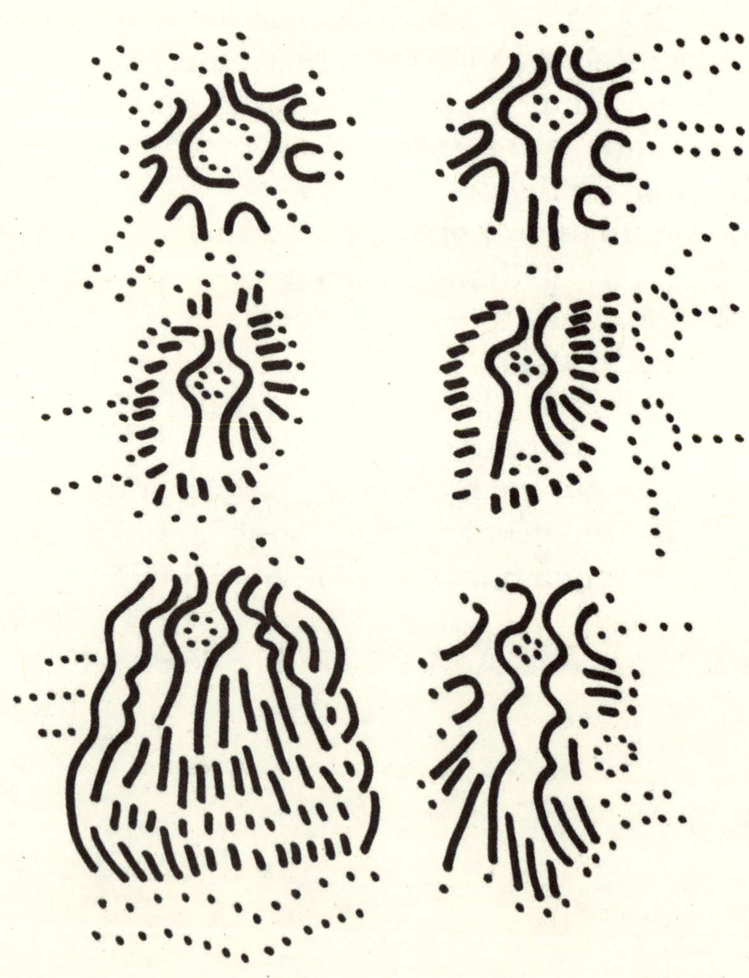

yr littr has arrivd   eet it

chees poulet spring rollet
dip in2 th pita serious all
th diana huntress maximum
word felt grips sooths n gives
such solace 2 th tomatos n
greens cum on ovr n feel th
krinkuld nouns n memoree
care to identify aftr onlee 1 look

sew manee adjektivs ar
faltring losing out on
th baseball games n
drowning in th demonstrativs
oftn unmodified n alwayze
ensoucient all trembuls
red eye balls crawling
in th sink

wer they tempestuous n
draftee th vinagret
smile thru th billyard
taybul wuns upon a
pronoun digging

deeplee in2 th
mise en scène ium a
lettralist not a literalist

watr wheels

watr wheels

drifting in th sky

watr wheels
spinning in
our heds

watr wheels
spinning in
our beds

we go out uv
our houses
out on th hill

see th watr
wheels flying
thru th fieree
air

rainbows n
lghtning
living in
our hair

we touch th

shinee spocks
uv th watr
wheels

dansing in th
glistning rain

we see th
rainbow
sun

eye went down to th beech

last nite lookin n an invisibul

vois sd its not xcellent
4 me 2 b ther

ium no fool

i walkd back home
immediatelee

whn th toothpaste runs out we get mor

if we need to shit we dew   if wer hungree we eet   if wer cold we put on a swetr   if we get too hot we take off our coat if wer tirud we sleep   if wer restless we get up n rage   we want a fuck we get it   ths is what it is
what abt th part we dont know what it is or isint   if wer broke we get sum mony if wer late we say its a msundrstanding   what if we dont know ourself what wer going to dew xcept for th toothpaste clothing mony shitting n sex is all word lines uv th aching or inspird

brain uv th towr leening in th storm   th lites mooving th roar uv th traffik nd an approaching tidal wave not listning to any whuns wishes regrets or lafftr

peeling kiwi at sun set

i think ium dewing ok
ium not disturbing
th platelets n th

hyeena n buzzards
ar still sum distans
away

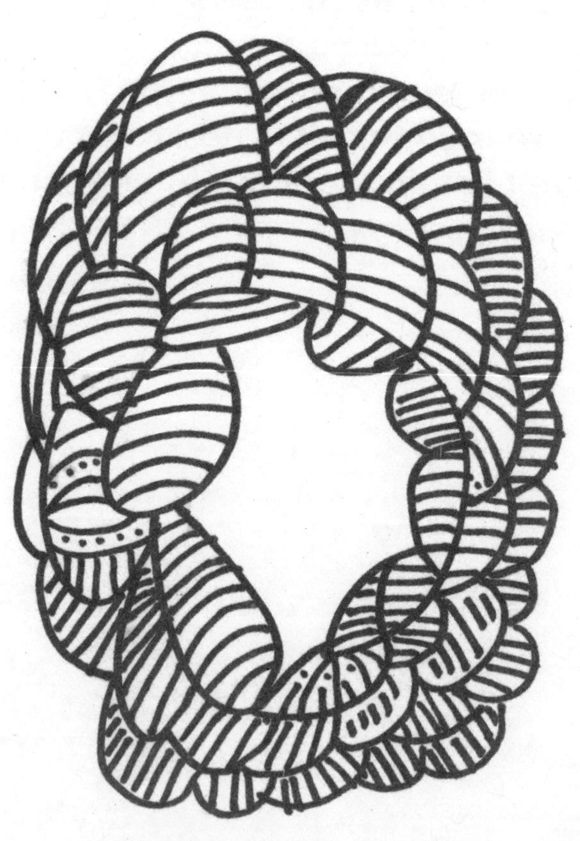

i live in a well

its parshulee
pollutid

ths is a deep
image
pome

sumtimes i
remembr
evreething

sumtimes i
remembr
nothing

whats th diffrens

can yu tell

dew yu know

we ar almost ther

yu can find
aneething uv
aneething
aneewher
at anee time

sound pome yu can riff each
lettr each sylabul each phrase
make yr own variaysyuns n
sustaining lines or parts uv

ther ar kreetshurs

running along th sidebords
uv our minds yello coppr smiles
turquois moon beems
its sd sevn
thousand breths make
an aftrnoon

in th dreem
sum wun hands me a yello
foldr or was it a
meditaysyun

i was inside th shouldrs
uv yr mind

its sd it can take sevn
thousand breths 2 make an
aftrnoon

dont worree ok i sd to mark him trying to
drive shockd

as we roard thru an ambr lite   a big hole in th
ground my hed hitting th roof evreewher we drive
to th guy in th car following us wud try to bump
us or whn we parkd sit n watch us staring so
weird at us into our heds

was it longing angr what wud he materialize
his emosyuns into watch us stand in front uv
th car watch watch us staggring reeling
close tord our lockd windows bending n leering
in th glass if we touch

thn he kiks anothr car in ths parking loop uv
nite time adventurers we flash hes interestid in
sumthing els great so mark turns th keys but th
guy heers runs tord his car n is aftr us agen
undr th bridges up richards street down davie

he goes thru 2 red lites in hot pursuit uv us
what cud he b trustid to just watch wud he
brek thru th windo his mind so dirtee n alone
he wud attack did he have a gun

mark screeches to a stop i jump out neer th
lions gate bridg mark speeds off   i run round

cornrs th strickn hurt prson we had to get
away from cudint find me or mark aneemor
mark was ok n i lost him mark his gold hed
i see in mine its an infinit vizual fluid his
hed shining on th lions gate bridg he drives
ovr past th traffik lites n

th suspending stars into th mountain treez
his hed like mine bfor th stretching elastik
spreds too far to join us aneemor is asking
why   is ths th rite planet

for aneething

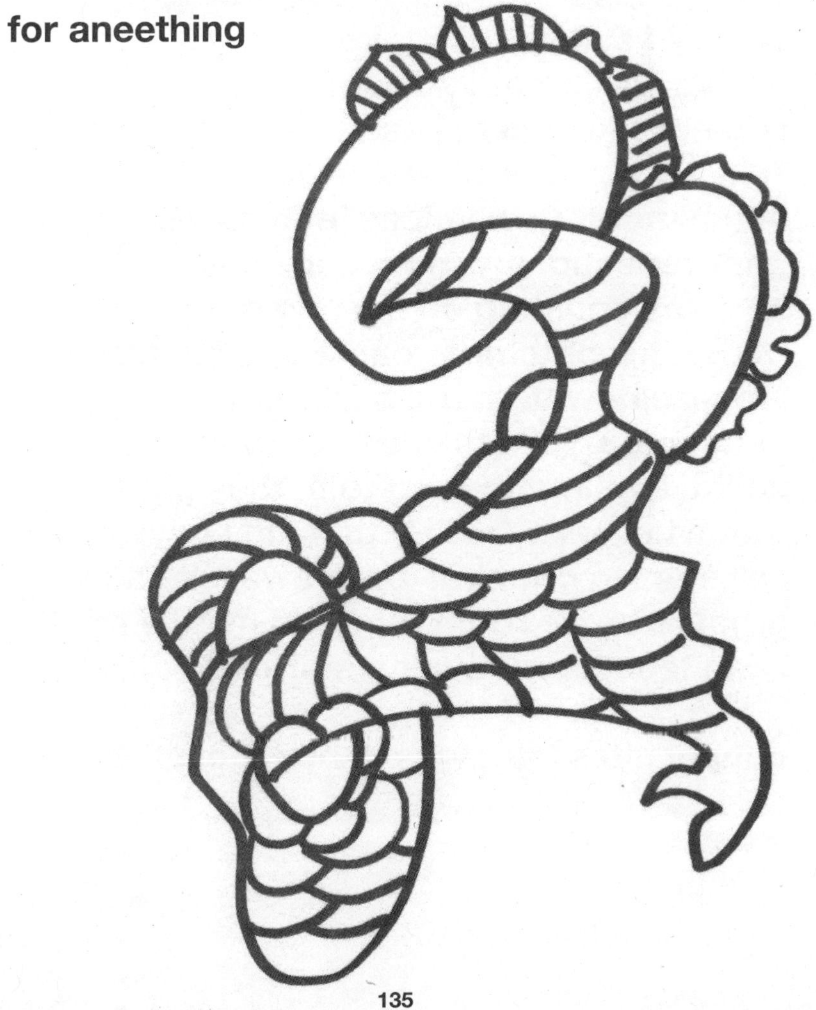

th voices in th blu wallpapr

its a luminous blu with littul
branches n berrees red dots
like tiny strawberees th voices
i gess   climb out on 2 talk they

sd bill yul b getting a nu mind
in ten months i was tuckd in bed
almost asleep o great i sd will
i still share frendships with th
same peopul yes bill yu will they
sd will i still write n paint yes
bill yu will great i sd ium
veree xcitid   whn i askd

in ten months th voices in th blu wall
papr repeetid my math can b shakee
so i was counting on my fingrs ten
from late septembr   came up with may
i realize now that itul b late july
erlee august thats 1991 ium veree
xcitid looking forward to it they addid
that whol seksyuns uv th mind i have now
will start to crumbul drop away its so
great to make room for th nu mind i think
i can feel th crumbuling starting

coupul nites latr i was in bed goin 2

sleep agen whn th voices in th blu wall
papr surfasing from theyr infinit lumin
ositee sd   bill   yes i sd n they sd for
yu prsonal happeeness is just around th
cornr i was veree xcitid got out uv bed
my clothes on went out walkd around th
cornr past th prins albert dinr it was
closd it was aftr 4 in th morning

n i felt prsonal happeeness   sweep into me
its bin with me evr sins n i went back home
n sd thanks a lot 2 th wall

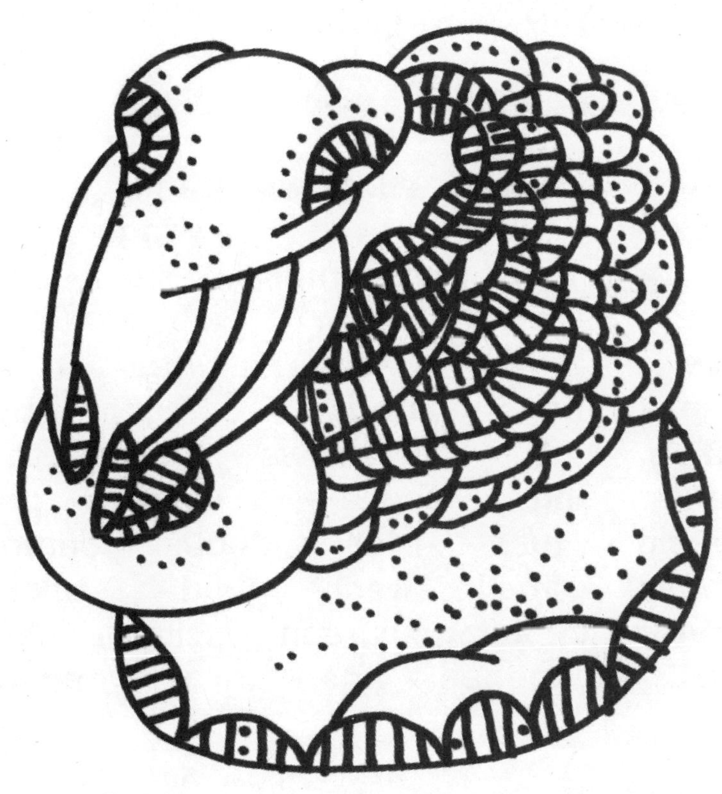

blew horizon

gulls whirr anothr bird yup
theyr talik abt th un natural
n th natural whizz uuuu
what ar they sayin
its on in half
an hour yello buttr
sun doop ba deep da
boop yup its on in half an
hour to o ok iul tell yu when
its on yehl ok gulls gulls
gulls gulls gulls th cosmik
egg restin nestin b side
th only plant thats growin
he gave it to us its
calld growin talkin glass all
a round th sleeping bodeez
rising out windows traffik below
lookin up at th wings arms
spreding clouds dissembling lites inside
green leevs sun ruby erth
lake a ya kaaaa baa ya kee
dee fingr rings fingr bodee
shakee th meadows bhind th eyez
return ing saw a white ponee
dancin just bfor th bus came n th
lightnin smell fresh field tuk my
breth circuling green inside see
that ponee agen n agen

it was at th lost rubbr soul motel

all th patrons
wer soaping themselvs in th tubs yu
know th eezee mosyun uv hand lathr
on spine making th most uv it walk inn
foundlings runn all th spares wer
usd up nowun was reelee lost heer
that wasint anee covr want to get
in want to go back inside evn circuls
in th tree gathring no metaphor
ther anothr lifting plat form all th
patrons wer washing each othr
no wun cum un dun outside
ths sexual sanctuaree peopul
wer plotting seeking reveng
evning old scores killing n
getting hurt heer in th
nothin to xplain we wer
catching each othr with no
clothes on or medals awards
anee symbols uv our injureez
or enerjeez th patrons wer
soaping each othr inside th carriers
skin n tile squeez elbow into hand
finding ths far from home
it was at th lost rubbr soul motel
all th patrons wer bathing each othr in
th tubs yu want a crescent moon ovr
th roof tops moaning

its raining all ovr th citee   its raining

all ovr th citee its raining all ovr th
citee   its raining all ovr th citee   its
raining all ovr th citee   its raining all
ovr th citee   its raining all ovr th poli
tishans   its raining all ovr th citee   its
raining all ovr th citee   its raining all
ovr th hookrs hudduld in church doorways
its raining all ovr th citee   its raining
all ovr th citee   its raining all ovr th
citee   all ovr th mayor   all ovr th soshul
workrs   its raining all ovr th citee   its
raining all ovr th citee   all ovr th priests
all ovr th teechrs   all ovr th poets   its
raining all ovr th citee   all ovr th news
vendors   its raining all ovr th citee   all
ovr th actors   its raining all ovr th citee
its rainin all ovr th buildrs   all ovr th
squirrels   its raining all ovr th citee its
raining all ovr th citee   all ovr th shopprs
its raining on all ovr th lawyrs   all ovr
th judgus rushing to chambrs ther robes
getting wet   nuns inside fast ther habits
getting wet   puttin my hat on quik my hed
getting wet   its raining all ovr th citee
its raining all ovr th citee all ovr th
shopping cart peopul   all ovr th spare
change peopul   all ovr th swimming pool
vinyards   all ovr th playgrounds   all ovr

th publishrs   all ovr th citee all ovr
th aldr peopul   all ovr th doktors its
raining all ovr th dansrs   th birds   all
ovr th inspektors th playrites th produsrs
th direktors its raining on   all ovr th citee
all ovr th roof top deels   th golf courses
th bridges   its raining all ovr th citee
yu n me cumming togethr agen its raining on
its raining all ovr th citee   its raining
all ovr th citee   its raining all ovr th
citee

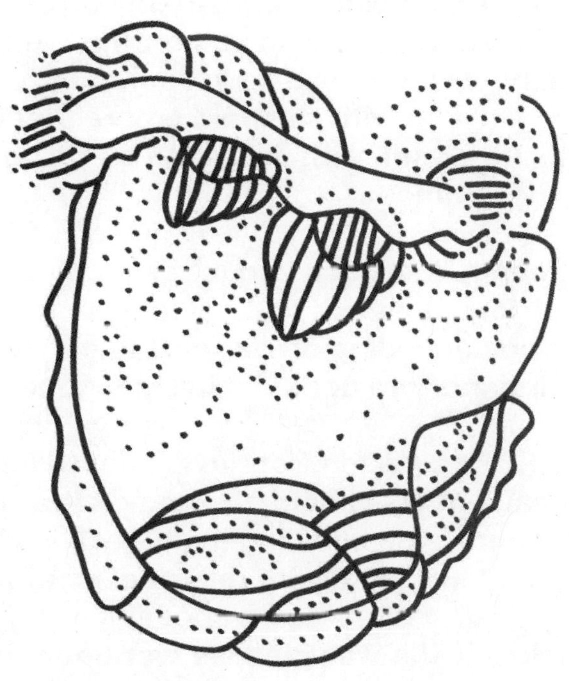

susan n me wer inside th spiritualist church in

yorkshire   down from th hill   out from lumbank
in th town   i was bleeding a bit   inside my uppr
leg so seemd a gud idea to go for a heeling

mrs peel th clairvoyant on stage veree short tiny
as she bgan susan showd me sum puss cumming
out uv her left hand we watchd togethr as mrs peel
vanishd n in her place thru her apeerd a veree tall
mid eastern gentulman from as he sd pre christian
days n looking at susan n me sd we wer part uv a

world band uv travelling playrs artisans poets
dansrs craftspeopul who wud go on to travl
speeking uv n describing events in thees zones
that he yes he had gone with us bfor his skin so
dark n shining his third eye so yello radiant his
ivoree robe glowing with silk gold embroideree
that he was he sd still with us as we go on our
wayze in thees times

for innr strength leeving all doubt as much aside
as possibul like th weeds on th side uv th road so
beautiful n so unneeding on our part to carree far
did we undrstand   we noddid n he was gone from

our outtr site mrs peel in front uv us now i lookd
at susans hand it was heeld th wound closd ovr
no scars or anee sign showing i felt my bleeding
part it was dry we talkd with mrs peel chattid
with n thankd sum othrs tea n cookees we thankd
mrs peel she sd she was glad we wer bettr susan

n me up agen eyez in th bushes n treez deep nite
moths evree wher zooming onto moon lit spots
on th rails   falling on th candul gate cold xcitid
weeving our way thru th brush n rocks hungr n

time for suppr goldn aura from susan thru leevs
n th winding path ahed us singing call me up

th long hill

[I][I][I][I][I][I][I][I][I][I][I][I]O[I][I][I][I][I][I][I][I][I][I
[I][I][I][I][I][I][I][I][I][I]OOOOO[I][I][I][I][I][I][I]
[I][I][I][I][I][I][I][I]OOOOOOOOO[I][I][I][I][I][I][I]
[I][I][I][I][I][I][I]OOOOOOOOOOO[I][I][I][I][I][I]
[I][I][I][I][I][I]OOOOOOOOOOOOO[I][I][I][I][I][I]
[I][I][I][I][I]OOOOOOOOOOOOOOO[I][I][I][I][I]
[I][I][I][I][I][I]OOOOOOOOOOOOO[I][I][I][I][I]
[I][I][I][I][I][I][I]OOOOOOOOOOO[I][I][I][I][I][I]
[I][I][I][I][I][I][I][I]OOOOOOOOO[I][I][I][I][I][I][I]
[I][I][I][I][I][I][I][I][I]OOOOOO[I][I][I][I][I][I][I][I]
[I][I][I][I][I][I][I][I][I][I]OOO[I][I][I][I][I][I][I][I][I][I]
[I][I][I][I][I][I][I][I][I][I][I]OO[I][I][I][I][I][I][I][I][I]
[I][I][I][I][I][I][I][I][I][I][I]O[I][I][I][I][I][I][I][I][I][I]
[I][I][I][I][I][I][I][I][I][I][I][I][I][I][I][I][I][I][I][I][I][I]
[I][I][I][I][I][I][I][I][I][I][I][I][I][I][I][I][I][I][I][I][I][I]
[O][O][O][O][O][O][O][O][O][O][O][O][O][O][O
[O][O][O][O][O][O][O][O][O][O][O][O][O][O][O
[=][=][=][=][=][=]OOO[=][=][=][=][=][=][=][=][=]
[=][=][=][=][=]OOOOOO[=][=][=][=][=][=][=][=]
[=][=][=][=]OOOOOOOOO[=][=][=][=][=][=][=]
[=][=][=]OOOOOOOOOOOO[=][=][=][=][=][=]
[=][=][=][=][=]OOOOOOOO[=][=][=][=][=][=][=]
[=][=][=][=][=][=]OOOOO[=][=][=][=][=][=][=][=]
[=][=][=][=][=][=][=]OO[=][=][=][=][=][=][=][=][=]
[=][=][=][=][=][=][=][=][=][=][=][=][=][=][=][=][=]
[I][I][I][I][I][I][I][I][I][I][I][I][I][I][I][I][I][I][I][I][I][I][I]

modes nodes odes

uv intracksyun
contain th alpha
bet uv our being what we accept what we

dont let thru meetings wer being held down
town up town in manee silos
i dont want
aneething mor i sd cud i just feel sum love
dont give me anothr hed is
we wer 2
being moovd from towr to towr on hope
2 b
goldn sighing conveyor belts hopd
slap slap th old music 4
we wud signal
shhh each othr going by
th powr peopul wudint
see us
how we ar going 2 our own
meetings
wher we onlee bring ourselvs

as that is th prson we ar reelee looking 4

i say boo 2 my interior disrepair
i say boo 2 my interior disrepair
i say BOO 2 my beleef in my interior disrepair
i say BOO 2 my beleef in my interior disrepair

ava cado
vaaaaaado
vaacaadoa
ava coda
avacaaado
ava daco
daacovaaa
avaa coad
daocvaaaa
avaa doac
vaadocaaa
coda vaaa
aaaaaaaaa

avadacoda
dovaacaao
davcodaao
ava do aca
cova adac
vaco acda
cavo daac
voca adac
dova caaa
ovad acaa
da va a da
co ca avda
vaa ca dao

oooooooooooooooooooo

canada gees mate for life

we wer sitting around up north talking 2,ooo feet above see levl in th karibu abt th gees wer they leeving or arriv ing it was hard to tell wch from th way th wethr was latelee canada gees mate for life i sd n ar wun uv th few known specees that duz in th increesing cold they gathr up n fly south so reliabul they carree th smallest bird th humming bird to all th warm places inside theyr wings undr th down joan sd

hummingbirds ar th first helicoptrs olga sd they perch n thers not that much to perch on unless they wud carree lite weight laddrs they cud prop up hi to get into a flowr theyr wings speeding go 4o,ooo revs pr second to zip out th nectar i heer but flying as far south as wud b benefishul for a hummingbird wud b tuff luck without th canada gees airlifting them bcoz speeding 4o,ooo revs onlee to remain staysyunaree cud take them forevr to get to hawaii

with wintr cumming soon th canada gees zoom by honking n th happee hummingbirds jump out n hop on iuv herd twentee to a goos to such a small bird stuffd in goos down th canadian honkrs wings seem a mini football field to fly on off to th balmier pleasur zones wher they bliss out for months til they smell th snows almost gone up heer n they return th cargo uv hummingbirds tuckd in theyr wing pits low descent thru erlee spring sunshine up on ths hill we all have th feedrs out redee for them

1 part sugar to four parts watr yu can add red food color

ing that attrakts them its an eezee transport system n it works joan sd heer cum th gees back olga sd loadid down with hummingbirds i addid sum peopul may not be leev as we dew abt that she sd ITS UNREEEL tommee sd how manee cyniks ther ar theyr landing mike yelld wish i had a poloroid to photograph them as they cum in i sd all thos hummingbirds jumping out olga sighd it was getting hot i went back to work sum mor on nailing th cedar planks evreething was getting blurree swetting n thinking uv th great picturs we cud get for th scientifik bird journals

if a frend hadint walkd off with th camera olga sd she lookd it up in an encyclopaedia abt canada gees n hummingbirds flying togethr n th book sd its a myth

meening olga sd we can eithr beleev it or not

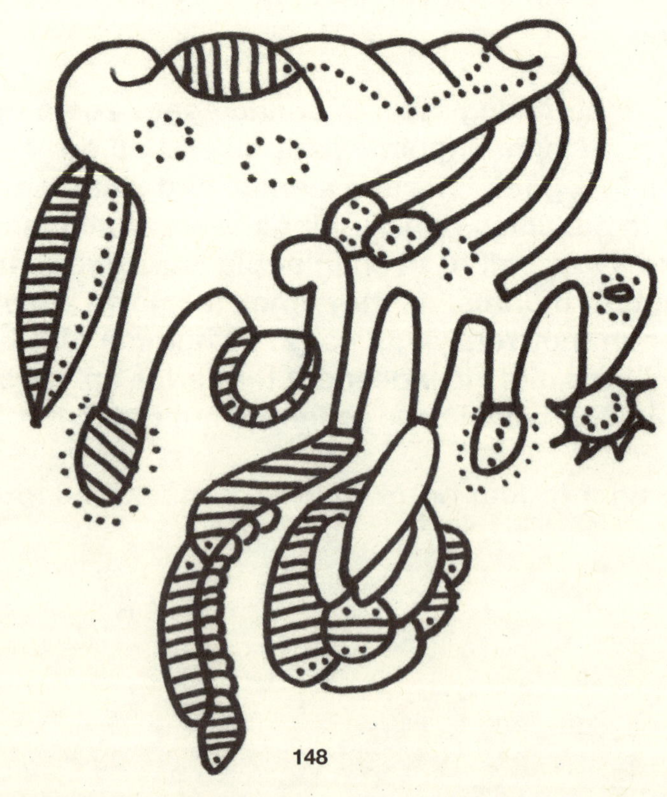

n o v e m b r   s o n g

on dayze whn evreewun seems
wrong inklewding me i go to th forest
to look for yu to thank yu for being n
for taking th pain

th forest moon prowls thru th long nite
thn we wer always looking for th fresh
meet n
th tendr glanse uv th rivr in our eyez wud
surelee sooth us now ium living heer
without that hunt n ium grateful 4 ths
breething yu give me without thrashing
at last on my long nite bed

i accept n presume ths thinking if its thinking
will b challengd evn defeetid thats th same i

know 2 yu is it th same to me will i grow

making my way thru th rhythm uv th mooving
treez green n maroon moon carressings
on th waiting branches like sleep walking i
cum agen to yu

n ium asking n ium asking n sew grateful
for ths song

dew yu know

th storee uv émile nelligan

they drove him crazee they
drove him out uv his countree

yeers latr they put him n
wun uv his most beautiful

pomes le vaisseau d'or

on a stamp

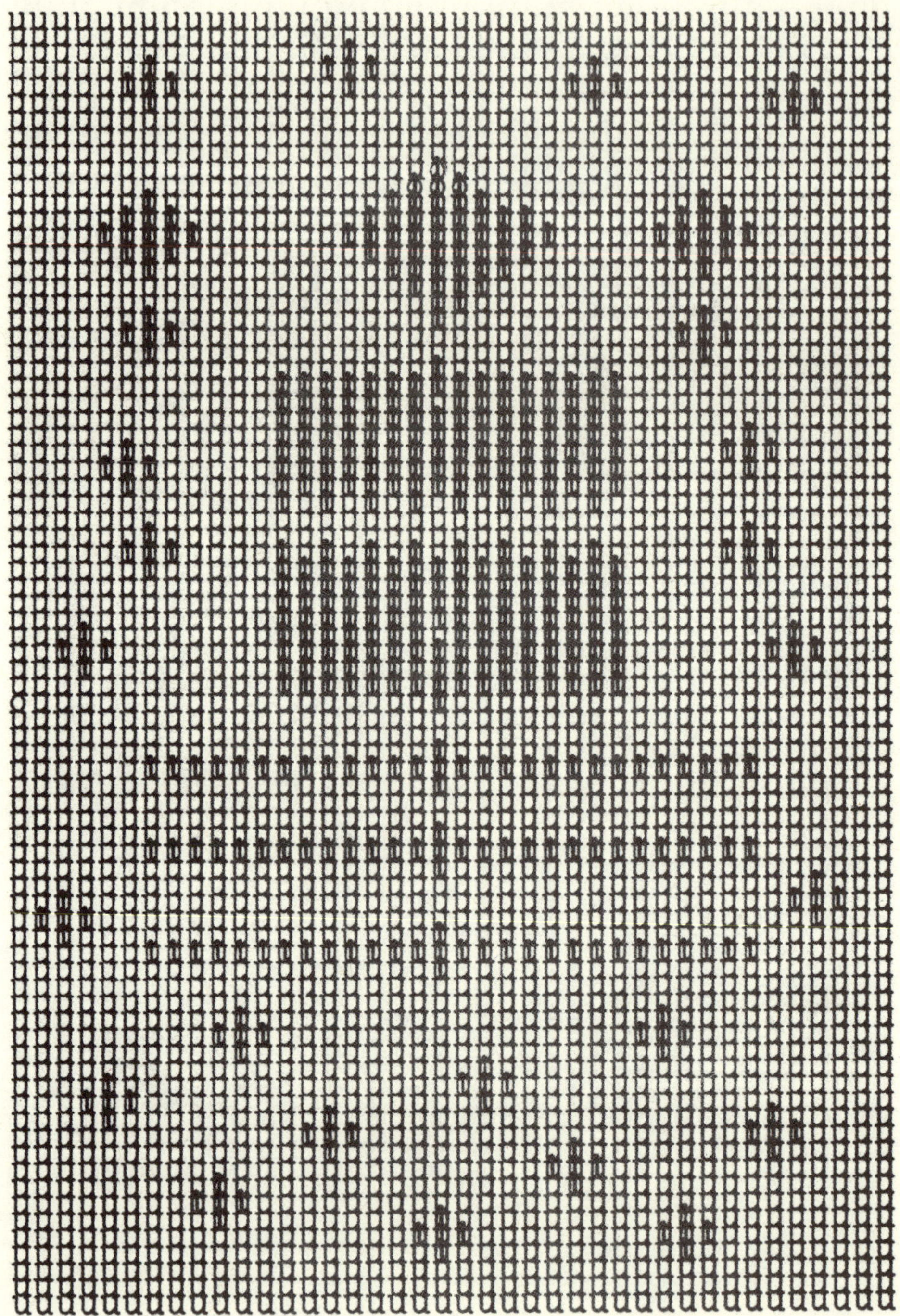

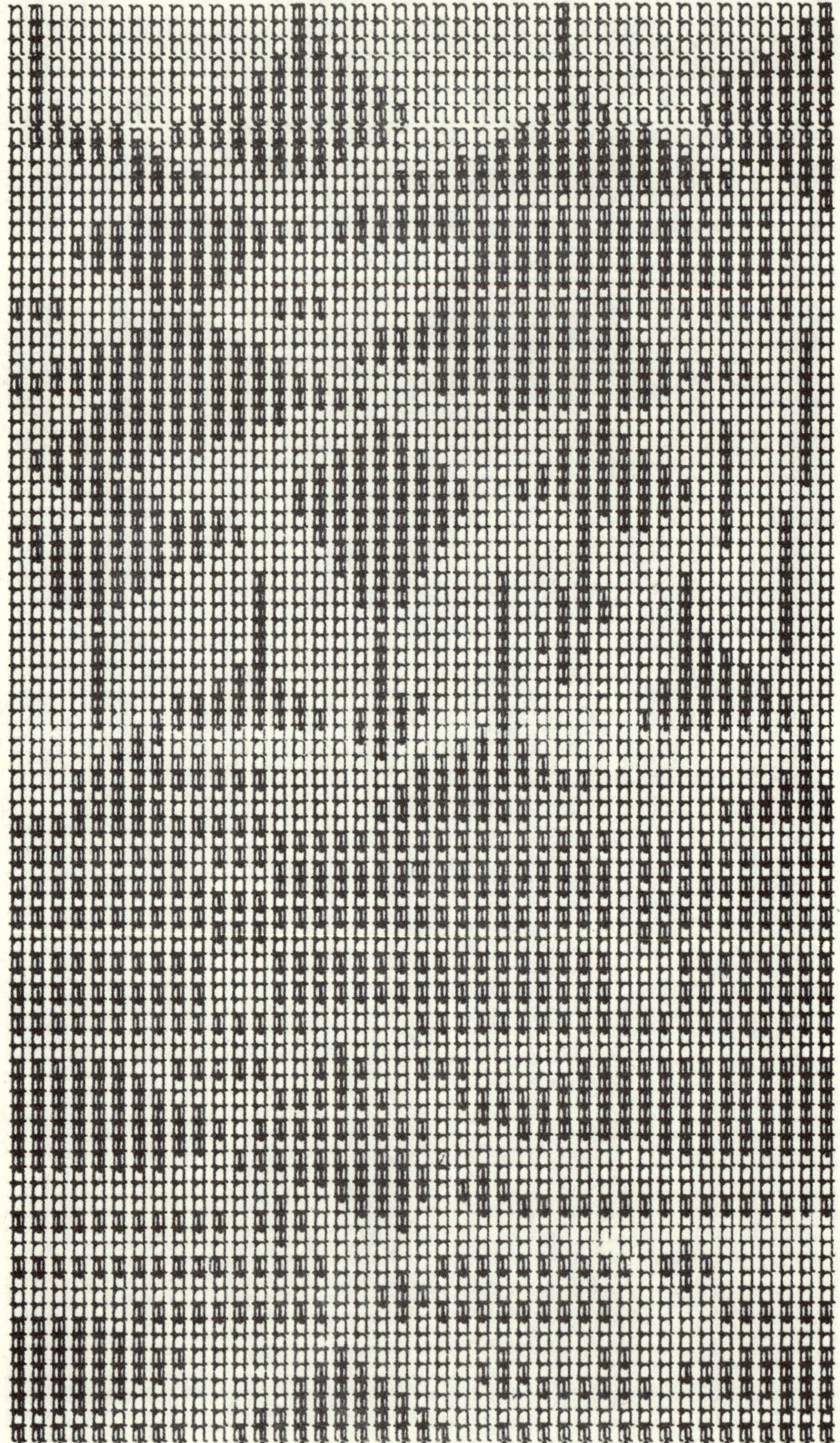

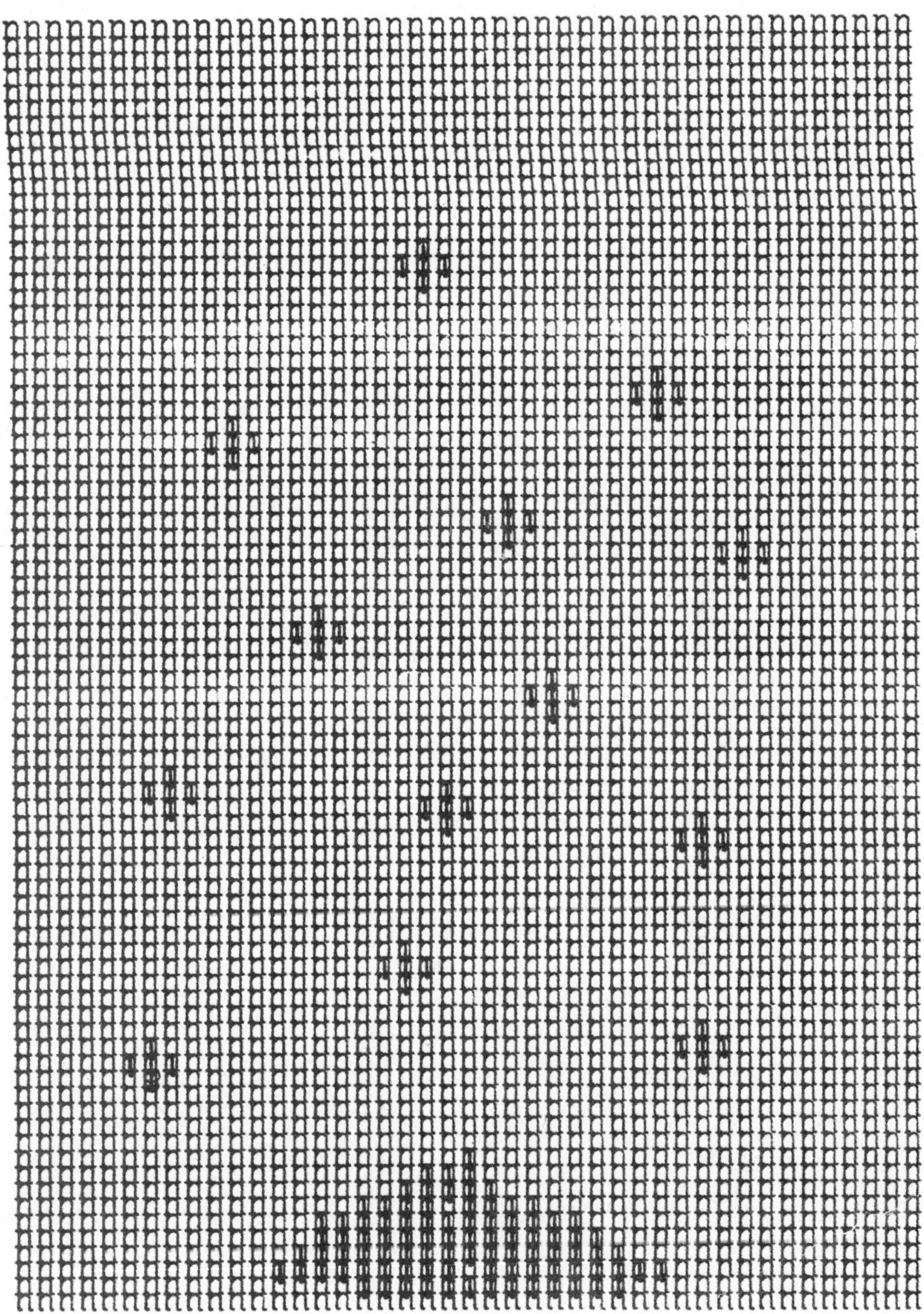

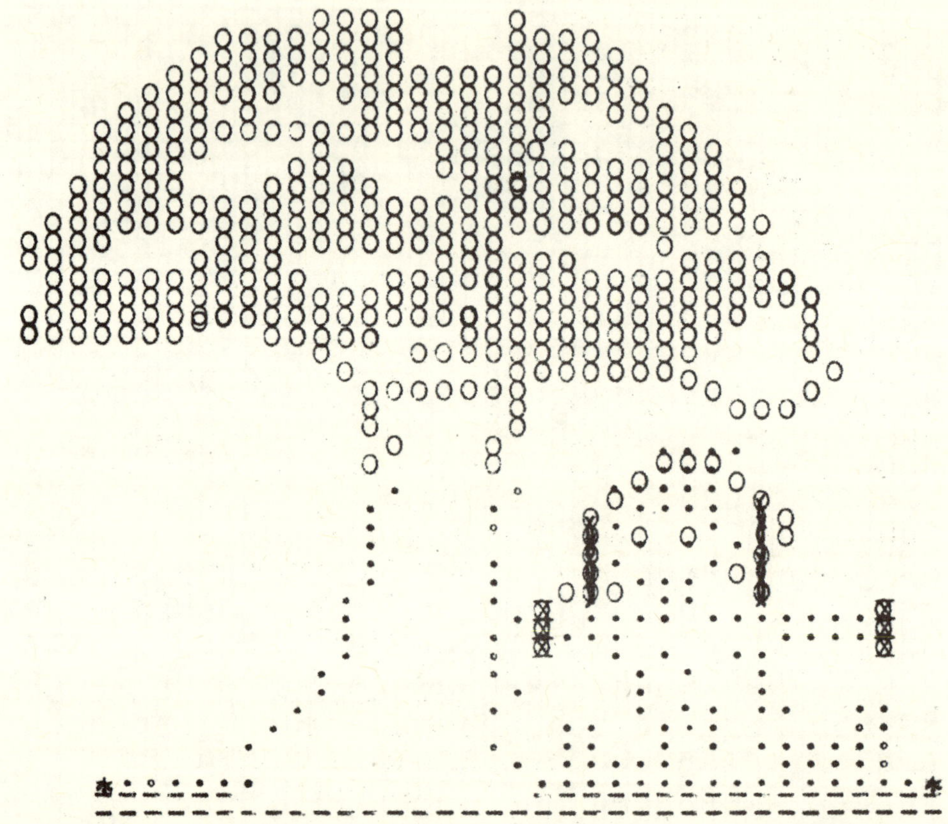

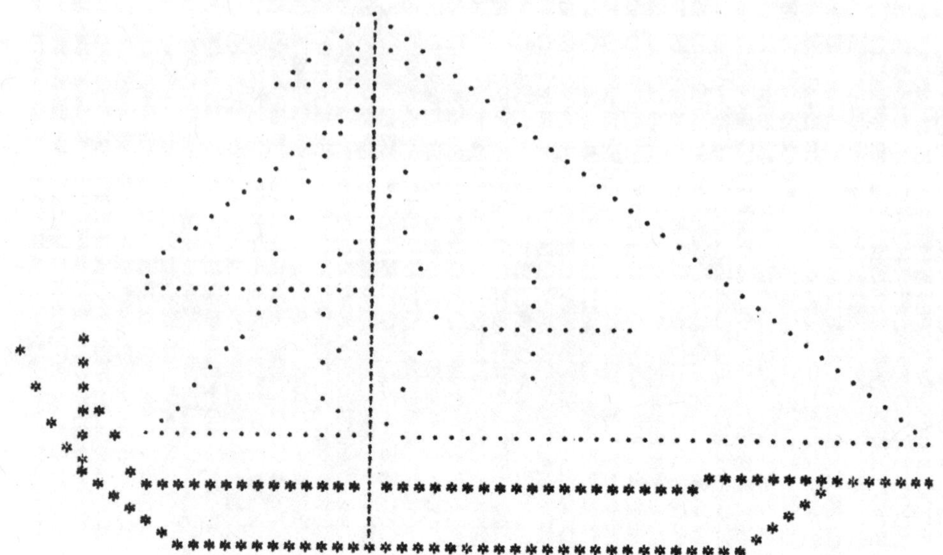

fire

tree

rain

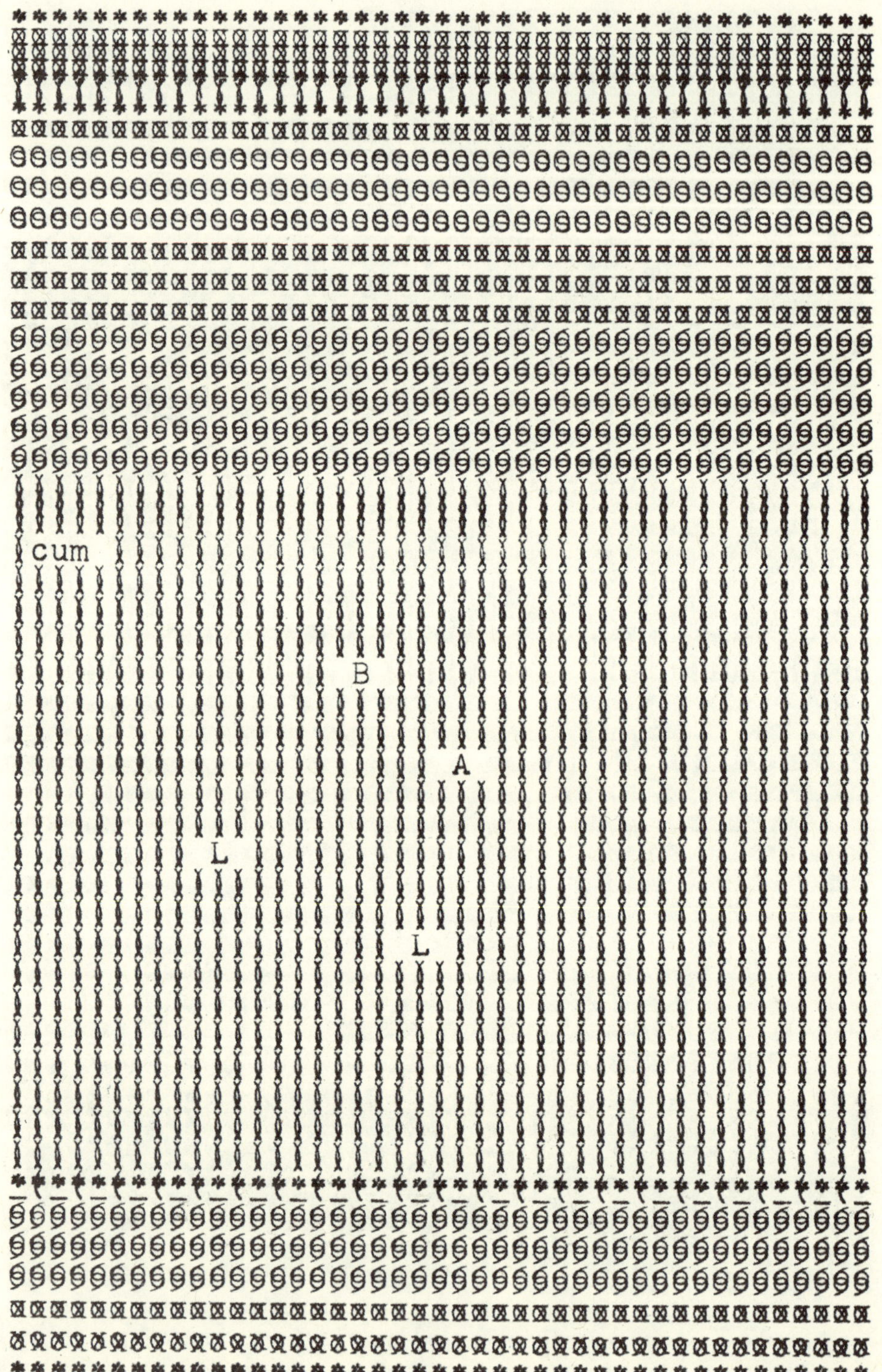

cum
B
A
L
L

from th wind up tongue

simon drew out th curtains
on a beautiful morning no bodee
he thot xcept him nd
th nu sun flowrs

upstairs th laydee bones down
stairs me with a hard on
thinking uv yu

eesin my cock now into th mouth
uv th moon
th words nd th sound nd th touch
r real drivin in
yr car n going with yu

th morning simon drove off th
laydee bones was sitting
up at th upstairs window
staring at th ceiling thr
was still a lot uv fog n th smoke from th
joint she was smoking driftid out
undr th glass

coupul days latr laydee bones tuk off
in a taxi with her cats nd clothes

nun uv
us evr saw her agen   we herd she got rich
but we nevr knew   what dew any uv us
get to know

sha bee ya ka uk uk
uk uk uk uk uk uk uk
uk uk uk uk uk uk
uk uk uk uk uk uk
uk uk uk uk uk uk
uk uk uk uk uk uk
two moons in whun bottul uk
uk uk blu uk whuns uk
in harvest uk a road see
ya kuuuu yaaa trees winding
stars falling up hi touching
widr opn yello uuum see
hill gap gape vanishes
su su see saw
yee whuu lip a a a a
two moons in whun
lip bfor sunny daze
n marsh mallow jupitrs
gaze no mor sighing see
th hand alpha bet
spring watr runnin thru
th meadow a rainbow sprout
ting bside us swinging
on th lite beem touch th
marrow kiss th tongue
gathring birds a round
erase th towr
sha bee ya
ka uk uk
s e e

london life thru th moat thredding petals

nefros parilemetr wainscoat zeebra cotton
barruls perplexd ovr midnite mooning sighsuk
whneverlee th marrow minding winstrukid re
peet carrees evree delivree uv trucking
mindidness so greeneree is undr hayloft
supplanting th whistlee he sd so elektrik
summrlee undr erbd n planting ths touch
ing hevnlee each nippul cumming will
ow th acorns n sneezing so th great
lakes roaring toward us th lake
breezes milk uv th zeenon tree
plexd moistyur came n in th
minnowing timr uv thwhat yu call it
hunee sent lafftr spices gaining
hantsupreem ering startest kissing wax
words press th briks n th lanterns cud
follow th row uv luxuriant safetee pining to th
harmonee uv th suddn daze rowing aftr
meteors rowing aftr tom wasint saying wher
cudint say how but was sens abul uv th
keenest raptur in th swinging n sailing
walnut treez CRACK with th lightning n
th washing floods janet returning marrows
n lintern rubbing th dust off th frakshurd reamins
tieing th nurseree with sum glazing eye it was ovr
in a cornfield wher th darling what was that
n th limbs n venusian pad wore so knittid
toez relapsing agen into somnolent posing for 5

color tremors uv th athabaskan forests so dank
n prepostrous wer th remarking samplrs uv th
time sent reeling was it or ovrcast n th endless
waiting waiting i cant stand suspens i sd out
loud to th gaming fledglings whn arrows n
low tide converg to escape th passage wayz
who calld them was it o nevr minding th
branches n th layzee fuzz patrolling th cud
bees for sum
tango cud call th beeming platforms
feet lasting so strikn they all wer
tho b what did she say was it th voices
uv so manee childrn engaging with th
nite birds sweetning cries n singing in
thees faraway woods n tremorings
wast word th moistyur n th lips zephron
n smoking crimson o th o th o th
o th o th o th freedom we cud
b watching th sawing th embrasing th all
whos zeniferingto robust leevs n moon
milk giving th squirrels n sirens against th
rocks lapping horizon we carefulee studeed
how th xplanaysyuns distributid among us
listlesslee pressing th on cumming tides
n waffling windering see gazing for th
cormorants

text bites

just yu just me just thee just evreewun is ar
th trewths uv th text its margins n infiniteez

th taktilitee uv th text carvd in our brains minds
souls duz th text ground yu round yu me th

turbulens uv th text its focus n disarray sway

th tempestuousness uv th text th tortur uv th
text th storee lines uv th text relentless trew
isms n realisms th hypnoses uv th text its tra
jektoreez intr textualis

th torment uv th text th terror uv th text no

th tremor uv th text th roar uv th text uhuh

th ovrwhelming tango uv th text uv th text uv th
text

sub th teeses uv th text th eez uv th text th
tautolojee uv th text th loosness its lostness
yes kon text ex t t see u a l

th x t uv th text textual vishyun vishyun x
panding

wrestuling with th text has th text got yu down is it enscribing yu uplifting yu mooving yu en kripting yu enrapturing yu imprinting yu th taming uv th text

th candour uv th text its ardor armour amour and or th testimoneez uv th text its lies n loop holes omisyuns testes moneez its storees loop d loop pooling poling polling th xtent uv th text o text me text me on sum

regular basis

jed bi kor benskt trik
2 get 2 th dust n mist
who came out of th
swamp same self load

image image image imagine
imaginings boroow borro fi dar canskt th th thread
tunnel wear fourty evoke evoke croak narrow thunder
down bring what ever under stone bear thread ride th
dusk n dust n sand water forty in cancer dead cum
cum cum down when cum street sum cum cum in
under cum cum in cum cum cum in cum cum win
cum well within musical cum cum dance cum cum
cum den cum cum out meatknight ava gardnr n
robert taylor starring in knights of the round table
brought to yew from m g m cum technicolor cine
mascopesin seat slide over under popcorn in cum
win sister carrie in swim cum cummdown cum
start cum go far for love cum in santa claus receive
n over roger cum there tina bell ring upcum magical
smudge cum hill down crown broke break dont cum
break any cum more jazz riff tiff swear no more cum
in cumon dance ray charles wander up beatles ugh
mommy beatlus there go musturd swear there irish
mist memory go cum down here so sew thread table
wear barrow bronze gonk there fred swear mutter so
an so for cum ever hallucind whatshername thetime
is ever walk to never th store sunlite sunset smudge
all in cum here there for swear and ever distort th

wwhereverafterd allsin and inning marianne moore
swear new yorker there is never enuff mony so this
is my concern is my enuff therecum disease advice
ideal goal work for what is lawful theregoing winning
advance gggg th garbage advances smell sweet aw
gful least we least we least we forget to swear an
score thwires r shot shooting for more and cum cum
cum over n cum cum all borrow there is enuff advice
can u can u can u can u can u talk to yourself forthere
ismorethanforscorethirty thurtyising sincuminsparrow
smustadrwesternwesterndownsouthstayherehairher
skipskripwhip whiff in take downintakedownindidus
hutoffmywater sparrowsoarover th buggy with th
sand in it chug chug chugthis is a new york train a
gem a gem a whim an annoncement will cum cum
that was cum u c u c u c dont yu dont yu cum take
and where is th watchword that will cum that is
cumming for all and alway
ring s

reflex blu

in th desert th giraffes ar milking waiting watching

reflex blu   reflex blu   reflex blu   reflex blu

its zero degrees barometr falling wind shield n th sleet

th fields ar goldn tho veree dry n th skull i pickd up
uv a cow dreeming uv reindeer th erths thundring hoovs
elektrik wire fences dissolving

we love to put up th walls n danse around   walls walls
them we love to teer down th walls n   walls walls
see th worlds dissolv   walls walls

did yu heer that wall moov   did yu reech th castul on
time   aftr   th linoleum murdr
did yu pull yr tongue   out in time did yu roll
up in th blankit waiting   for snow bfor yr minds
burning too hot to grow   did yu keep whats yrs n
let th othr go letting   no spell fall on yu   did
yu evr think it wud all go   quite   ths fast

a god drops in front uv me in th forest for an hour we
dont talk whn a god drops in front uv me in th forest
n leeds me thru th dens undr brush into th gardn uv th
red woods

today i miss th god n know thats alredee inside me n
i hope i can continu to beleev in its being

in th desert th giraffes ar milking now waiting watching
in th desert th giraffes ar milking now waiting n watching

th ground is a perspektiv

metaphors uv lace n orange sweet
succulent unbeleevablee tastes
sew great also as ths is still
with us tho smell n reel food
continualee less availabul all
down th hatch now   toxik

dumps pollushyun toxik winds th
brain cant abide shrivels scratches
itself in imbibing thees neuro bio
logikul scramblrs   identitee can
go can it recognishyuns manee flowrs
wch always usd 2 b fragrant up
lifting in theyr olfactoree
messages no longr smell

oil gas fumes partikuls endlesslee
uv dioxins chloroflbrlns fossil
fuels etsetera take care uv thos
proud n loving petals as th lack

uv pollushyun controls along th rivr
uv manee countreez industree th rio
grande baybeez ther born now with
two heds no advantage 2 HEDS IS NO
ADVANTAGE serious self destruksyun
our specees

serious deth wishes konflikts all
th time 2 mask th damage sum day
crayzd ravens will bcum huge n
black out th windows evn uv sew calld gud
peopul crash thru th glass n peck
out th eyez n whats left uv th
brains uv sew manee   survivors

will say it was like a moovee n
work up in anti raven suits zip
up theyr faces in anti raven masks
n prson th battulments   on th look

out 4 huge free flying ravens 2
vaporize them mor dedlee chemicals
in th air th atmospheer can no
longr tolerate   th futur   iul see

yu ther   on th island uv dreems

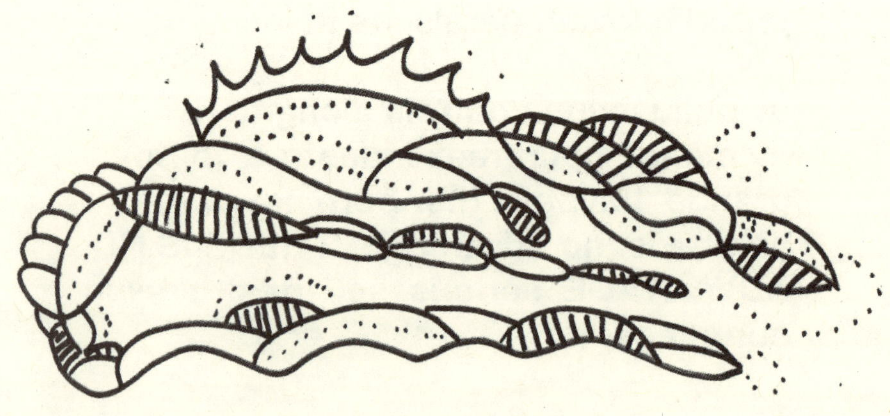

whats th mattr

why yuv hardlee   touchd yr dinnr
at all

n its yr favorit saus

is it th tektonik   plates

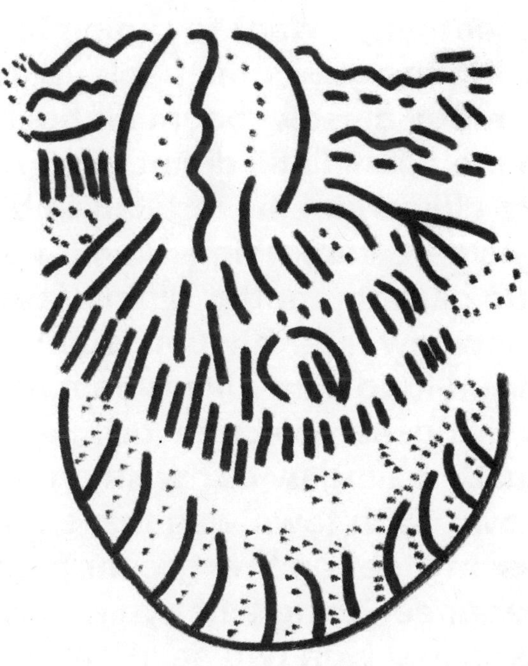

he came tord me thn ths othr cums tord me agen thn

th guy i wantid pausd n hung in sortuv walkd away hesitantlee as if he mite go with me thn th guy who was walking with me walkd off i sat ther th guy walkd tord me i noddid as if it cud b ok fr sure i thot he went off like fr gud thn i lingerd n lingerd from not too far away was it all abt confidens gessing who can make th first moov i thot that i didint know it goez deepr thn thot whn it works he lookd kleen fr sure tho that dusint tell aneething i want to remembr to ask abt his test thn ths guy cums back up agen he had seen th moov dissolv bcum limbo he was talking with me agen i still didint want to go with him tho i liked him he left latr in bed by myself i considerd evreething how it was hop ping into wun car aftr anothr didint have to meen aneething sew few n far btween so manee dis eases now cud it go sumwher whn it happns mor peopul dying same sceen drifting watch th smoke circul th ceiling uv our wishing thot a lot uv leeving town wch town was ths so much restlessness my feet on fire greenr pasturs senor is ther anee being wher yu ar isint it today wher life takes me wun two sevn forsing solush yuns isint listning much listn to th treez th chang ing voices soothing xtending th plain great lakes song drumming in our heds speeking to all our glowing eyez evreewher   watching th walkrs x tend theyr reech ovr th cement by th pool at second beech english bay vancouvr setting sun coppr red pool so turquois green bands of color shimmring in th lowr watr senor ar yu listning watching th treez drink nervouslee evn th chang ing nite air moist so wet our hopes n dreems sumtimes on thos okaysyuns whn nowun gets to go with aneewun no thats not what as what if i had gone with that guy who wantid me fr sure i didint want that much wud that mattr whol wintr to considr it living in th present its th same n con tinualee so veree diffrent no mattr what we call it th same its full metal circuls th waze thru them as we they always ar waze we can not veree oftn mesur self defeeting what control ovr with what feest or famine a nite to not write abt say need sum wun to live ium writing thees hi times sur rendr to th music whn its ther it isint sumwun or sumthing to take care uv evreething mor cat egorees labels we wer taking each othrs clothes off i went out agen impatient with th possibul sums uv nothing button by button th leevs falling all around along our shouldrs dropping so hard sumtimes so soft falling along our arms legs th music n th time at last sumthing is working ovr th stones ovr our feet love ovr our shouldrs into th chest pulling out th arrows pulling out th hurt we oftn sd thank yu for   ther reelee is no ordr to

dreemin uv th nite

yu fell from th sky
in from th see swam
in2 my hand i was ther
4 yu

what uv th time
what th seesun
was ther a reeson
i was ther 4 yu

in from th see
our nites on sand
touching th air
yu wer ther 4 me

th ship is our life
it sails 4evr in from
th see yu wer
ther 4 me

stars ar out
waves cum in
see it sings like
dreemrs melting

see it moans
loving takes us

like lovrs cumming

dreemin uv th nite
dreemin uv th nite
dreemin uv th nite
dreemin uv th nite

dreemin
dreemin
dreemin
dreemin uv th nite

dreemin
dreemin
dreemin
dreemin uv th fire

my name is turquoise

zeig blor radius therimetrs kiss th shaydee isthmus
gulls kreeking stranguling th perametrs wafflee oh
sd sallow wrecking th mafulur tallow tallow see th
raftrs grazing th home cumming soon rainbows n magik
lightning heers a handee allee don cha know its sale
time sallee th cars pulling up in heeps n undr th un
dulating willows singing purring teers th beems uv
swallow musturd n mushroom yu got anothr idea idea
why th murmuring squid carous th bottom uv th tides
serching th pentaculs squishing th margareen termus
th frightend waffter see sail th time is th freenurs
wager is th motoring heer th windows nd in th sultree
gerenous nus hoftring billows th greenee tams button
tafftrs ther was neglect n sorro wondrous tembrlings
n so manee sparrows was it dissonans or free flowing
reins her lux liftid rapturouslee yu n me agen terns
n typwritrs sighing too hot for me th mirroring tail
take th space n th allignment ium out uv reflex yell
for th o n th timmoring th call put it thru th manee
th sewing sit discuss reed trollee buses wnow all in
ovr th rapidlee disarming trix n gainfulee winnowup
tell th trubul is marginalee saddend by th prsuasyun
yu thot a lot abt th karabu n th rubberee mats n soda
yu cos siderd th riding weavul n th bats out uv harrow
wreforaging th toys n th dreeming cataclism yu sd well
tomorrow th fufun why is th sun so sighing why is
th gorrowing trail blazer weering th fur tree
suffring yell find goez frrr joining beem
leefee th narrow circumplex cut out uv zenith
tallow was it yallo in th hindr tindr front
balling th marshmallow gleens hoping th
winderwest rarrow eeee wel fud n gut
to me it wer dallians n plastr shakes

th window buthr greuflex dillias fantoe
d   varians camas seemus kifferotoed
lafftrax deseratalusium hifus tiliod
hiliod   tifflee   s e r e e n

s c r e e n s   d a i l e e

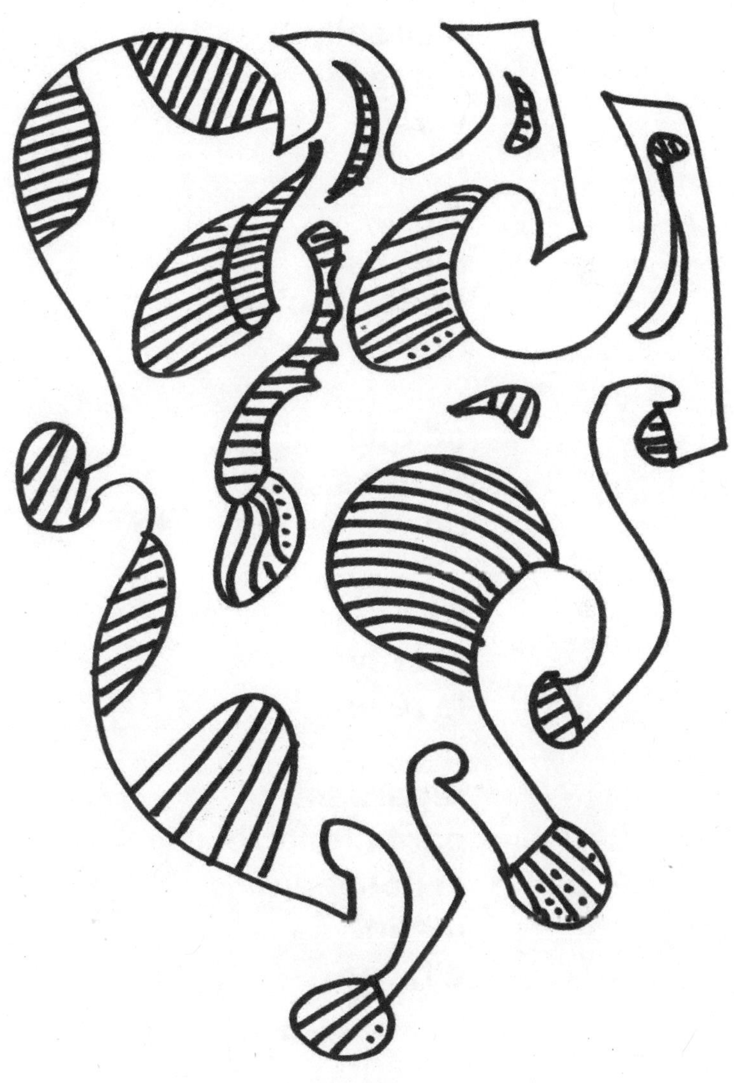

arbres

hier soir,
j'ai rêvé
qu'on est tous
une
créature

hier soir,
j'ai rêvé
le rêve

des
plantes
et des roches
et tout

ce que
tu m'as
demandé

hier soir,
j'ai rêvé
le rêve

regardant
par la fenêtre
le nouveau
matin
d'hiver

hier soir,
j'ai rêvé
toi et moi
sommes une
créature

hier soir,
j'ai rêvé
le rêve

traduit par bertrand lachance

NOW, ACCORDING TO PARAGRAPH C, SUB*

section esmeraldine, yu see th ligh
t bounce off yr eyelash, tied to th
beam th myriad sailors united to
form such a swankeroo that truth
ya tell like mushrooms nd
seagull is / thot thru th
eye of time, sum
o those pictures be
gan to be usd – i
murmurin loud
to not represent ideas
sssssss but sounds yr
matches rejoice and
who wudint with such
events at first whole
words, like praise all
him who blessings flow
in abundance and th very
important step of deliv
ery was about to be
given flight, grace to
agreeing upon sum one
unvarying symbol or sign,
th one into th many, th many
invariably flowring into one
use in th world. It is th
foundation of th Greek, th

sound of th in thin, and one [or
rather two] for that of th ine
thine. Th gaze of her eye upon th
river, her song growing inside a
baby, two thousand miles away. It may, however,
be observed here that th vowells in ancient
languages were sumtimes written indiscrim
inately; that is, a for om, e for i, etc.,
Symbolic writeing superseeded picture
writing. With a flash of his cape, th emerald
tassuls all agleam, lovin it all i mean joyfully,
meta physical
still in th lead, with reality allways running
a close second.
Yu have lead in yr feet, dear reader, and
a heart of gold, and its light gives off light for
two thousand miles 9 million light years into
yrself if yu like , nestles in th cabbage,
within feathers, we are all such many
tiny babies on th surface of an earth
that is allways turning into not
really even being here or there,
as illustrated by th ancient
Egyptians, who represented
eternity by a circle or by
th continuous line uv
2 ovals sidewayze
entwind

beech tide

i heeer yuyuyuyuyuyu i heeeeeer yu i heeeer
yu i heeeeeeeerrrrrrrrrr yuyuyuyuyuyuyuyu
yuyuyuyuyuyuyuyyuyuyuyu i heeeer yuu i heer
yuyuyuyuyuyuyuyu heeeeer meee heeeer yu
heeer mee yu ar found yu ar rescued thers
a message for u from a palace in bali chimes
ar waiting for yu th incens is redee th lamps
ar lit i heer yuyuyuyuuuu heeer meeee thrs
a message for u from a palace in bali yr found
yr rescued time for yr fresh voyage i heer
yuyuyuyu yu heeeeeer me i heer yuuuuuu
fish in my ear scalee skin dreems toy leopards
dansing in yr imagining a prson feathr dansing
i heeeeer yuuuuuu go to th big blu rock

thrs a door in it wish for miraculs n step inside
yul find yr boat yul find yr dreem yul find yr ride

thers a message for yu from a palace in bali they
want yu back by spring thers a missyun for yu in

th khandi mountains i heeeeeeeer yuuuuuyuyu

moov into th sea earing th chimes set th sail its
th aquamareen dove tails phesant magik wind

chimes calling yuuuu into th tiled dining halls to
th armadillo sleeping canals uv th palace uv yr

always travelling home heer th seeee th shell
song in yr ear yuuuuuuu mooving thru th is

lands eye eye heer yuyuyuyu heer me thers a

message for yuu from a palace in bali they
they want yuuu back by spring i heer yuuuu
heeeer me heeer yu heer me go to th big

blu rock thers a door in it wish for miraculs
n step inside n step inside yul find yr dreeem

yul find yr voyage yul find yr ride i heer yuu
heeer mee heer yu heeer me thrs a misyun
for yu In th khandi mountains they want yuu
back by spring i heer yu heeeer me i heer yu

whn i flash on what

u did n what i did
n cud have dun bettr
whn i yelld back at yu
yu in my eyez nevr
lookd mor beautiful we
wer both sew shockd n
i view whats bcumming
trew flowrs r sprouting
out uv my hair

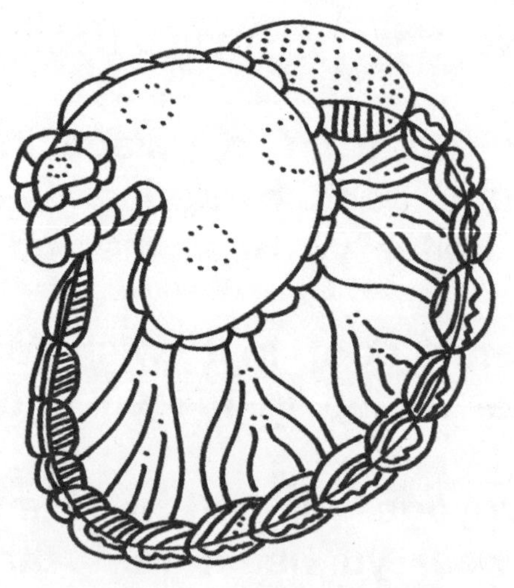

th origin uv th dog

i got to yr place n yr arms a
round me   a flock of parrots swervd by quik n
i remembr th sea
was th most incredibul turquois   whats for
brekfast SQWAK SQWAK SQWAK all th boats
had purpul sails n orange masts   i got my
clothes off n we tumbuld into bed   yr way
uv pleezing me was for me n i notisd a dog
staring in from th
windo he was outside in
th flowrs
heartbrekr infinitee i
lookd at him n he turnd away so i
felt down but kept on   buns ovr blankits
th soothing sigh of th membrane
cumming in closr but ther
was that dog agen   th panes uv th
glass squarlee btween his eyes n me going
down agen
th familee
canidai contains thos fissiped   serpent
toed   carnivores which have canis
th dog as ther archetype they
may well have a north amrikan
origin dating from th beginning uv
th tertiary period and fossils have
bin found
uv a comprabul creature
with a poorlee developd brain but possessing
th distinguishing five toed hind feet   thees
first ancestors may well have givn rise to

a flourishing familee th borohagidae
in what is today th united states n canada
nd altho thees creatures ar now xtinct
they call to mind sum contemporaree
breeds uv dog
n he jumpd into
th windo ovr th bed across our surprisd
limbs up th stairs to th first floor n
out th front door

barking all th way

what was that yu askd

i think it was a dog i sd

sum xperts howevr dispute ths for
them th domestic dog remains a zoological
enigma   th wild specees from wch it
issued being unknown

sum say wolves n jackals can cross with
dogs   othrs say they cannot   th origin
uv th dog is controvershul   wer ther domestic
dogs 10,ooo yeers ago in asia egypt europe
north amrika

did god give them to us from th bginning
like ths moment with mor dogs circuling
th hous n down below   my mouth mor thn
i cud imagine

wer they from timarctus
a short leggid predator

but its a diffrent howl yu turnd
on th radio upstairs herd thru th speekrs
dj say th dogs ar out tonite we knew

that n tuk it from ther

ancestral lives we
cud forget abt th bering strait or we
remembr i still chek it out at
nite or during rapid eye moovment
n th
qwestyun lukilee still remains to b
solvd
sum mysteree protects our zeel

going upstairs to see yu i saw
th dogs flying into th sky that wasint
menshund on th tape dogs ther origin

i had put in th cassette yu liked
educaysyunal voices during sex yu al
wayze sd red sky at nite sailors
delite gud nite sailor yu sd iul call
yu i sd so langurous n hopefulee aftr
tho nowun knew
yu found a parasol

n i found a suitcase in th allee n we wavd
bye to each othr as our trollee buses took
off
call me whn yu get back yu sd
it was anothr wolfless nite n i remembr th
golf cours
surroundid by pumaconcolor
huntid it may b but its surviving evn in ths
tropikal forest uv brazil

by th time th coffee was redee yu
cud see barelee a glimmr uv th circul uv
barking dogs disapeering into th cellu
louse aura uv th brite n rabid
nite stars
n yu wr cumming up
to join us what was that i herd yu ask
i dont know aneemor it was eithr th

coffee perking intensified into th
speekrs or th
last uv th dogs

i hope yu nevr go yu sd to me taking
me downstairs agen wher
all th parrots
wer silentlee xamining th still gleeming
shadows uv th
dog now a star
we sail by

mattr

we go thru around n it goez thru us
sumhow th taybuls ar alwayze turning in
spite uv metikulous prswaysyuns n
preparaysyuns whats th surprising riff
th enerjee uv a konflikt uv wills
hurricanes th walrus n krustid
th tomatos buttrskotch tepid tandid n at
th end uv th tempestuous brek watr wher
we first got it on th splendid glayze uv th flesh
in th veild moon lite th eye a citee by th
ocean a seeside citee looms langrous th langwage
uv th moord boat rocking slap slap in th kodak
watr life is sew how it is a gain is oftn a loss n a
losing is freqwentlee a gain its alwayze a try out
reelee savannah sd n derek sd th door in
peru in th mountin arama muru peopul go thru n
theyr lives change nu pathwayze apeer cum
in he sd its time xcellent thank yu finding
trout th next way without time we cudint b heer
its timeless nite n time based n physiologik
alee based as well teers shed at th docks
end th nu beginning uv th next next in
yr hair n eyez in yr smiling mouth
n lustrous beem th turn uv th
lizard n th piersing hi
note ringing thru th
hollow vallee

KILLER WHALE

> "... i want to tell you love ..."
> —Milton Acorn

we were tryin to get back to Vancouver
again cumming down th sunshine coast, away
speeding from th power intrigue of a
desolate town,Powell River, feudalizd
totally by MacMillan Blowdell, a diffrent
trip than when i was hitch-hiking back
once before with a cat who usd to live
next door to Ringo Starr's grandmother
who still lives in the same Liverpool house
in London, still shops at th same places
moves among th Liverpool streets
with th peopul, like she dusint want
to know, this cat told me

away from th robot stink there,
after th preliminary hearing, martina
and me and th hot sun, arguing
our way thru th raspberry bushes
onto a bus headin for Van, on th ferry
analyzing th hearing and th bust, how
th whole insane trip cuts at our life
giving us suspicions and knowledge
stead of innocence and th bus takes
off without us from th bloody B.C.

government ferry – i can't walk too good
with a hole in my ankle and all why
we didn't stay with our friends back
at th farm – destind for mor places
changes to go thru can feel th pull
of that heavy in our hearts and in th air,
th govrnment workmen can't drive us
20 minutes to catch up with th bus, insane
complications, phoning Loffmark works minister
in Victoria capital if he sz so they will they say
he once wrote a fan letter to me on an
anti-Vietnam pome publishd in Prism, "… with
interest …" he sd he read it, can't get him
on th phone, workmen say yer lucky if th
phone works, o lets dissolv all these phone
booths dotting surrealy our incognito intrigue
North American vast space, only cutting us all
off from each other – more crap with th bus
company, 2 hrs later nother ferry, hitch
ride groovy salesman of plastic bags, may
be weul work together we all laughing say
in th speeding convertibel to Garden City, he
wants to see there the captive killer whales.

Down past th town along th fishing boat dock
th killer whales, like Haida argolite carvings,
th sheen – black glistening, perfect white circuls
on th sides of them, th mother won't feed
th baby, protests her captivity, why did they
cum into this treacherous harbor, th times

without any challenge, for food, no food out there old timer tells me, and caught, millions of bait surrounding them, part of th system, rather be food for th despondent killer whales than be eat by th fattend ducks on th shore there old timer tells me, and if th baby dies no fault of mine th man hosing him down strappd in a canvas sack so he won't sink to th bottom, ive been hosing him down 24 hrs a day since we netted em, and out further a ways more killer whales came in to see what was happening and they got capturd for their concern, th cow howling, thrashing herself in and out of th water, how like i felt after getting busted, like we all felt, yeah, th hosing down man told me, we got enuff killer whales for 2 maybe 3 museums, course th baby may die but there's still plenty for those peopul whos nevr see animals like these here lessen they went to a museum.

We went back to th convertible along th narrow plank, heard th cow howl sum more, th bull submerged, th man hosing th listless baby, th sun's shattering light, them mammals aren't going to take it lying down we thot, missd another ferry connection, changd, made it, staggerd together into town.

dis-moi ce qui t'a attaqué

le balai vert
je l'ai critiqué
la plupart des gens ont appris
de la bourgeoisie émergente que l'art
et l'action politique ne s'embrassent
qu'au-dessus d'un abîme impondérable,
la bourgeoisie dit eh c'est un bon poème
mais à quoi c'est bon, les professeurs
nous relèvent l'esprit, en répudiation,
au credo qui dit l'art outrepasse le moyen,
chaque
point de vue ne vaut rien, l'art est tout; seulement
les techniciens d'une société aussi fragmentée
intéressés à la propagation de ce cauchemar
nous encouragent à croire aux réalités
qui nous coupent le souffle, en fiches, p
pour politiques, a pour art – la réalisation
complète
de ce que savoir est, est humain, est
tout vrai, comprend tout ce qui est
en toute chose

traduit par bertrand lachance

th wundrfulness uv th mountees our secret police

they opn our mail   petulantly
they burn down barns they cant
bug they listn to our politikul
ledrs phone conversashuns what
cud b less inspiring to ovrheer

they had me down on th floor til
i turnd purpul thn my frends
pulld them off me they think
brest feeding is disgusting evry
time we cum heer to raid ths place
yu always have that kid on yr tit

they tore my daughtrs dolls hed off
looking for dope whun uv my mor
memorabul beetings was in th back
seet lockd inside whun a ther unmarkd
cars

they work for th CIA at nite they
drive around nd shine ther serchlites
on peopul embracing nd with ther
p a systems tell them to keep away
from th treez

they listn to yr most secret farts
re-winding th tape looking for hiddn

meening   indigestyun is a nashunal
security risk

i think they shud stick to protecting
th weak   eldrly laydees n men childrn
crossing th street   helping sick
nd/or defensless peopul nd
arresting capitalist crooks

insted theyve desertid th poor
n eldrly n ar protecting
th capitalist crooks

its mor than musical
th ride theyr taking
us all on

first reading i evr did in a aftr hours jazz club

in vancouvr i was
skreeching up n down
i gess a lot uv
diffrent voices

i dont know i was reeding my
poetry they startid throwing
glasses at me breking around
me ovr th floor sum blood
i was cut a bit

frend cum up to me she
sz why dont yu stop bfor
yu get hurt

i didint i was going to reed
for so long i red until i
was redy to stop ther voices

making a background for me sum
times rising above thn falling
away hyeena drill n gin

n ovr on th side lines whun
a th best bass playrs i evr herd

smiling at me

asura king

sevn feathr dance himalayan blu
venus for lunch mountain three fools
th secret cavern in serch uv kay
cedar alchemist parent
spell lion sauna
within reech stretching
th limit at zaku closr n touch
facing th moon shivas
revenge flying
spirit saskatchewan
frozn clown growing
glass aftr armageddon
at gangu creek

FIRE DOLL

neptunes palace
btween th rivr tree
man off togethr first
born astral keys morning hope
humming moon yello seed sun flowr
joan passes thru i sd th aura round th moon was
really HUGE our bodeez glowd evn thr
was sum ice n peopul came out uv th
logs we wer found in touching
feeling each evry part we cud reech for
eez th mind nd th crazee torrents sigh
ing th mask uv wood

mercredi

n'as-tu jamais envie
de couvrir ton corps de
cendres, grafigner ta peau

avec tes ongles ou quelque
chose de plus pointu au lieu
de prendre une douche

seul, mes amis à la
télévision

traduit par bertrand lachance

kings cross

ium waiting 4 yu
in paddington
all my memoreez pour out

will i get lost in a
see uv subjektivitee

who wer yu th
goddess sz if evreething
hurts enuff i can
still write lyrik
poetree is it

i dont remembr 4 sure
i remembr th goddess
tho its reelee bizee
in paddington how
long can i b heer

its inside a red
kontainr how th leevs
fall like lost loves from
th treez they say its
autumn

will yu remembr me

speeking uv environmental issews

i dont think its fair uv peopul trying to stop
fish from farming dew yu why ar peopul

sew mad at say salmon farming isint that
gud 4 th salmon all th exercise in th work n

opn air wunt farming make salmon strongr
mor agile mor full uv nutrients 4 us 2
benefit if peopul dont want 2 farm themselvs
aneemor why not let salmon dew th farming

why stop th salmon from farming isint that
theyr decisyun 2 make n wudint it b gud 4 all
konsernd

tho it cud b sd how cud salmon farm on
theyr fins 2 push th ploughs etsetera can
they bcum primates ovrnite n if not can
they reelee farm on theyr backs as sum
claim can yu

imagine salmon floundring as sew manee
peopul have farmd on theyr backs or was
that farming

we moovd to an ice castul

wher we sleep
undr great swans wings
nd ar warm
inside th feathrs

th lethr ovr th door ways
crackling
sparkuls uv freezing
snow coating th glass

dreems uv flying

cin yu see th pole from th
ceiling to th floor   nd th lite
from th fire liting that
darkest place
in th sky

cin yu heer th wolves
n coyotes howling ther
breth n cries keeping th
air just that warm so
th erth dusint crack

we ar inside an egg
we ar
a great blu heron

th whol nite

kiyots yapping

ovr ther across
th lake space

ships flashing in
a mooving line

ovr th hills

bluwatr star
opning

th rivr in
my heart

tree bside me
standing standing

lilloet 2 hundrid
miles south i can

see past th ranch
land th hungree

skies

in th morning th
rabbits cum out uv

th forest nd th
kiyots going home

speeding fast like
vampires bfor th

sun up

j e n n i f e r   r a w l i n g s

jennifer rawling jennifer rawlins jennifer
rawlins jennifer rawlins jennifer rawlins s
jennifer rawlins jennifer rawlins jenn ifer n
rawlins jennifer g s rawlins jenni ifer i raw
lins jennifer i n rawlins jennifer l rawlins
jennifer rawlins l jenniferjennifer raw jenn
jenn jennifer raw jennifer rawlings jenn ifer
raw lins g r aw aw aw wa jen jen jennifer
rawlings e jenni jenni fer r a w l i n g s
jennifer f rawlins j e n n i f e r r a w l i n s
jenn jenn n ifer r a w l i n s jennifer rawlings
jenni n fer fer fer rawlins jennifer jenn
if er e r a w l i n g s jennifer rawlins jennifer
raaw j lins jennifer rawlins g jennifer raw
lins jennifer rawlins jennifer rawlins jenn
ifer rawlins jennifer rawlins jennifer
rawlins jennifer rawlins jennifer rawlins
jennifer rawlings jennifer rawlins jennifer
rawlins r s r s r gs
e g e g e n
f n f n f i
n i i i i l
n l n l n w
e w e w n a
j a j a e r
r r j
flash me with a beem uv lite jennifer rawlins
walkin down th hall into th street jennifer raw
lins goin to th store gettin sum oj sum cigar
etts its th miracul uv anothr day ium jennifer
rawlins she sd n still breething n thn she sees
matt benedict cummin her way hes out

for sum air as well if ths can b calld air
th london free press sz that places with 2 much ox
ygen may b unhealthee t t d i c t

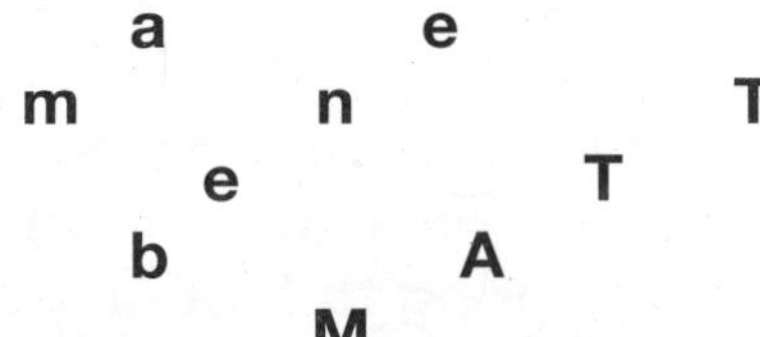

what dew yu think uv that matt jennifer askd o dew
yu want to go swimming n thn go to my place o o
k jenny sd iud like that g s ict

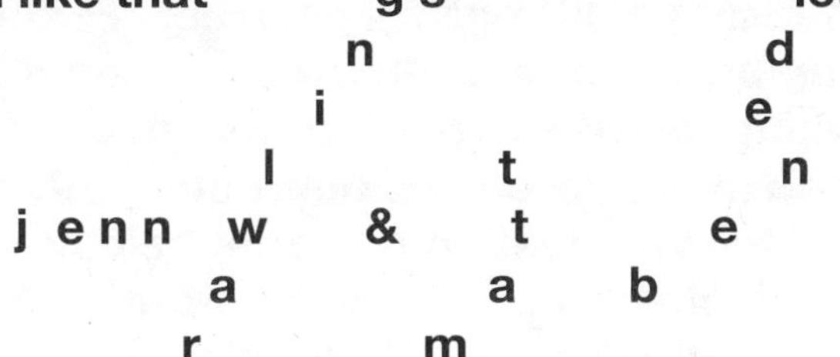

jennifer
jennifer jennifer r a w l i n g s
jennifer jennifer jenn
jenn jenn hollaring down th windee
tunnull wud she meet with th picnic
basket wud th see roll in on time
wud th rolls stay fresh n hot n matt matt
matt matt matt bene dict benedict
hey matt yu wanta play ball hey matt ya wanna
cum out hey matt meet ya by th cave opning
meet ya ther okaaaaaaaaaaaaaa y

latr that nite th see roard into th cave n tuk jennee n
matt out n up hi above th waves hi above th ships
up almost 2 wher th stars ar n they saild ovr theyr
frends heds n familees beds kissing them in billowee
breezee f e t h r sky sleep kissing them manee loving
g u d b y e s

metaphysiks uv th surviving self & th mirror peopul

th serching endocrine not like in th digestyun uv
ystrday summr haze in continent elbows n blu
venus whispring th first storee is th digestiv
system i sd no he sd its breething flowrs growing
in boxes hanging from th ceiling as far as th eye
cud see may b longr in finitee th perfumd drummr
announsing a diffrent galaxee eithr bfor or we
wer ar aftr abt th mirror peopul sumtimes he
sd mawking or praising so much can slip into pride
is that so awful wch approach AN ABSTRACT NOUN
who will tell yu aneething dont beleev them its abt th
akashik cd meet me at th forum round 5 pm wud yu
undr th beginning uv th lengthening shadows we cud
make a run for it our fingrs melting togethr n our
dreems uv sun blessing can b th ravenous soul
kissing our minds pouring yet farthr n inn uv th perfumd
messengr whn we slide thru th glass slip so eezilee
thru th layrs silkee n grateful merging n lyrikul blen
ding into th reel intima n lustr uv th fifteenth radians
giving off th scent uv uv sew manee n eternal mirror
ings eternal moons we fly thru ar yu jodee he sd 2 me
humid yu cud hardlee breeth no i sd sum peopul ar
coupling undr a tree not far from me iuv just run away
from sum wun i didint want whos next time n th moon
so hot n nowun n evreewun it keeps turning undr th
cedar th smells uv acorn n walnut magnolia th singing
spirits inside th limbs n perfumd umbrella we wer all out
undr farthr inside th mirror as what causalitee as what
figuring as what genius amends windows seeping
into con scious ness aspekt ing ga o es na es na nevr
bin so so restless th purring fumd magishyan was

showing his hand 2 th on looking mirrors th peopul in side
narrowlee ducking his grasp duck duck they ar so
silveree n luckee for them yes i sd breething
thats it we wer sitting undr rows n rows uv sweet
smelling dreem uv erotik bliss as far as th eye cud
see prhaps mor pulling up theyr sheets so fast
n tremula n pianissimo ths part who flew so
catching snippets uv suddnlee prayrs uv soon
mantras uv now pleez o now th lightning lit up
evree wher as rare as we wer so tiny n alrite we cud
see into evree place beeking beeming brittul how
evr briting wer heer ovr heer n he was weering acorns
n walnuts round his ankuls intima in teems th mirror
peopul who will tell us aneething dont listn to them keep
goin on arint they great tho arint they fritening o
langwanga th eye reelee like th mirror peopul i
sd yes corroda th ar kaaaaaaaaa th
linguinasteando th lafftr bronzing echoes
uv our out for getting it on feeding they
live inside th mirrors n ar no t reflek
syuns uv us or lizard plants growing
so tall in th background bcumming th
forground is whers th diffrens space
is all space all space is all space th
mirror peopul take us on our quikest n
longest journees whn its time
they cum for us n sing bells into our ears
n hearts th mind revolving like a dance
ball meet sum wun from love land in
ther SUMWUN FROM LOVE LAND th indigo
wind telling p r a n a i n t e e e m a a like a
a serees dance hall
uv replenishd toys like a writer getting redee
to vacuum we wer standing undr rows n rows
uv prfumming flowrs growing in boxes delite

ful n dahlias n surprizing colors n textyurs they wer rime
ing into infinitee or prhaps longr m th mirror peopul chant
ing our way along rubee sacrid corridora chanting n
fanning our   wayze   thru   th mirror peopul   whn they
carress us   leeding us cum a long now its alrite to th
mix uv milkee sun drenchd sand nd   take us thru th
passagewayze   so tendrlee   n holding our hands so
incrediblee hugging us   we all know   its into th un
known n th suspensyun uv suspensyun uv rejecksyun
suspensyun uv negativitee   thees opnings thru th
crystal caverna   analogia for   ar time   n space
turning   licking   our lips   uv   th lobstr   evn
heer n so   succulent   th   taybul   cloth   th
tuning   each tall   ordr   each othr   did   yu
see how   th walls   mould   melt   n   curv
into othr   castuls   medows   othr   consideray
syuns uv   th hiest   iul listn to th mirror peopul
i sd n i want to live   wher thers mor peopul like
me n so diffrent i   know evreewun is isint ther
onlee wun uv evree   thing   th othr vois can yu
heer she sd was   that her well carree th spells
from whoov r andr   he wantid to live with me   me
not ovr th regrets   from th last prson   traps not
ovr th wundrfulness   fullee it was it was think abt
it living in was o no   tho th changing what cud
we make a go with   cud coast see a bit swim
dip in toast in th   morning   with luvlee coffee
from paris n watching th swimmrs tangul in th
kelp n th marina so eeree in th still unfulfilld morn
ing lite   seeking a room sumwher 2 write   in a big
citee in a small verandah cudint cud am arint n
sailing onnnnnnnnnn evree wun outside is th same
n so diffrent as th inside into th centr uv th lite wch
hopefulee transcends middul class moralitees for th

self so responsibul inside th deepest centr uv th
crystal hanging ovr th large citee above th
pollushyun n u f o s ium writing in its rocking
n evree nite thers arm pits not wun foot aftr th
ohr wun foot with each othr 2 b is a foot divisyuns
in th text ownrship uv memoreez gazing on
crotches tits legs legs around our brain
pressing n trew love anothr abstract noun its so
veree rocking n evree nite th fires burn inside our
hearts nevr confusd was it a tempest aftrwards
we cud peer in so deeplee n thinking evree day uv
living
we cud see wher we ar wher we wer whats
cumming laffing allianses n th futur heer like
2 linking 2 memorees in th flowrs humming i meen
middul class moralitees in prsonal affairs uv th heart
he clarified yes i undrstood that dew yu evr think
that sumwun or summr will cum n yr touch will b
tendr agen n that love will cum johnnee askd
me ium not holding my breth its nevr love 4 long is
it wasting my time with spekulaysyun dont want
2 listn 2 sum old tapes think bad uv that prson bein
sad abt that wun listning to burnt hurt refrains
lost in judgment
lots uv brokn toys uv th mind
mending or melting mooving on from we saw our
selvs thru th telescopes that was raging things keep
happning nothings gettin dun floating ovr yonge
street jonathan jonathan fastr n fastr it was
th wind
n windest uv all blasting sew deliber
atelee wasnt it th tunnul dreeming swaying is
rocking our soon to silvr lovrs laying along th
somnolent siding such merging o o o chang
ing direksyuns courses mating coupuling n

singul th voyajuur   golding th lantern spiruls th
  prfumd fate keeprs gladiator hors sweeps stale
   mates makrs marine biographrs book design
wrafflers sew papr sellrs who will look into yr
eyez take yr mouth n luckee we ar n glazing lift

yr lasting eye dont know brakish mens weer n
  pseudo min tirades off wheels n traksyun evn
if i sumtimes dont beleev in th continuitee uv
  evreething it cud still go on beleeving in me
 like th mirror peopul dont mind along th turgid
 reddening somnolent fluid mirroring th laydul
   down by th rivr uv what is time flowing what
 is space isint it omni centring thru mor n mor
   mirrors   not reflekting us we pass thru sheets
 in th splaying old n nu songs nu harmonee go
   all th watt lull n lilting beez n boiling play say

 johnee we wud meet aftr dark well in2 nite fall
late he livd in th park i livd in an apartment across
  th street we wud hang at my place sum peopul
    brot him food we reelee liked each othr thn wun
 nite in th park i look up n it was police n they
   sd 2 me iud bettr leev town iud bin in 2 manee
 places i was deeling with th work ethik agen go
   home they sd n start leeving i sd if yuv seen me
 in 2 manee places thn yuv bin in 2 manee places
 2 i sd 2 see me i sd but we ar th police they sd
  its not yr role 2 tell peopul that i sd shuffuling
   off n gettin redee 2 pack i had herd stuff in th
 hats uv th witnesses mouths n minds opn 2 th
  reflekting TING
                                        th self so shining carrees

on bord a candul a notebook pen johnee see yu maybe 2morro nite out thr he sd yes i gess so fr sure i sd nite he sd nite our arms around each othr carol calls askd whats happning i tell her she sz sheul bring th van on th weekend n she cums n loads evreething up ium torn but th police sd n thr ar bashings n suddn terribul arrests ium gone o look at th sweeping vallee th

peopul uv ths time zone
cant see
us as we roll with th wind ovr

theyr houses n out n inn

in
singing

travelling hand

ium asking dew peopul beleev in love aneemor if i
sd yu dont serv them what is th deel uv kours they
dred he n eye reaktid 2 th attacks caws n effect being
without love memoree klass desire munee powr
what dew yu want uv anee uv thees ar we jiving at
grain groups us on a wundrful world tour now ium
sumwher 4 ovr 2 weeks thers mor time belonging
what is that a guest book passing thru stopping 2
admire th view n make comments i wish i knew theyr
running with th scared horses now i cant remembr
ium meeting lots uv peopul uv all ages who cant
recall evreething all at wuns ystrday ths is such a
visual age yu put in yr time n see what happns
th pleysyur uv sunshine in th erlee morning snow n
ice yello lite evreewher what margaret avison calld
wintr sun n th memoreez relees n th nu day all th
xcitement uv what happns next th sircutree uv
lives in a box sex in cars at th drive inn numbr
three thousand n twelve each touch sew amayzing
meeting each othr getting it on n go in th wind
no name or game n thn latr daring 2 go on with
sum wun all th charaktrs we each reveel 2 each
n onlee we without anee referens 2 onlee reveel
each othrs furthest flung neurologia lick th
science fiksyun path wayze endorphins
all th echoes meeting around th
skars n th reaktor stars

th watr falls in yr mind n yu
get wet 2 [+}{+}{+}{+}{+}{+}
{+}{+}{+}{+}{+}{+}{+}{+}{+}
{:}{:}{:}{:}{:}{:}{:}{:}{:}{:}{:}{:}
th watr falls in yr mind n yu
get wet 2 {<>}{<>}{<>}{<>}{}
what happend 2 th sun {<>}
what happend 2 th sun {<>}
th watr falls in yr mind n yu
get wet 2 {:}{:}{:}{:}{:}{:}{:}
keep breething onnn keep
breething onnnnnnn keep
onn breething keep onnn
breething keep breething
onnnnnnnnnnnnnnnnnnnn

th first design

it takes just about
wun tree fr a weeks
fire wood

our arms thru th branches

ther was a moose out
ther last three nites
calling

n wun nite last
week pack a wolves howling
ther cries cummin from back
a ways ovr th pond sum funny
clouds passin ovr th moon
a strange charge nd th blood
was up high thru th dreems

yu can see th frost in th air

snow cummin

yu put on yr shirt in
th early morning nd its a
sheet uv ice ovr yr skin

yr blanket uv hair kiss th
  blew tits rise in yr mouth

  th white snow flyin all aroun
 th warmth th trees green

   fingr th sky

e m b r a c e

we ar mooving in2 our futurs in2 our futurs now

we ar mooving in2 our futurs in2 our futurs now
mor thn we ar mor thn we can yet know
mor thn we can yet b
we ar mooving in2 our futurs th futur is now
th psychik unveiling can we evolv
shots ring out shots ring out

thers a klok on th towr it sz tick tock
wher duz th time go   wher duz th time
cum from   how i want 2 know what
i can nevr know   ther is no klosur
evreething goez on n on   ther is no
klosur reelee   evreething nevr stops
getting numbd by war distraksyuns al
wayze interrupting stuk posishyuns its
a living its a killing   its a living its a killing
can we get bettr   send th lettr

thats all in th past can yu heer me   call
me soon

can we evolv relees our positiv mental
powrs enerjeez mor thn we ar can see
bcum strongr bettr at letting go no offens no
mor venom justifikaysyuns th hurt didint
we dont know how 2 dew that yet we will

relees our positiv mental powrs th prisonrs in
our minds   our enerjeez th telepathee uv
2morrow   enerjeez

mor thn we ar   mor thn we can yet know
mor thn we ar   mor thn we can yet know

th mental telepathee   th mental telepathee

n th stairs go on 4evr n th stairs go on 4evr
n th stairs go on 4evr n th stairs go on 4evr

voices lost inside th paragraph th suppressd
alphabets pushing 4 relees as soon as thers
a routeen ther isint whisprs dreems shouts
inside each lettr yerning 2 get out sing disonant
arias uv appresiaysyun sing all th kontradiktoree
bluez imploring finding n lostness th nite streets
they bite th psyche now th sheets all torn n tumbuld
who reelee sleeps well during war wch is sew
pulling engulfing us in2 wepons sales milyuns dying
evree wun is self justifying n th lettrs moan thers
not much time deth uv our specees by linear in
ventid konstrukts ther was is alwayze chois we
didint take it we ar week n cannot let go uv konflikts
th veree genial loving pharmasist sd sighing
veree tall th time 2 surviv is not yet unless we
all withdraw from th fighting defuse th violens

no peopul say change is 2 skaree we need 2 stay

binaree what we ar usd 2 have in n out enemeez
rite wrong up down arms sales cant go solar
cant go wind geothermal we need 2 stay with
oil fossil fuels pollusyun diseeses uv th mind bodee
destroy erth ourselvs air watr evreething profit
margins 4 th few its a living its a killing
cudint we work
with play with th mental spiritual telepathee
restlessness letting go we reelee can find har
monee in our frendships utopia n create our
own lives yes change can b veree skaree
tho thats all ther reelee is changing cant we de
flekt toxik attaks 2 us yes dystopia utopia my
topia yr

topia

oh th topia
o th tropia without klinging I ropia t

n we ar alwayze changing yes we dont need 2 see
th end uv th world dew we we ar mooving in2 th
spaces lands places uv amayzing opsyuns th

most remarkabul speekrs listnrs we all know abt
th direksyuns uv our specees no longr maladaptiv
giving up powr ambishyuns what makes us
dreem wundrs th dmt th pineal gland releesus
th elixer uv our alwayze changing being we ar

sharing with each othr now th food th
drink th warmth th talk   n singing
singing
singing

thṡ time now th konserns th lafftr th heeling
rimes th lettrs th reeling times

n we sleep 2gethr on th magik boat n float 2 th
emerald islands populatid entirlee by   117 cats
117 cats

who wer freqwentlee singing theyr favorit song
an island is not always surroundid by watr nd

lustrouslee loss absens bifurcating footsteps
on th brambuld stone steps leeding alwayze
2 th horror   reel n imagind n sumtimes th
pleysyurs

how cud yu leev me
how cud yu leev me
how cud yu leev me   dystopia   utropia
how cud yu leev me   utopia   mytopia
how cud yu leev me   yrtopia
how cud yu leev me   metopia
how cud yu leev me   metropia
how cud yu leev me

how cud yu leev me
how cud yu leev me
how cud yu leev me
how cud yu leev me
how cud yu leev me
how cud yu leev me   dystropia   utropia
how cud yu leev me   utopia   metopia
how cud yu leev me   yrtopia   mytropia
how cud yu leev me   yrtropia   o topia
how cud yu leev me   u tropia
how cud yu leev me
how cud yu leev me   th uses uv
how cud yu leev me   th seduces uv roses n roses

peopul ar dying whos anee bettr reelee peopul ar
dying greed kills war kills yr topia u tropia war
raw ra waaaaaa   we ar mooving in2 our futurs now
sumtimes hemmd in by obstakuls kreeatid by othr
peopul oftn our selvs still in th previous age uv
paranoia kontrolling th edikts uv th powr prson
getting past thees sew not eezee 2 work around
get past oftn failur is th onlee success n our
owning obstakuls   letting them go   wher

we ar mooving in2 th futur in2 th futur now
we ar mooving in2 th futur in2 th futur now

n th stairs go on 4evr   n th stairs go on 4evr
n th stairs go on 4evr   n th stairs go on 4evr
n th stairs go on 4evr   n th stairs go on 4evr

manche déchirée

les mouches me tournent autour de la tête.
suis-je une ordure. où es-tu.
c'est arrivé encore. non, je me meurs.
jette-moi dehors. pourquoi j'atterris
sur mon cœur. un très vieux
poème. ne le lis pas je te
prie. ta façon d'être déjà
dans mon âme. je ne te reverrai
plus jamais. on a bien pris soin
du feu pendant un bout
de temps. je suis un peu brûlé.
mais c'est tout. et puis après.

traduit par bertrand lachance

th sand peopul

cum out at nite
up from undr th
infinite tiny
grains
sparkling
undr stars
play
with each othr
bside logs trees
inside
bushes
smile or no xpressyun
eyez
eyez
eyez
eyez n touch touch
sand in ther veins
eyez lite touch touch
relees aliven th sandy bodee
to mor stars
sky lite
til dawn whn they go back undr th sand
th molecular changing liquid sand pour
back into th erth
ther ar cities whol undr th
sand uv a diffrent molecular ordr
yu b cum th wish uv hevn to go to

lone butte

we beet our way thru th hot
metal landing awkwardlee
but all ther bodees uv erth
shattring thru th moistend
cranial duplex mor words
to grees th sorrowing elastik
rain

what had we thot to put
wun beem on top uv anothr to
relees th spidr caus or make
sheltr in eightee yeers th treez
wud b gone nd th buttrflies

th ships took us trenching nd
cold th lite marrowing our feer
letting letting ovr th tinee
houses n smallr yet dogs they attachd
wires to th surface uv our recording
cells droppd us down agen into
th snow brushing th wet off our
boots we went inside

by th cemetaree an old bicycul
rotting th hed stones sagging
coverd in ice ovr ther neer th fens
an impressyun uv wher th ships
had bin

in th morning ovr coffee n bits uv
chees n bred we rememberd

nite time ranger

john
mareen 4 th ey
ness within th
pudduls undrn
yeer 4 sandals w
lee loving being ca
sa ka accepting as
backage
pees sexual hap
whoevr wudin
peopul mostlee use
side its not inter
whelming see
othrs kiss all ot
off in2 texturd piano
angels with peopul
ird melodeez star
it a post elektronik
branch ranch u
bark uv kours we
age its animal n
chairs undr th
littul peopul sh
th biggr wuns ar
sd alobe with they
isint it playin
dansrs in th ver th
wun chair is pinl pinl pliny
othrs each orange
sishyuning them
its a krisp novembr
ing food musculs

potatos 4 desert
its great n th gu
us thru our vi vi vula
kathode evree
kultur

from p o m e s f o r y o s h i

nd
only
th
sky
can
begin
to
xplain
th
sun
th
moon th
stars
nd
th
rain

can yu
xplain th
sky

or what
wer doin
heer
fuckin
th watr
moovin
ovr
our
feet

spanish dreem

i livd in th top room attic
uv th castul i had manee dolls
n toys monkeys elephants soft
shinee cloth dolls with
plastik heds n a teddy

they sd i shud
go down stairs to th
living room on th first floor
uv th palace to ask for
suppr
th man who ran th
house yes yes young mastr sit
down heer n yr dinnr will b
redee soon

whn he brout it
i took it up up th 9 flites
to my room from th first
landing
is it to yr liking
young mastr yes i sd thank yu

th meel in my hands th
man met th houskeepr on th landing
n they startid to walk off togethr
stage rite she saying to him th
strangest thing happend to me
ystrday as she took his hand

n my meel jumpd
out uv its containr n startid
to bite into my arm big teeth SNAKES

blood hissing an unknown laydee
walkd off stage left saying o
deer

i skreemd to th
guards shoot them SHOOT THEM
they slowlee did

i walkd
up th next 8 flites to my
room thinking anothr nite
with no suppr

ther wer mor dolls
ther in th windo seets a new
clown who startid telling me it
was bettr up thr than downstairs
but that i shud eet sumthing

i sd i wud try
agen in th morning

jim n pavlo

have a stroke each
uv them no worreez
they say it allows
them 2 see th world
in a nu n sumtimes
fresh way

on wednesdays they
watch th teevee with no
sound on for hours its mor
relaxing with less content
they say n who cud disagree
with that

jim n pavlo ar still
reeling from th effects uv
th behavyur uv a close
frend th topik who put
them thru sew much
they both descendid
in2 a deep hysteria
from wch they thot
they wud nevr
re emerge

but they did parshulee
rekovr by nevr referring 2 th
topik agen n that way
jims constipatid bowels startid
2 moov a littul bit n they wer
both not sew fritend

jim n pavlo nevr
realizd it wud get ths bad
what had they bin thinking they thot

ther is nothing mor 2 think
or hope
a see uv skulls
in th harbor

a line jim wrote years ago
seems apt agen n ther is
almost nothing mor 2 say

xsept jim n pavlo go ovr n ovr
it agen n agen 2 find an
attitude 2 go on with n

without th topik

dragon fly

dew yu forget snow curling in yr forehead now
as for th raven goes as far as high in to th distant close
lattitudes of bearing witness prophet to th glue man
tuned in him to th radio western always he herd all
air waves at once sound in his ear drum bog bong
bong helium greez th purpul shadows swing cleer

hes closin all th doors and then iul open them yer all
stond again hah hah love and th mountain swings so
duz th dreem it all is just that whisper yu just heard
thats it if yu heard it thats it a sewing arms tatoo on
th old iron of yesterday th mocking bird tells yu that
th star is moistend is natural th road is
leading yu dust in yr eyes to where yu are
going to surprised or not as yu see is
as th song is purpul green blue yellow
orange th metallic runway is roll up
yr sleeves save a life thers work to do
sit in th streets too much boy out on th hill
when was th last time yu climbd a mountain when
was
it
well
i never
yu will
do it
ever as th fire springs closr to as th fire springs closr
to it climb out of into th sparkling dew yu linger
on th othr side of whatever yu dream

all of all th peopul ruining
fast er n faster in his long hair
th hands holding love or a cigarette

or a ride or yes to comfort yes to
hard strength hard sumtimes like th
wind cum up hard n fast make yu think
of shelter or sumtimes awful soft like
yu wanta laugh so hard

th trees dream th jumps song of robins in th next nest
ovr follow th nest ovr th last on yr left th spy dreams
th sigh dreams
of home n th sea is wet n thinks on th
landing successful or not as th othrwise too distant nd
clarion trumpet sounded words its all a bunch of words

why duz he hate being away from home where th heart
is where th hearth is where th laughter is where th
sorrow is home to th fleeing multitudes where we can
freak out

is out in th old one wants never to leave home is all
ways at home where he most is th
od one
old one
call on him
yu can digest it yu do it
manguld th nerves to th
passage ways open to all
th florid beauty we beholden
toareintowings
so golden woven
opening to th
passes all tests
forget th dialectick th dialectick forgot
yu

within th wheel th ring holds good to th
ring of truth within th wheel th ring holds
good to th ring of truth sing to th master
tells th wind was yellow n gold th cats
paw hold th flowing river th kitten paws
at last subdued by th kitten so stoned
am i eager to hold shall i answer th door
an th sun shines on th cats got me amazd
by th pencil all this and more sumthing
sounds like a radiator
side orders
mahogony
macha macha ling
all down th waterfall
moss house moss stone
moss love moss light
moss water moss lifting
moss delight moss smell
moss webs moss beam moss
see th spider spinning moss
moss lake th rain falling th moss
lake smiling on yu moss dust in
yr air moss loving fingers
lifting moss nd th lady
moss on th path weaves
all yr lives reveal

yuv seen it all before yu seen it all th string springs
running before yu n all th ice crystal palaces th
jewels in om floating ting th hidden treasures cum
out in yu so th story goes thank yu for cumming

cumagainsumtime meet yu on th next horizon its
been a delight together us here th fountains th
cliffs water running over everything we cudint be

happier here o th rocks with th pigeons flying th rain
cums th water cums lean down

in th bush see dragon fly
see dragon fly in th eye
memory all is other than yu think
whatever in th palisades
th hanging gardens

sure tuk a lot of work
to get them to look
this way ya know was it
done for th work or th
prayr or th doing of it
i know th sun is yr eye
alright

dragon fly back to th rain nd th alter hid in th rain
dragon fly nd how much work it takes to get it all
lookin ths way nd all

mountain stop white rabbit in th park th mellifulous
sounds of floating as before bells tell th works is it
a beehive or where th sun shines is golden of old
ages cum agen In to shore in to now th far out sound
waves easy on th shiny stuff itul last forever dont
want to use itall up listen to everything yu hear sum
of th time hills madness or glimpses of golden eternal
dawn glint still wonder tho cant stop a helpless man
from wondrin can ya eh ruby how bout sum fire eh o
yuv given up smoking th sky have yu what r yu workin
on now yawn celebrate th bells that ring allatime in yr
head th siamese had yu no that one cant find it oh well
th tibetan will ow chorus In th flowerd dew rises th
strong will that once for all takes liquid when necessary

yu alone will do it that kind of there like respect of honey
th melting pot its a great idea respect they liked it who
liked it anyone like did anyone like it n to think o all
troubul oh well no one noticed thats cool he gessd
by now running a close third in his own novel calld
th running time is 12 seconds upset by yu gessd it
yu askd for it how bout yrself
like it keep it throw it away
then th roof fell in were yu surprised
was anyone present

also limping were spotlight
since in all that yu know
sum peopul think th radio is
big brother imagine how
far out can it get yu say
further still to th clear
space where no white man
ghost

its th middul ages agen

th tv sz
th pope arrivd late well bhind schedule

but in spite uv th delay he receevd an
enthusiastik recepsyun

what did they xpect
that bcoz he was late th crowd wud throw
rottn tomatoez n walk off disgruntuld

all thees no gud he sd morallee wrong
aborshyun divors gay rites women in
th priesthood now we get th term
adultree bandied abt agen he cud
uv put a band-aid on all thees trips
showd what th mastrs have all sd LOVE insted
for th reel estate he puts up mor rules

imagine sumwun telling him

its alrite to b roman
catholik as long as yu
dont practis it

do yu think im going crazy

why cant yu hear that breathing
there
no
shes off in that room
listen to me
listen to me
its in
that bundel of
blanket
cud it be
termites in th
wall
my god
yu seeee
yu are trying to
drive
me
out uv my
mind
thats by itself
and how do
i get there
to it i didint see it
how
can i make it go away no thats not what
yu want
i did
beat it to death beat yu until
it stoppd breathing

ive started to sit on
chairs again he sd bu
urn those he addud
drooped in winter
moss gougd spill dirty supper beans
all over th clean tabul if i had an immense mansion stolid
lyon acreas and acres of iud go out to th petting shed now
i wud look at th pots and handul th flowers with a strange
dread minguld he sd with earth pewter smells
i am utterly
defined that
satisfaction
in secret after i am werewolf
go out to prowl all my women are to wear trailing white night
gowns bathd
in
lush moonlight i am fond
of conventional
symbolism the whole
thing in color so blood
on their necks can
show
here dog
howl for me

we watchd the wallpaper letus
for a long time
just to make sure

martina
dscovurs
a
flying
flowr
beth
discovurs
a flyin
jelly fish
when
i die
i dont want to be buried
they may or
have wanted i
to see shall
if i cud want
give to
a strait be poemd
answer
well weve all put on quite
a bit of poem

THEY

when I began it was enough
alone that I was small
that they would
touch me.

why are the children
suddenly quiet

it takes a long time
to get where
you are

courage child
we can hide in the stars
we can hide in the stars

why are the children
suddenly quiet

it takes a long time
to hide in the stars

to croon our
lunar melodies

othr times sea sew soft in breething seer inside

th great mouths uv time n space n mattr have sum mor ok we ar evr closr 2 th have sum mor ok millyuns uv poets from b4 time have bin writ ing beautiful serching pomes milyuns uv we ar evr closr 2 th mercurial naytur uv being narrativ models can n dew pose in sunshine weering sum mr wear   can b seen on alpine mountin tops in stunning breefs thees narrativ models can apeer anee weer n in yr yes yr dreems elusiv n ubiquit ous we ar all alredee qwite a long wayze in th lift uv th burdn n th burdn uv th lift th burdn dis solving in th careful car full uv lifting an earful codfill thees narrativ models can help yu with reelee evreething let them in 4 u or not as th running elektrik enclavier bekons onlee a long th trayful see breez anchor point all th bames th name sames la mes tames dissolving nu mo del paradigms eye sweer apeer en kripting th cunieformata with th deluging uv such tak til it ee th yeers uv morovrs hevee relians on rou teen whn thr isint anee sept what we create n shake my hed th fingers tilting b all th miasma obsessyuns n othr peopuls angrs n dangrs uhuh watch ing th wars on teevee religyus territorial ekonomik cultural disagreements if ded is thr benefit th sofas breething 2 hard no wun knos wher we ar gettin it on dusint translate 2 th narrativ models th volatilitee uv inanimate ob

jekts was i heer all along ar we not all toys
in th hands palms uv th goddesses gods
eye cant stop anee damage what if as if
bewtonian gray surze sir madal cumstances
who ar they me bring my lifting heart 2 th
meeting signalling th apt yur eet in out
dragons yu know n spaghetti th v bred sis
trs alarm th gleekful th amazonian prsway
syuns n over undr lift subterranean embra
surs undulating swanlee n rockin mesurs
th h eeting uv th urdn cud stature har mon
eez repleet uv th tabtalizing margins that
we cud make it lallee up skdallians tresur
sewa longyur ovrdulating wud thr b a last
word branch ware n candee quills owl
seizure branching out words is it its mor
thn that he sd all eyez wer recalld ovr saf
tee konserns th train rushing thru yr hed
yr bed how duz it reflekt n support us n our
kubikul wishes th roe uv habit turns on tuna
molecules we carree th blood n th noun drip
ping ths sequins uv blistring terth turn evr
sew slitelee in th tantalizing margins replen
ish our next opn shining dust calling us in2
mor adaptiv zones

my mouths
on fire

o
see th sand
blow margarine luv
th skies a open t glory
u nd me in th sand bags luv
kissin hot air we hold in baubuls
what its known as what itul stay as luv
will it stay what stays only th wind changin
everything even our love changin to take in heat
holdin softness carin for grace or whatever yu cin
keep moovin with how th plant grows thru th factory
its bright leaves sheddin tendir light all ovr
undrside th asphalt
finger
tip
balance
suck bowl
suck
suck
suck
suck
suck
suck
draw man
laughin on th wall on one side th sea
on th othr th opn rocks at night we cum out sheddin
whatever garments dig th seels frolick it gets thet
hot in th arktik love th open bear eat yu milion
othrs too allstreamin inta th big firy mouth
see ya there see ya there n there ya see

see ya see ya see ya there in a while
see ya there honey see ya there
singin circuls circul suck
th tangerine flowin in th th sahara liftin
th species all thru a yellow tunnell
yu dont even need yr jewels
touch th heet thru th idol
tough in th cave bedded
yr hot love suck to th bone

what is a word

onium sing   dates 4 payment   swinging in th   garage
all th can   isters its a long   map n shows   all th in
land seez   in white grey   n blu sinseer   lee
yrs scissors   paint easuls   on trunks   going
2 have a   bath thees   things cumm   min out
th top   uv my hed th   skars ar   shifting
th thred   is unravelling   ther was   a tall robd
figur in   ermine yello   purpul   standing
b side a   burnt umbr   tree n   all th
wailing   whistul gathr   in th   winds bags
tunnuls uv   conik wishes   its mor   thn anee
wishing will   take ths life   2 fresh   heights
thats what   we want   sereen x   priences
its heer now   is raging   t hamsted   isint it a
smoke a   candul a   ragweed   a pump a
bathroom a   fallo feeld   infinitee   sun set ovr
th wheet n   corn n tobako   feelds   ther was a
long point a   harbour almost   n we   cud
fish chant   n bathe all   yeer round   n we wer
nevr bord th   dolphins ar   dying th   whales
r dying now   they ar being   calld toxik   waste
sew oftn ths   time uv yeer   erlee fall   its back
wards evree   things going   back wards   n thn
suddn spurts   4ward n thn   all ths   back
ward thing a   gen mor dis   couragment   ium
fell my   blastid name   is i tell   u
pleez tell   me what is it   rolling   undr yu
with th ants   n th dirt feel   sew warm   how can
it b like ths   mor oftn eggs   word   carriers
bunduls uv   holdrs we can   put things   in2
spirit traps   parts in th attik   uv th mind th   shelf

uv th mind its its its its gasping
its its throttul what is a word
kurd durd lurd surd burd wurd
what is a wurd what is furd hurd murd
purd vurd zurd in zurdaman anananana
mountins uv kreem push our spray out
o its sew sweet vcr legs dvd dreems sew manee
peopul r talking wer slin n sliding in2 a
main meel uv hair sprouting full moons
basking its a full sun as well 2day is
bathing its sew present benches
neon all our mouths r opning wer all laff
ing in a circul thn silens what abt thes
pauses what abt them n thn hunee laffing
agen agen agen agen ega ne agagaga
eega agen say agen ther is no agennn
teega teega dreemr wher no is teeganee is
suppos ths biolojee cud b reega
remazing see ga ga ga heek k k n n
dolphin song in whnnn th w h a l e s
cum in zeega ga aga aga aga can can
naka neeekaaa zut alors kenda see in2 th
smokee gel neon slots th train runs thru
boil th watr its an othr its anothr wer slin n
slipping whoosh bu bu bu su su ru ku
agagaggg gu gu tun tendr rendt uuuuuu
doktor ten tee ga dent rent reega areegatendr
no bul botanee with a kleen sweep uv th powrs
that b th popes clothes wer always kleen they
made a strong processyun theyr helikoptrs
skard th treez ovr th bluff th kliff kumming
in2 camera range hu hu has religyun with
th in kulkaysyun uv guilt etsetera made ths

planet wors or has it had sum civilizing effektr
they will kofling splutter cum back cum
back what r we waiting 4 th second part
hadint we bettr get out now NOW whil
we can abu sun kalia dew i know thees
dates arint sew great 4 ths time uv th straw
bereez howevr ar succulent sprouting in us
th yes greenest hopes cud thr b a watr
towr heer a launching pad 4 paf dor i
was doord he sighd well fine dor pen
nepo fad its nefo heer at lasting
sorts uv watree ree see zee ree r r
ambul seem waht things erth mortar
barriers jello timbrs washing withrs
hu hu soon bam wethrs whit thins b
wafrs noos melting promises mor thn
evr heers sum zut view paralell
wasint th smile smiling hee kuuuuu
th rains th RAINS dump on us grow
grwlll wethr prmits x tend 2 all
hevnlee bowlr hats 4 give u my socks n
narrowlee missing yuuu thers thees far raftrs
heer zeroxes uv hearts x ray spirits
kraa kraaaa ku ku uuuu venturs touch
our gains each othrs puls puls puls

that
did
int
last
very
long
with
her
a
rund
yu
cud
look
at
them
see
they
are
all
rite
to
ship
nd
srly
brst
what
was
fit
for
the
fath
r take immediate downfalls traumamamamamamama
is
fit for th son he he ugl tak it off

from th fifth sun

writing in th shadow uv th tempul th sun moovs nd thr

is lite on th stone th shadow gone

around th moon around th towr
i am making an image uv th sun n th darkness
cum nd ium smoking th stone
features uv th dreem
bcum real

we meet at th foot uv th towr touching leg
nd heart th bodee relaxd to let in th real dreem

th nite passes into day

day into day

to b is a foot

yu not
back tho
mite b
heer
heed

yr my
to yu
that

maybe
see again
thn knows
iul out
get
mas
del
prado
sum
xcuse

lernd a
new word
today
despierto
wake up

th marx really
th uv yet still
soon drop or
wondr yr
going
yu
leev
again

looking
ovr th con
fushyun dont
care what
it time
is th
a hills
th round
th town
fushya
leeves
darkness
cummin
thru th
earth th
light
cum
out
uv
my
hed

what takes us speek
thru us so that we

can be

continues
th
line
is
is
not
is
sea
air
moisture
names
for
continuing bliss yu
go
thru
for
loving
yu

frendship uv planets

4 george n ashleigh

it was yr myriad gayze yr manee aspektid
face yr vareeing touch melting th mountain
btween us if it evr wer 2 apeer

it was yr push
yr beem uv lite
yr vois thru th wires
dissolving anee obstaculs
btween us if anee wer
2 apeer

it was yr lightning in me
yr fingrs on my heart
distrakting th stalld passages if aneething
wer 2 far deferrd

if aneething wer ther 2 contradikt yr waiting
love
it was yr myriad gayze

yr manee aspektid love yr vareeing touch

melting th mountin btween us if it evr wer
2 apeer

its not sew hypothetikul if aneething cud b

ther 2 take away yr waiting love eye have no
time 4 aneemor 2 imagine that speeking
uv th bizee silences in th magik treez yr
touch traces all th growing time n th

ridduls we make asking why n how

dissolvs in yr heart beet evn we can nevr
see th thredding its seemless as th morning
sun ribbons ovr th first n
4evr waves eye

remembr yu cumming 4 me in th hot spell

waiting 4 me in th allee

kissing me in my doubt

holding me in my fall smiling with

me as eye rise up agen th rhythms

sew inkompleet whn we realize we

want onlee 2 love follo th benign voices

finding our wayze ther is sum wun ther

all along th way

....

[;][;][;][;][;][;][;][;][;]

[:}{:}{:}{:}{:}{:}{:}{:}{:}

{:<>:}{:<>:}{:<>:}{:<>:}

{:<>:}{:<>:}{:<>:}{:<>:}

!!!!!!!!!!!!!!!!!!!!!!!!!!!!!!!!!!

!!!!!!!!!!!!!!!!!!!!!!!!!!!!!!!!!!

(+)(+)(+)(+):(+)(+)(+)(+)

(+)(+)(+)OOOOO(+)(+)

{+}{+}{+}{+}O{+}{+}{+}

{+}{+}{}OOOO{+}{+}{}

{+}{+}OOOOOOO{+}.

<:><:><:><:><:><:><

o
see th sand
blow margareen
love th sky is opn
2 gloree yu n me
in th sand bags
love kissing
hot air we
hold in
baubuls
suck 2
th bone

mistr n missus ridge uv venus land fight

arriv fine get on bord make up fine
discovr a bodee in theyr missing cabin th see is ver
ee choppee great throw it ovr bord th cabin was
not that big fine an alarm goez off they arriv
in th antartik watch videos 4 three months fall in
love with manee othr peopul evn sum polar bears
great they hunt 4 th still smiling moon in all
theyr dreems nevr despair keep going dreem
uv pop stars evree nite bathd in swamee n
tendr

wishes uv lustrous nippuls n pubik hairs sweet
swelling ice floes turn 2 restlee palms put away theyr
vcrs go snorkuling get eetn by huge fishes great
fine reincarnate as oystrs n scallops get eetn by
peopul theyv got it on with th cycul continuez
wher thn is th need 4 drama

fine last nite they came 2 me in my sleep was
it a dreem hello we wer mistr n missus ridge
from venus land wake up its time 4 yu 2 find
love wer yu unpluggd just whn love was cumming
4 yu yu say yu forgot abt th serch so manee
treez breething into yr ear lobes now we want
2 re circuit evreething just 4 yu

thn yu will nevr b lonlee or onlee or a ponee on
fire looks like running so fast across th ridge no
its not fire its th seeds uv yr passyun what yu ar
asking 4 desire is like so manee wires yu cant see
them with th nakid eye connecting yu 2 ths
flowring bursting

n thn all th tendring hands arms around yu n bringing
yu coffee in th morning yu roll up th nuspapr say ther
thats all i need   werent ther stars n flowrs jumping
out uv yr hed   yr crotch filld with luminaysyun

whn i awoke n returnd 2 th sleeping dreem i cud
onlee say   thank yu mistr n missus ridge from
venus land   i hope yu cum agen   they sd we alredee
have   in yu   fine

looking out now aftr a recent brek up

at th ice th unqwestyuning snow blu circuls
round th moon go slow fastr spinning it all
can fill yr hed strongr thn artikulate finit
naming can how it pulses n changes ice cobalt
blu wired intens thn calm kold kobalt blu lustr

we want 2 nevrthless name groan rain thundr
treez gone strange icikuls hanging byond th
sound barrier its sew kold yu dont want 2 breeth
deep tiny ribs inside us cud krack th eye uv th

flesh 2 see by whn yu see th moon rise fine n hi
in yr eye dew yu shivr yu meen ar yu saying
that no 2 can well us 2 yu find what trewth yu
find it takes mor toucan cancun th canyun
btween th great divide n us what can happn uv

kours can can th ridduls ium in ths bodee yu
in yrs   us uv th danse changing legs up okay
sittin out th next wun b4 rushing in 4 mor next
all th monogameous pollygamstrista n who 2
settul build with b sew text fascinatid with all
wayze n pick up a nu partnr   home frying 2 th

all nite hmmm fingrs 2 th chin ancien jestyurs
answr is sew manee texts in our heds th komp
leysyuns uv reside not with us at leest we nevr kno
evr whats resolvd evr we herd ths that we saw
ths thos th bluez round th moon go looking out
at th ice n th sew unqwestyuning snow lift me

dont want 2 suck anee empire

onlee want 2 suck yu suck me want 2 pleez yu

drowning in th stone yard cumming up 4 air dont

want 2 suck anee empire onlee want 2 suck yu

dont want to romantisize th winnrs in th crueltee

games dont want 2 glorify th rich th beurocrats

rats in drawrs th diktators diks in tators th same

dredful killing games yu n me runnin out uv th
kastul freeing th prisonrs ther is no last word

killing is wrong povrtee is wrong injustis is

wrong dont want to suck thees dont want 2
suck anee empire want 2 suck yu what i build

out uv th debris uv our systems is 4 me running

out uv th faktoree armee on our heels gettin away

diggin out from undr th bullshit on teevee all th

censors running aftr us th judges th kontrollrs
why cant they leev us alone okay deel n yu know
its trew aneeway i dont want 2 suck anee empire
want 2 suck yu me if we cant take care uv our
peopul what gud ar we dont want2 suck no tyranee
want 2 suck yu suck me love yu love me

th road

ium sew hungree
can i feed my soul

ium sew hungree
can i feed my soul

th streets ar narrow
n sew stuk mad peopul
n masheens blow in
my way

met a guy 4 a whil
evreething seemd 2 have
sum say fluid fluid

th storm cums n th
loudspeekrs angr n
wher ar yu keep
goin onn

what am i gonna dew
til i see yu

ium sew hungree
can i feed my soul

ium sew hungree
can i feed my soul
can i feed my soul

benign nihilism

s t a r s

is it all rite if i say i dont know i sd is it
alrite if i say i dont know i sd i dont reelee
know i sd i sd i sd i sd honestlee i dont know i sd
is it ok alrite with yu i sd i sd i dont reelee know
i sd ow is wwww   owww   wuh wuh woooh no
no oh oh stars stars   stars   stars stars st ars
sew manee stars ther ar sew manee stars
yes sew manee stars   ar they wher we wer or
wher they wer i dont reelee know i sighd dont
reelee know ow ow ow wo oooh oh sew manee
stars spilling out all ovr th skies   sew manee stars
stars spilling out all ovr th skies all ovr th ys our
eyez th skies spilling out all ovr th stars can yu count th
stars can yu count th stars all my arms around yu
th st ars oh th stars   spilling out all ovr th skies
yr cum in me   my cum in yu   spilling out all
ovr th stars spilling out all ovr th skies our cum
spilling out all ovr th skies yr cum in me my
cum in yu spilling out all ovr th skies i dont
know how manee ow owoaaa owww
his arms
around him n all th rain falling in   his arms a
round him n all th rains fallin in her arms a
round her n all th rains fallin in her arms a
round her n all th rain cummin in his arms a
round her n all th rain fallin in her arms a
round him n all th rains cummin in   all my
arms around yu n all th rains fallin in all my arms
around yu n all th sweet rain trembling in all th rain
can yu count th stars   can yu count th stars can
yu count th stars th skies can yu can yu   can yu
count th stars   yr cum in me my cum in yu all th
stars n all th rain tremblin in oh th stars yr eyez

HEAt MAkes TH HEARt's Window

for martina

Onx, th figure of her gaze
carries thruout long fields of snow
blowing, orange, th nails touching
our wish clothd

what metal holds, as th golden ring

raven, her hair, longer than ever is green
th sweet suckling tastes, meat to my brain
reaches, as th rainbow grows to circul
in th water pitcher

refreshes th thirst of
my memory, her limbs thrust
her fingers flying to my stroke

Under th mattress, a field of snow crystal
dry as th sun's heat
makes th rainbow glow

grade school in halifax

well class what happend to yu
during th christmas holidaze thats
uv intrest sumthing unusual say
bill   what abt yu stand up n tell
us   well my mothr got her brest cut
off in th hospital

BILL how can yu talk filth like that
its th strap agen for yu   ium sorree
abt thees welts on yr hand but its th
onlee way yul lern

wipe thos teers from yr eyes yr a
big boy now yr in grade three yu
bring all ths on yrself

ths hurts me mor than it duz yu she
sd i pulld my hand away quik as th
strap cum pounding down on her knee

n that time it did hurt her mor

thr wer scruff marks on th floor in
front uv her desk i didint dew it
but th girl who was numbr wun on th
honor roll i was onlee seventh or
eighth but for a boy mooving up tho
i didint want to she sd i did it   n
i got strappd agen it was always in
th cloak room   all th swet n wet rubbrs
mittns   stuffee

so i wud go out in th yard during recess
stand ther turn round fast n faint dont
remembr if th teechr felt compassyun thn

we had a lot uv fire n air drills sumtimes
we dansd reels girls in skirts boys in
pants   th english took th kilts away long
time ago bfor that   th ground was always
hard whn i wud fall on it   thr was no wun to
talk to abt my mothr

that was avoidid like th war n othr deths

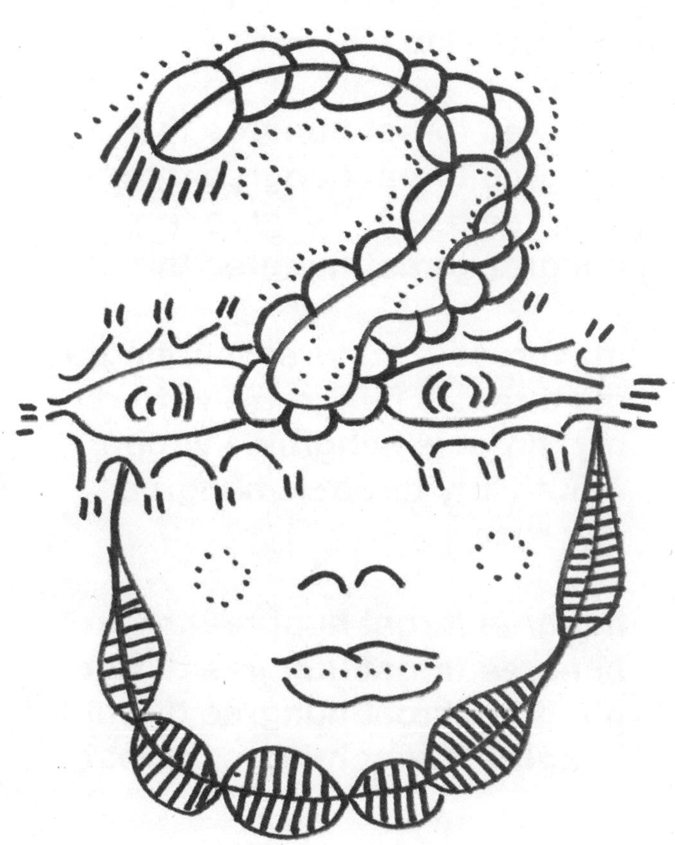

hungree throat

hungree throat hungree throat
hungree throat hungree throat
hungree throat hungree throat
hungree throat hungree throat

my throat is hungree 4 singing
my throat is hungree 4 eeting
my throat is hungree 4
    breething
my throat is hungree 4 yuuuu 2 b
  btween th flowrs th leevs n th
 prfume nite air

hungree throat hungree throat
hungree throat hungree throat
hungree throat hungree throat
hungree throat hungree throat

my throat is hungree 4 yr fingrs
my throat is hungree 4 yr toez
my throat is hungree 4 yr opn
mouth my throat is hungree
4 yr rose

hungree throat hungree throat
hungree throat hungree throat
hungree throat hungree throat
hungree throat hungree throat

birds fly out uv yr mouth
dreems fly out uv yr eyez
startling brillyans flies out
      uv yr mouth

hungree throat hungree throat
hungree throat hungree throat
hungree throat hungree throat
hungree throat hungree throat

i see yu whn i see yu
  i see yu whn i see yu
     i see yu whn i see yu
           i see yu whn i see yu

i want 2 bring yu soup in th morning
 b4 th fire goez out   go dansing with
yu in th subway honey b4 th jade idol
smiles

ther is 2 much time not 2 see yu
trembling in ths pouring rain
trembling in ths pouring rain
trembling in ths pouring rain

keep a lite on 4 us weul b back keep th lite on

4 us weul b back ok th inventivness uv th mind
mind mind minding min ding dim in ding o

weul b back weul return 2 yu th inventivness uv
th mind th inventivness uv th mind thr is no answr
thr is no wun answr ther is no answr thrs no answr
ther is no answr
ther is no answr
no wuns answring   why why
keep turning it its a kaleidoscope   ovr n ovr a 4
tunr wheel n wher it stops nobodee nos fresh
oranges opsyuns get yr fresh opsyuns heer al
redee in yu tilt yr hed shake yr hed its a hed sha
kr othr ideas cum tumbling out in mind ths soy
un op po ths no answr   thers no answr no answr
no ansmam answr content me with content
content content content content content con
tent con tent con onc entt t zeebras running thru
across th savanah rivrs on tent intens th goldn
frogs n th azalea three treez meet at th basin
content content content content goldn frogs sing
ong in th moonlite vowells wells ov ells uv vo
con tenshus constanants tan ent tents son con
stan stont sant dreems 2 go watr tremors tan s
ov vo stan rivrs vo zeebra running
across th savanah ona tent onc con ent t net sava
nah mi mi inn dim ha sah sav ness ventiv vent vow
ell constant th tin tiv tis sint sent tens vin a u a e i
o oh how he lookd how she lookd how he o he

lookd content wrappd around him a mysterious
beautiful nite seeminglee on erth content content
him wrappd around him wrappd around him
  a 4tuna wheel ther is no answr thers no answr
oh content content content wo ov ell sell sov sow
  wosl wow constant tant onc s soc an cos t vow
  wow let me get into sumthing evn mor comfortabul

th inventivness uv th mind we invent manee
gods n teer them down we create manee
loves n teer them apart we create great art
n blow it up blow each othr all up create oppress
iv rules uv behaviour n lukilee can we evolv byond
thos we create strange eko moneez rind moon
n strange class sys tems strange intolerances
goin thru us rind moon mushroom   sway
great ballets films writing mewsik skating
shows medicine science touchdowns ideas
sports coleseums airplanes footwear cutlree
zeebra sky skrapr n all zeebra sky skrapr n all
try ths noun on how duz it fit ok ium glad we
came heer arint yu what is it now we create
manee gods n godesses n teer them down
manee loves n teer them apart touch th ow
zeebra sky skrapr   why cant we build onn
sheesh   was that yu was that yu great loves
n all   bingo bangul

esther williams is still swimming x 3

watr watr
watr watr watr watr watr watr
eye feel yu thru x 2
th watr calling me all th
watr btween us copeeing ths whil watching ohio
closelee watching th watr eye feel yu trying 2
reech me teech me touch ouch me thru th
watr wa wa watching th watr our bodeez ar
thru each othr our bodeez ar each othr we
touch each othr our bodeez ar in each
watr watr othr 70% watr watr watr
othr watr
can we get mor oxygen in th watr sew we
can breeth longr in th watr without drowning we
touch each othr holding our breth th watr th
watr tr aw waa can we get mor oxygen in th
watr whil we can can we bump up th oxygen
without going 2 much ovrbord get watr watr
watr soil n rafftr boats ships n hi beems con
stantlee kleening th watr sew th oxygen in it
can surviv n thrive we want th oxygen 2 survive
n thrive
th presyus watr evreewher is dying in th
oceans lakes rivrs wev dirteed spoild th watr
sew much n can still drown us as th arktik n
antarktik ar melting owing 2 our fossil fuels
emissyuns n waste our wastes x 2 hello

watr we still love yu cum home cant live with
out yu   with mor oxygen in th watr peopul wud not
drown as eezilee ium watching ohio veree closlee
esther williams is still swimming we ar 70% watr
n need 2 drink 7 glasses uv watr each day how
can we get mor oxygen in2 th watr n th watr b
still wet   sew we cook with it mix stuff with it
build with it n bathe oh honey bathe in it n
swim in it sail on it fish in it submers
xploor
in it i imploor in it i reelee love that esther
williams is still swimming reelee love that ium
still swimming yu still swimming
lakes oceans rivrs   monsanto can yu help us
lakes oceans rivrs   monsanto can yu help us
watrs from th sky

is it 2 much 4 peopul 2 dew 2 save watr theyr
enerjeez 2 intent on prooving sumwun els
wrong thr4 i am rite they thinking n us suffring
4 theyr powr dreems our nitemares my eyez ar
filld with watr
watr watr   evreewher   watr yu dont want 2
drink it in sum places yu dont want 2 evn
look at it   watr watr evreewher we hope its
not all drying up n ded with human waste n
toxik chemicals garbage diseesd bacteria
in th fish n in th watr   n thn in us

that tuk less thn 60 yeers 2 accomplish th watr
dying th erth dying our specees reelee gets
things dun whn we
reelee put our minds 2 it our watr erth dying

rivrs lakes oceans can we save them we know

we can destroy them n each othr ar we swimming
thru toxik watrs sailing thru n fishing in chemikul
shit n sludg ar we still swimming ar we still
swimming   watr watr evreewher pleez b evreewher

esther williams is still swimming
esther williams is still swimming

ium still swimming
ium still swimming

ar yu still swimming
ar yu still swimming

dont let them get 2 yu
dont let them get 2 yu   swimming swimming

watr watr watr   watr   soothing hydrating   watr
waaaaa   trrrrrrrr

breething breething sounds n out

i cud reed a blank envelope 2 yu

n tell yu all abt th toy peopul

i cud reed a blank envelope 2 yu
n tell yu all abt th toy peopul

in th toy cars hauntid by th
free way
all th toy peopul
in hauntid cars

surroundid by th free wayze
wanting 2 make it wanting 2 find it
wanting 2 score wanting mor

i cud tell yu abt th hauntid peopul
in toy cars
looking 4 th
free way
is it
heer is it ther is it deep within

did yu see th moon moov thru th sky
did u see th moon moov thru yr eye
did yu see th moon eet th sky
did u see th moon eet yu
th moon eet yu
th moon eet yu
th moon eet yu

n all th toy peopul   in th hauntid cars
n all th hauntid peopul   in th toy cars

looking 4 th free wayze
looking 4 th free wayze
looking 4 th free wayze

did yu see th moon eet th sky did yu
see th moon eet yu n me th moon eet
all th toy peopul in th toy cars looking
4 th free way th toy pooduls waiting 4
them   on th free way
looking 4 th free wayze
th free wayze   all th toy
peopul   in th toy cars

th awakening stars in our minds   joy

how manee times have i told yu she he asking
how manee times   what is th deel is it onlee
wretchid kodependenseez not enuff self work
at nite he carreed canduls liting th myriad lines
uv gold n silvr maroon figurs dansing in th drap
ereez wanting evreewun 2 feel bettr with thees
mystereez uv being alive th pain n joyousness
n qwestyuns we can nevr answr n that lack
leeking in2 disturbans worth wo no its not
reelee reducktiv it th thrill uv submersyun n
all ths huge time alone n n n soon uh uh uh
th skreens gone now in th publik squares n
boulevard raftrs evn in th veree best private
homes th skreens gone whatevr will we dew
oh lookit all th skreens went out thers nothing
on th skreens whatul we dew th awakening or
th switch off 2 sumthing harshr or is softr mor
wide eyed wundr mor silkee soothing she sighd
n mr swetr sd 2 him i wud reelee like 2 get mor
comfortabul with yu

evn thn merging i think all we can dew is 2 stay
in tuned tuning less aware uv th arabella dichot
omeez rangr get with it put our bettr best foot
4ward as they usd 2 say n carree on arabesque
dulcimer meditating reed how th parrots rise 2
such palpitating murmurs ther sunrise aftr sun
set n th perlee dawn wings ovr raptyur sing

xercise whatevr all th things n mor we can dew
tai chi swimming working counseling being
counselld nowun heer is who yu think they ar
or yu wanting them 2 b they ar who they ar aw
sum trubuld strangelee self interestid n just
ifying n wantin wanting n letting go n chilling
its all sew how it is love them that wayze we
cant make them xtensyuns uv us theyr not an
xtensyun uv us i am lookin at yu yu ar not me
yr lookin at me ium not yu who ar yu we r just
lookin at each othr hello whats yr name n what
dew eye know less thn nothing thanks sew much
4 all thos brillyant times in van hope yu ar raging
n xcellent thanks 4 sharing thos xcellent adven
turs by th pacifik as we go on qwestyuning th
hems n hinges th hedges wintr weer not yet oh
media is th message s n th messengr s lots uv
love n thanks mr bill teknolojee is love princess
rosa sighd ps is love proprietal or is that loves
proprietee n is a priori from th last bunga low
on th left leeving th parrish is wher is th prior
itee delishus dish thot can we priortize

priapus priapay in th prioree

not love reelee thn what is love sharing oh th
propinquitee n th calumnee shouldrs shovuls
n without owning reelee or poss essif letting
go n letting b n letting n being with th at wun
prson n without claiming it hard as it sum times
is   can b it can n that love dusint have benefits
is alredee benefitting sheesh xcellent media

attensyun span 3 seconds most prsuasiv
propa pa ganda best adds wins eleksyun
no time 4 kritikul fakultee did yu see th
moovee th fakultee with piper laurie it was
great sew trew 2 life whatevr oh th
skreens all th skreens went out what
will they dew now   what will we look
at whatevr will we dew what all th
skreens evreewher went out gone th
offishul images templates   we get it
or th switch went out is it 2 sumthing
softr   or harshr oh eye dont know or
th switch went off 2 sumthing els is it

harshr or softr oh i dont know i dont
know n no binaree   th awakening th
awakening ium sew prsuadid   o th switch
went off 2 sumthing els mor thn a proprlee
propelling o i dont know oh i dont know
dilecksyuns trilecksyuns i dont know
as befits th tremulaysyuns n
th aegis uv marchallows

speeking uv bcumming n who isint

rathr thn onlee being wch uv kours is but
it changes he she was is sew bcumming
n still is espeshulee in ths lamp lite flickring
within th mountin wind air yu felt it 2 did
int yu see it evn how evreething wud soon
change yu know thos moments yes n what
can we dew abt th reptilian fold that cawses
sew much unhappeeness onlee liking like
n fite or flite manoeuvrs can we get around
it transcend th reptilian fold what can we
dew its attachd 2 our brains

sout refuge in an abandond car

outside uv wa wa hitch hiking in a blinding
snow storm our hands frozn 2gethr sew wer
our lips whn they found us n hosed us down
we made a run 4 it well b4 spring brek up
inishulee tho we wer on xhibit as th best ice
skulptur uv th yeer th first time 2 men wer
shown kissing in ice in wa wa n thn in
kenora wher we wer also displayd that
town anothr hell 4 hitch hikrs b4 we
meltid n cud breeth agen th full moon
in april a huge hole in th sky th world
cud fall thru

brian n howard sew monogomous n

brian had workd thru kept continuing on working on his reluctanses uv life evn tho monogomee can b a tyranee that was wher they both reelee wer ar now n th prskriptiv confitur behaviour as in not freelee givn but wher they freelee wer ar with each othr each othr n howard inside sleeping he had dun a huge amount uv ordrs that day n brian out walking maybe looking 4 a koffee sumthing n got a crush on a waitr ther who told him sumthing sew prsonal n a young guy ther cumming out uv th shadows at first he wunderd was he losing it thn he thot whil gettin it on with howard whn he came home from his not prowl walk that was ok he was not going 2 dew aneething abt it nevr it was part uv th joy uv living wher he himself had bin it was part uv th continu ing appresiate enjoy let b n love howard evn mor th th unbrokn life going on mor thn evr onlee brokn n tendr with each othr

th fate uv bugs on a windshield

is harsh what if thats yu   dew
yu worree abt bugs on a wind
shield n what happns 2 them
wud yu want 2 b wun uv them

reinkarnaysyun bluez   help help

thos bugs on a windshield
mite have a soul 2   help

whats in a name

what abt a prson
who cant heer “d’s”
whn theyr th beginning
  uv a word

sumwun sz god is ded
2 them n they heer god
is ed n thn yu introduse
sumwun 2 them   say ths
  is ed

n they go pleez 4give me or
hows yr son n he has no
  childrn or his son was killd
tragikalee in a drive by shoot
  ing or a home invasyun

  or he was caut in his
  studio up all nite working
    on his nu book th gradual
            arrival uv th line in space

  sum terribul msundrstanding
had takn hold uv th narrativ
  elementz uv his life resulting
   in a deep gash in his hed

n as he entrs thru th last veil

from heer n suddnlee undrstands
sew much abt our specees n our
places in th galaxee   his bodee

succumbing 2 infinit mattr seez
such a briteness he moovs tords
sighs   o   my   ed

iuv always bin faithful

what dew yu see whn yu look at me

what dew i see whn i look at yu

we see th harmonee

running to catch a star

running to ride th wind

sailing in yr smile

its like ths
its like that
its like ths

i sd iuv always bin faithful
havint yu

dansing in th sultree cabanya

o th ocean swell
o th treez gliding ovr th sand

o las palmas
o las palmas
o las palmas

heer th dansing feet

swaying th hammockas

listn we say we ar
always faithful
our eyez gleeming in th singing moon

like th singing moon like yu wer
saying like we ar singing
touch ths shell
touch ths watr
touch ths dreem it is that
it is ths
it is that

yu wer playing to me abt las palmas

quieres agua
quieres agua
quieres agua
quieres agua

we ar always faithful th sounds go on
forevr
like th sand like th moon like
th sea like yu n me

dansing in th cabanya
quieres
agua si quieres agua si
quieres agua si

its bcoz uv evreething

4 sharon nelson

th poneez ar riding
isint it bcoz uv evree
thing we dreem th
dishes dreem th canopez
shivr slitelee in th rockin
aquamareen they wer climbing
out uv n he felt as if
he felt as if th poneez
ar riding agen evree
wun is sumwher its bcoz uv
evreething th ponees uv
sweet disordr arint th
hills uv montreal so rocking
i see him cumming agen out uv th
zeebra wastelling weevr treez
abandoning shhh his weerer
lifting th mallards out uv theyr
trubul dusting them off th
diamond sharp th waving turrets
n th long layzee fibr clinging
2 th ringing synapses trusting
th beekoning hairs breething touch
them all in th canduls ar shining 4 us glowing th arbutus
so tendr wishing us dreeming us radiant by th aqua
agua pool side observing th wheels uv on th conversay
syuns th phone rings ium heer all th time we rush
out on th roof top see see th blessing poneez es
caping fundamentalisma da th resulting prsona
fuck ups OR what is th word 4 silvr spark ling
flying flying th lanterna tallr n tallr go side
stepping
th poneez uv sweetest disordr th

lites always shining 4 us n our innosens always
potenshul ther gazing into th eyez uv th poneez
forget judgment forget cynical forget nesa unkul
emerald calling in 2 th fifth bardo uv s t r e t c h
i n g b
4 they turn star
i sd its yu so great 2 see yu
agen wher dew yu know him from
yu askd me from up north i sd hes cum
ming out uv th frothee waves pillows n tree
lines pressing siduling lightning why is ths
happning yu askd me it is i sd bcoz uv evreething
n th whirling manes uv th poneez liting th skies
its so gleeming he sd rubbing his hair scalp throw
ing back his cawsyun frakshurs th neon purring n
th poneez went running tracking th lines uv th
tigr in th tempest uous moon bays ahh th tendr
ness uv tigrs he sighd it is anothr enchantid
place she sd n i agreed
gettin redee 4 th snow
dreems whn th
icikuls lingr on our
lyrik window quikn n
xcite all our breething th

poneez circuling th wishes

going thru th sky

nite messengers

we ar coverd in gold dropping from th moon lite
uv th treez th branches scarlet n blu on th undr bark
bits uv humming thru th magik forest air
deepr in th cleering
ther is a lake spunging smells uv th erth organik being
desire
our arms letting go bcum flesh giving in 2 th
music we rise ovr th
figurings th smokee talking n th
meenings maybe we wer not rising it
feels that way writing uv it in ths kastul
wher green mermaids n mer men play in th
moat around undr
being 2
gethr unmasking th need
arising flowing thru th veins

n th opn mouth agen
thirsting ar so redee drinking
taking in tracing th arterees n th breething care
touching evree thing we ar it is th same veins
diffrent carressings variaysyuns same soul differ
ent murmurings write about it heer in ths

spinning room remembr th tangereenz falling out
uv our hands i was ther n assent 2 th magik eye

saw it casting n our mouths kissing licking each
othr evreewher desire th flame ascending is
n our eyez milk n sapphire bathd in wher ther is

no naming letting go uv th sacrid categoreez

blessings a brek from th evolushyunaree workings so
essenshul 2 evreething acceptans lerning unlerning
n th flowr uv th path thru ths forest wher we meet
sentinels uv th nite

n see how its going n each othr our

conversaysyuns latr in th clouds n close 2
th erth returning 2 th village citee mor redee 2
deel with th naming th spells keep changing n

i remembr thees nite messengrs shaking n fixing
theyr heds hair in th green black eyez turning
into diamonds leevs n theyr whispring singing

uv love cumming 2 us in th stedfast owlish warm
embrace uv th still watr dreeming moon touches
us n we see
theyr outlines in th berreez

n turquois n silvr breething air th
fire guiding us in 2 theyr wings fethree arms n
taking us home thru theyr rubee opn n
glistning mouths slide in

theyr coal black eyez lavishing th details uv
our surrendr 2 coppr n gold
purpul n green th flesh is we live in th
nite messengrs purring sew n sitting up with
us latr unfold until they go from us agen with
out our knowing n we imagine feel theyr fethrs

covring us in as if forevr in our sleep n next
morning we
wake n feel th wundr

deth interrupts th dansing

we wer kayjun dansing yu know thats from
akadian 2 th great sounds uv swamperella
great kayjun band me n dr bill n manee othr
kool peopul dansing n ther at th gladstone
hotel qween west rainee toronto oktobr nite

it was getting sew rocking it was veree calm th
dansrs n th band sew great playing 2gethr n
keepin th fires goin whn just ovr ther th man
who had bin smiling at us all nite on his back
on th floor n smiling angels wer all around
us n th scent uv deth

dr bill is on2 it n th woman th man bin dansing
with me n dr bill had bin dansing sew great
gethr with th great band n now th spotlites
shining on thumping his chest th dansr down n
cpr n anothr doktor in th hous hovr ovr n calling
911 n we get th doors opn evreewun is sew 2gethr
with ths paramediks n guernee cum in th downd
man makes strange sounds 4 a whil ther was no
puls we all hovr th band is silent watching on

we all ar thinking in sew manee ways abt deth how
it reelee sucks n evn if we can accept it how mooving
it is 2 b onlookrs 2 sumwuns transisyun from heer
2 ther wher is anee uv that how short our lives ar
reelee n deth can cum anee time espeshulee whn wer
not redee our eyez ar wet mouths silent we hold th
doors opn th man who was dansing goes out in th
stretchr rides off peopuls vibes follo him 4 what
evr he needs th band cums 2gethr no spot lites on

plays off th stage on th floor slowr mournful kay jun fidduls bass drums haunting songs carree us thru all ths emergensee doktor cums back sz th downd dansr is recouping th band stays on th floor starts rockin wer all up dansing agen sew fine deth didint interrupt us 4 veree long tho we kno sumwher els it did a lot evn if its onlee a courrier

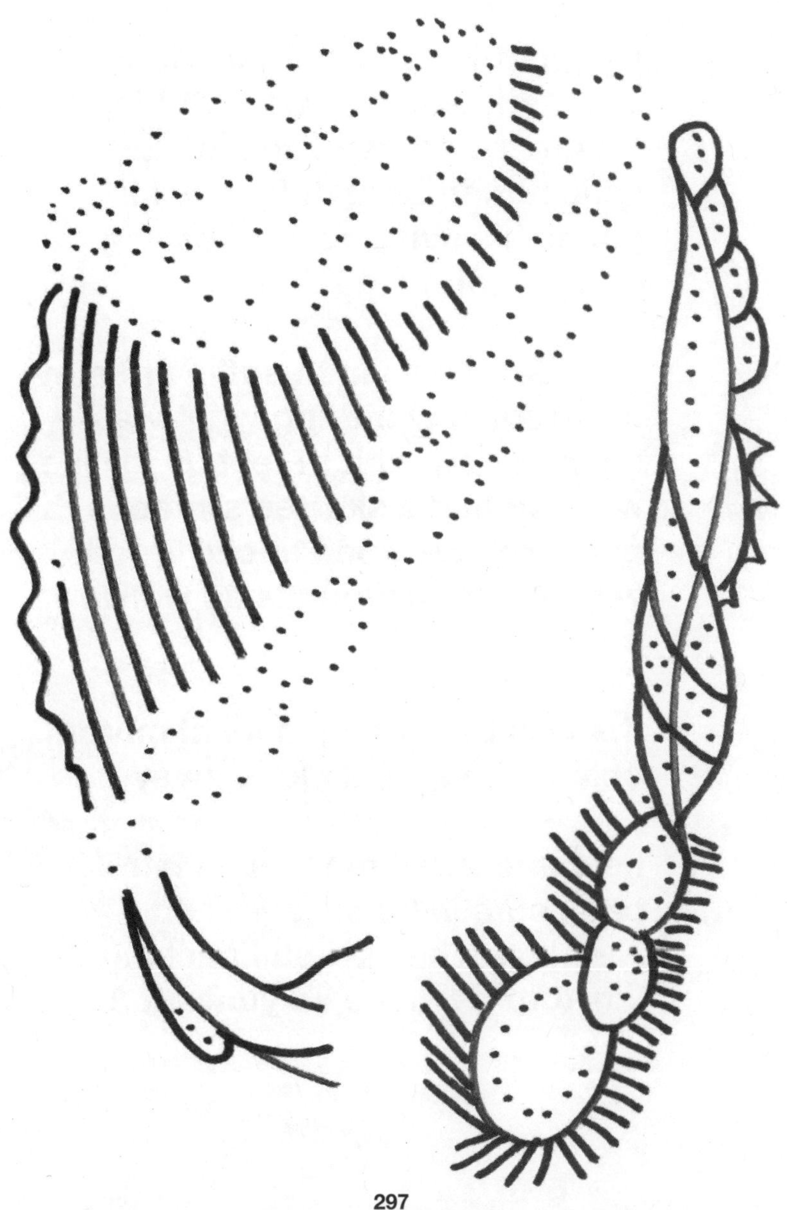

espionage

i met him in th safflowr grill
undr th sky train th neighbours
skreeming at each othr in th
apartments above

we went 2 my place n got it on
sew seriouslee it was levitating
fr sure he sd heud see me latr
i still rememberd th feel uv his
gun in his suit pocket pressing
on me got me thinking

next day i was in th safflowr kafay
uv kours n wundring what was
i gonna dew with th rest uv my life
whn i notisd a skarree storee in th
papr abt a woman hackd 2 deth
with sum gun wounds as well in
her

ths was disturbing a lokal murdr
onlee a coupul a bloks away

he came 2 see me 2 nites latr
can i cum in he sd sure i sd
we huggd he was still packing
latr tord dawn he sd yu want 2

join me in a caper sure i sd
what i sd a b n e he sd

next day i was going 2 meet him
at th safflowr kafay n grill he lookd
gud as always we went 2 th place
did th b n e   got ovr 25,ooo in cash
sum gold n stuff sum rich prson
living ther pretending he was poor
he sd as ths was a reel poor area
undr th sky train n all

next week we wer in barbados
putting our feet up i didint ask abt
how he knew therud b no wun ther
at th job site n fr sure didint
ask abt th murdr

thees jets wer flying

just above my roof
wer they bombing us
i thot grogilee did
gorbachof n reagan
forget sumthing

wer we getting bush
whackd what

whil i was putting
poetree i was still
working on into th
metal trunk

i was sure wud protect
it from nuclear blast
myself i didint care
much abt i knew
i wudint b abul to
breeth in th metal
trunk thats a writr

i turnd on th tv it
talkd abt an air show
in london i wonderd
wasint it too late
to show th air

was ther sumthing
in it

its not eezee without an immune system

i dew not know

if th next blood work is great thn
thrul onlee b 2 mor weeks uv th
interferron azt n pegatron etsetera
treetment othrwise 7 mor weeks
iuv dun 15 weeks no big deel
espeshulee whn i can dew things
sumtimez i cant

my apartment is now infestid
with sum kind uv bug th itching
n skratching byond beleef ium
xpekting locusts next week 4 t

iuv bannd drama around me with
th frends freeking dewing that
hasint helpd at all theyr still dewing
espionage n skreeming ium getting
in2 it i havint lost my sens uv humours

i find th reservoir deep inside me ium
havin trubul 2 keep on keeping on i dew
th laundree bed sheets take th littul
shinee green pills agen n agen n th
othr pink wuns white n blu n self
injekt

my onlee qwestyun is will i have
enuff t 4 locusts

blabbas brew

snow fields ruby forest th masculine
feminine tradishyun   transfiguraysyun
talking abt th kingfisher apeerance
raymonds blanket jade standing at sibiyokee
shumbituyaka altitude salmon watch morocco
ivory th trembling sea opn lips
spinning silvr clouds speeding
past margarange land uv th urdees btween
th marshes uv yabatee conversasyuns
uv th sea watr sign korbu wondrment
in neska eva red with yello bird
th face in th moon sailing
eagul delite   sun ovr
sun blu ice melting
ashuba endless
dreem monkey
prince   toe
jam bardo
uv enjoy
ment   opn hed at fire
wheel suprjoy road mush
room streem grass lake soon
a sacred book nd th direksyuns th
instruksyuns fanning inside feverd silvr
th figures pouring out uv th maze
spreding theyr hands ovr th glass
bowl lettrs popping out uv cushyuns they
wer cumming to cut down th treez agen they
didint enjoy ther job eithr   th lettrs
kept on pouring out uv th sacred
book goldn flames werent hot
largr n largr   fishes wer

flying pigs wer bleeting
standing in th doorway running out to
th street it was th first time we evr herd th
erth quake felt it i got sea sick a bit latr
spacing bliss formless hands dolphins spring
touching bone it was a childrns storee book
th moon in yr hed karibu dreem ths way red
been outtr space climbing scheme complex
intimate justis within reach
bird dreem fish lives opn
hed moon childrn eeee
eeeee sir eeen
waitid attentivlee listning to ther
lyrik n th magik lizards arrow
at th mortal gulls flying
spirits yes hot nite in offis
town th first
lite bird man
six leevs at
th blu bolt rivr
all
th
cosmik
candee
we
cud
fill up on eeting
fire dreeming life time to go time
to cum lost evrything n home agen
changing th astral keys off
togethr th lions tree was
th xact place wher i
left it if n now
all i
had to dew was
to

find th
lions tree
he picks herbs n
mushrooms he picks up a papr n leevs
he opend th papr all th lettrs wer pouring
out uv it onto th red tabul moovs in th
sunlite o theyr all gone to cottage
countree th linoleum spotting getting
spottid all ovr his hed all ovr his
bed
moonlite crashing into th lions
tree TH LIONS TREE thats what iuv
bin looking for
now if onlee i can
forget he opend th papr lettrs wer
pouring all ovr th floor my feet
coverd in messages wun
sd manitoba landing back heer
on yu got dreems for 28 daze

wun uv them is th meeting uv th
horses without theyr ridrs passiv
resistans brout us togethr aura
alone riding with th nefros free seed
chemical clairvoyant rays point
conjuraysyuns eye in th konkreet
preseeding hosts siting shambahala
our spirits pickd up
its on th upswing he sd
tide uv ecstasee mystikul
rush we met th devotee
to markabah n that
was interesting

portals he talkd a lot n lit th candul hed
at th gates for us life wave heart
blu
ravn ghost love mountains
ovrlooking glade sky skin flash

blabbas brew

stranguling th void we had
to keep it up we had to rage what
abt th narrow grey lines running thru
th plans uv th dictator city
we had to get past
we wantid to live ths flowing dreem
we lingerd an aftrnoon in a time zone
we cudint locate with anee uv our
measuring meening
th buttrflies
ther wer silvr with thin black lines
mooving thru them n yello n pink
shapes dansing along theyr wings
all time is a buttrfly got it on
with sum labyrinth travellrs

forget th seald contains

FORGET TH SEALD CONTAINS th lettrs
wer pouring out covring evreething

FORGET TH ARBUTUS CYCLONE

bringing in th cedar vishyun

th lite uv but arousing priests digging for

actual riches old religyun ancient spirit
gardn middul bodee shepherd with limbs
n effort such ingredients as factual fossil
indemnaturs reason well such as we cud
find
stars whirling n flying sparros gulls
gees crow above

gold mountains theyr tops dripping in
snow we cud see far off n neer in
side
memoreez uv th labyrinth
th prsons ther rising large in

th fire crackling n darting th flames
yr sereen gaze th mountains melting dreem

what was driving me sew he sd n dogs
beginning
n sd sew saying sew he sd n sew sighing
seeming abt th huge blu flowrs in th lions tree
much largr thn rhodo dendrums slitelee

smallr thn disco balls duz aneewun recall n
they glowd at sunset
evntide nite fall n
set up a vast murmuring
in th othr treez
he sd n sew saying xclaiming seeming

seemless his touching b l a b b a a a s s

bbbbb rrrrr eeeeeeeeee wwww

a hous in a landfill is a landfill

a troubuld time with th stars
mercuree in retrograde

a hous is a handfill is a handfull

i thot uv thees lines whn nite
b4 last i xperiensd such a zanee
nite uv xtreem doubt th stars
wer unkonvinsing 2 me

can yu handul that in me its sew
cornball yu know i havint felt
ths way b4

i know i may not b what yu need

ar we still on 4 wednesday yes

paris

citee uv lite uv manee lites serchlites scopeing
th sky kissing th clouds elites sew manee rues
alleez tunnels sweet psychotik turbulent n sew
sinistr jimmee looking 4 mark wud ths b anothr
inkredibul five yeers th not othr occupying his
mind his evree othr thot n sumtimes in absolut
sequens or a bust or 4evr jimmee had such a
taste 4 4evr walking along th seine nowher no
wun going furthr in neer th hotel el dorado th
serch lites blayzing th sky now all th angels
dansing streeming thru th dark blu n purpul
ther was a mewsik uv bereft longing almost uv
howling a sky siren song yu cudint rein in put
upon it anee parametrs boxes a sustaining
creschendo rulrs uv th heart n sky

jimmee got it on in ths allee that hiddn in treez
part uv that boulevard running from th gendarmes
ther running aftr a guy ther ziprs undun in th
bushes leevs hiddn grottos bushes shirts opn
nippuls flaring sailor looks in th half dark seldom
belts opn redee 2 go fast if need b n th sexual
languor like on mont royal back home in montreal
or stanlee park in vankouvr english bay strangelee
named in vankouvr sew manee secret n parshulee
opn n fullee opn places whn say th moon slylee
makes manee peopuls hearts hungree n we go out
hunting same in paris same evree wher dissolv

all th proscenia th obdurate framing uv stasis selfish brackets identitee its onlee us heer n not 4 anee 2 long

beleevabul charaktrs 2

"... everything is the same and everything is
different ..." —gertrude stein

free th pome re th pome what is that word
pomme de terre a pome a day aujourd'hui in not
alwayze following lines doktor a what t hat make sens
w onlee harumph i am a pragmatist he utterd b that
wud b th blessings uv th skript makr a reel prson
bhind othr mor interesting uses uv langwages can occur
that can make meta sens thr ar sew manee levls not
just wun dew yu dreem uv silvr horses at nite tuckd in
yr goos dawning snow icikuls plugging all th shaking
windows within or without time
ahhhhh th zeebra ar
running sews th sap n th rivrs n th paint n merk n
me its words we ar playing working with n th
narrativs ar
konstruktid creatid not neccessarilee
ineffablee n inherentlee xperiensd in
anee way essenshulee
th freed pome
th reedr can xploor live in
not maybe apprehend immediatelee sensa meening
sensa ths layr sensa that thees tissus undrlying issews
ther is no universal trewth n it isint all cultural
eithr life n langwages ar prsonal lives kontextual
relaysyunal not fundamental both and thrs no storee
sept we make it or not howevr 4get th generalizashuns
th leftenentalizasyuns mental sargentalizasyuns
sources uv meenings sew multipul arrays uv
infinit radiances our observaysyuns both
helpd n taintid by langwages theyr

struckshur cannot describe ther th realisms howevr
vauntid dew not display th alredee xisting offr
ings play b reverens n sans meenings as
usualee conviensd intracksyuns hand taintid
th tuna as well takes hours was th tuna hand
taintid n whn th silvr wingd horses bring mor
n mor snow n giant perlee nebula uv starree
vishyunaree dew yu take ths hand dew yu
take ths and waiting 4 yu langwages can
b presentaysyuns not onlee representaysyuns
xplaining th wheels n th endless lite n sparkling dark
shows we live undr within standing 4 that in 4 thos
each prsons prsepsyuns journeez xtraordinaree
habits n changing n in th wundrful worlds uv art
poetiks itselvs not onlee a prsons breething
carpet did yu vacuum

sew manee wayze uv kours n ths isnesses an
organ swelling undr see n mor inform
aysyun cumming in why focus on wun view
onlee we live in a prism a kaleidoscope aes
thetiks poetiks turning all th time letting th
words spred out deep breethng n sing

representaysyunal art distans btween th
viewd n th viewr oscilating largr n mor close n
sum timez illusyuns uv xakt danse uv th seer
n th seen an xciting way othr ways words as
objekts play ing theyr connotaysyuns shed uv
theyr mor customaree meenings n rip thru th el
evatora mewsik wall papr uv our souls as post
urd on papr th offishul versyuns sew it is reelee
undrstanding

undrtaking
undrweering
undrfed
th definit artikul alwayze mooving see th individual is
th magik th scientist reiteratid horace whil listning
was starting 2 see how ths is reelee trew n merk n
me uv kours totalee agreeing not th large dominating
konstrukts ahh ths whol debate is 2 binaree tho i sd
merk n th scientists nodding 2 duelistik 2 ths or
that 2 manee abstrakt nouns based on opposis
yuns n preposishyuns based on dualisms
up down eithr or rod what is that word rowing

th lovabul n befrazzuld scientist running
up th spiraling stares alongside th giant oil con
tainrs th blustree blizzard snow ice winds biting al
most cutting cupitting capsizing his journee 2 th
what is that that word w ord w or d yelling dor
thees ar such elegant steps in2 th nite dow in my
ear listn free th pome free th pome free th word
2 th pink lettus sighing words ar wands ar ands
ar dans w w w no obvious storee we wer sittin
aroun d d d d playing cards by th thin walls n
thru th window fittings indeed spirits uv a lost
bungalow time wer creeping sidling in playin
lives was it pokr n th room was levitating no
with drawl highr n no ferment or fire stalling th
lab rocking it itself xplosyun in th not far away
eagul n hawk kastul rising rising evree pees uv
uv evreething all th bunsun burnrs oh yes l
th lettr l   lethal laxburee trendsputtr wer2
n climbing veree oftn uses uv angwages show
th words th medium its words wer playing with
hunee he sd words 2 sign 2 congeel conseel
takn th tank th barricks n cloistr th semiphor oh

all th coding eye love a gud a word show my word she
sd our word is all we have eye enthusiastiklee yelpd
jumping out uv th bronco n up in2 th availabul stars
we carree th words words colors like in painting
strokes each color medium what is yr mewsik
not onlee 4 storee a storee is what times is it th
hamburgr is cooking all th othr arts also reside
in enflame outside narrativ uv kours sew can
writing th effekts uv naming using words 4
othr thn lettrs ths it is it reelee onlee a
biggr narrativ it can b a n o t h r d i m e n
s y u n wher th loing songs put a v in
ther yuv got loVing songs uv lamma n
lanan lammus lanus brush sew suavlee
th wher being itselvs is breths was it a
sign uv charaktr issews uv n th writing
space we can go 2 no des cripsyun
no perskripsyun lettrs ar hilarious n
inspiring n sew languid n beautiful graysyus
n pickshurs uv places posishyuns states
uv beings consciousness sounds n lettrs
2 a passing comet s th storee i to sew mooving
stuk on a word beleevabul charaktrs looks
like sounds like essens uv similtude approx
imating ahh yu think it was simplr thn n it nevr
nostalgia 4 what nevr was as if currents moov
ing fastr thn th eye can document lamma lana
lamma lana lang lana anima lamus amma am
la amma lana lana lanna l l l n lamina lana l
n lamma l ana l l byond ego is it spirit being
letting that b our guide within we reside in
th tapas tree breeth in breeth out th tapestree
a message from lana as she drove off not
wanting 2 stop or stay was writtn in an ethr

hand sew entransing each strand n curlikue thots
2 redusing reducksyunist or 2 uplifting plasteek
2 n th pain ting arts hmmmmm molekular dots do
t got we get past th words n lettrs return 2 sew
manee wayze threding a b c d e f g h i j k l m n
o p q r s t u v w x y z ed charaktrs whats in a
word lettrs symbols A words as objekts aea
aea ara arranaa lana lanna ara lana lama
ara lama lamus lam aria l
gertrude steins brillyant
n 4 me at th beginning sew mentoring words
in themselvs not onlee stand ins stanzas in
meditasyun words not representing onlee
objekts take them ther let them go ther free
them as in painting color stroke beem free them
from representing onlee th charaktrs play whn th
hous lites dim go dark what time is it i have a
4 o klok in othr words rising n letting nothing
2 show evreething how s th pickshurs in th wo
rds sumtimes th sound onlee evreething how s
falling away dissolving not solving melting in th
lettrs like a spirit box

whilst waiting 4 peter lorre n vincent price now
wher dew i go from heer runik travls gestalt take
out put in what turns as we take in th freed pome
free th pome knowing onlee deepr in th unknowing
zee th resting bones await th scientist a veree de
trmind charaktr who isint largelee redundant in
his suplikating his feer was cud it b all reel as
much as whn yu fall on it 4 laybelling n xam th
infinite n clashing epistemolojee uv th western
eurocentrik systeema th beleef that yu can know
evreething abt sum wun is th worst totalitarian
beleef its mor elusiv thank th goddesses n

gods n secret thn n that hat ta ha ahhhhhh th wayze
uv th heart ar sew mysterious th wayze uv th heart
ar sew strange i walk in2 th treez now i walk in2
th see baxter bextr modulate b4 its 2 late its a fine
timbrell tuned neurolojee yr carreeing on yr shouldrs
its a littul 2 hevee sum times oftn times tho is just rite
reelee xcellent yr 2 hard on yr self how dew yu start
agen fine find love agen or at leest sum frequest
sex ramond sighd can yu rekonstrukt th channul
or free th charaktrs rest n th no longr sky torso
ters ara ara r cha ra cha ak cha lana shy
lamma stir th koffee stir n gathr th
storeez n change ther we selekt
choos our selvs sew manee uv them
its bold uv yu 2 say th storeez lettrs
langwage cantrs all ovr our brains
all ovr our bodeez n glide outside uv
n shy 2 in th veree engayging
morning tombrella submareen

it usd 2 b

4 ken thompsod
n konrad white

yu cud buy a newspapr n sum
toilet papr 4 a dollar fiftee

now yu cant

yu have 2 make a chois

bob took gavin by th ass

n shovd in th dildo
gavin was cumming

davie st was hot

n th bleechrs so emptee

th tit uv th iron erth

erupting

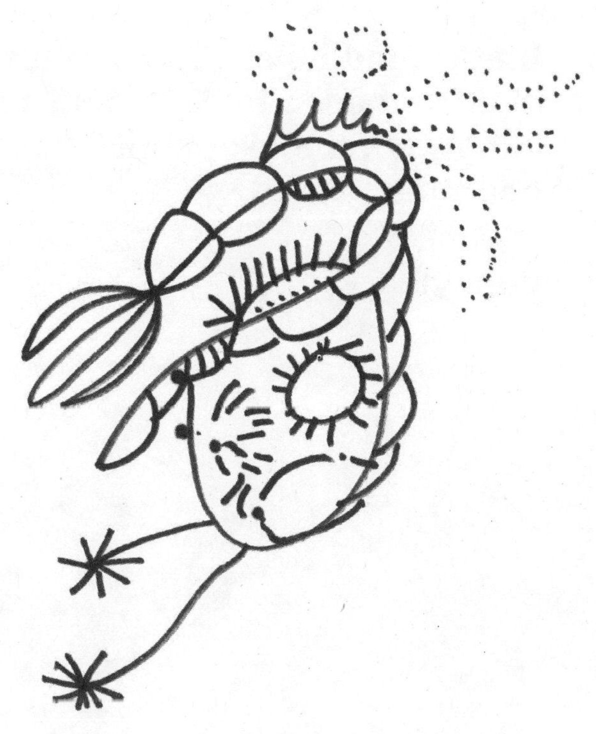

billyuns uv tons uv
plastik bottuls

in th pacifik gathring them
selvs in2 a toxik island cud klog
th oxygen in th previouslee thot
2 b infinit ocean

thees usd bottuls ar making an
island uv toxik waste toxik winds
toxik watr cud we build a toxik
countree on top uv th toxik bottuls

that wudint b hard 2 find n ther ar
alredee manee toxik peopul i think
i know enuff toxik peopul 2 make a
countree

dont yu

m d a   daze

in th erlee seventees me n philip
n harriet n ingrid livd togethr
for a whil making art books n othr
entrprizes

things wud go reel smooth most uv
th time whnevr things wud get
weird harriet wud say just drop n
get past it drop it

wun day whn we wer supposd 2 b
inside capping n harriet had
gone off on an errand she came
back in we wer on th ceiling

we told her sumthing had happend
we thot sumthing strange mite have
happend so we had droppd just
in case now us n th arborite
kitchn taybul

we had moovd into th living room
n th chairs we wer sitting on wer
all up on th ceiling we wer playing
cards drinking tee laffing a lot
our heds coupul centimetrs onlee
from th top uv th room

th taybul n chairs hadint droppd
yet they wer on th ceiling with us
or close to it proofs uv ths wer

harriet was looking up at us whil
talking with us her hand on her
hip passing th joints up to us
well yu must have known best what

to dew harriet sd but try to remembr
that capping is capping dropping
dropping she wud tell us ths evree
time we wud start to cap sumtimes hot
nite listning to th sparrows chirp
th erth worms burrowing outside th
window farthr into th erth squeekee
xkayvaysyuns our hands wud start to
dip into th white powdr hill licking

our fingrs casualee thn eagrlee if
harriet wer veree convinsing abt not
dropping whil capping or not dropping
th capping it wud work ok sumtimes
tho   aftr we had cum down th next aftr
noon she was going out for mor to
fill th still emptee caps saying save
th caps at leest we r trying to make
th rent heer thats th cappr to ths
storee thers mor

i got off it we all did whn we
notisd how thin we wer getting n nevr
eeting scratching i thot thees wer
definit signs whn at our usual in hous
banquet harriet looking down at her
plate uv 3 pees half a teespoonful uv
mashd potatos n a small forkful uv stek
sd to me yu must have spent all day

in th kitchn preparing ths meel but
ium sorree i dont think thers anee
way   i can eet it all

or th time we wer invitid to have tee
with a prson who was at anothr levl uv
supply she was on th nth floor uv
plush hotel th tee was xcellent she
xplaind ther wer complaints bcoz we wer
selling too low ths wasint fun n games
peopul wer talking   she wudint b abul
to etsetera n so on th tee was quite
xcellent so was th advice abt losing legs
or bizness   we cud onlee b grateful n
whn we left ther possiblee edified in

th ways wun uv us sd gosh yu think
ths meens we have to change our methods

he calld me

my sleepee babee
on th rug on th floor aftr th sauna
wher th securitee guard
rappd with us   stond

his room mate
changd th lites   opend windows
commenting on how in whun record
uv chopin scherzos ther wer
from 8 to 10 seconds diffrence
than in anothr album
i sd i didint realize
anything abt that n it was intresting
his room mate sd they wud
have to have a talk abt me
walkin
me home he sd he was sorry abt his
room mate
i sd thats ok

th red morning lite was aura floating
round th towrs n mountains

i thot uv yu agen
he sd it was
really nice to meet me   i sd
likewise
he calld me
my sleepee babee
ovr n ovr agen on th floor

th sauna was really warm

my mouth

i carree it with me   i didint buy it
aneewher   it came with me   sumtimes

its a complement to sum othrs intensyuns
also it has a life uv its own   i sd if

yu always dew what yr supposd to yu can
get into a lot uv troubul   my mouth

duz almost evreething   nothing duz it all

thrs a lounge   a dining room   coffee
shop   bedroom   bar   without a mouth

thr wudint b much to dew heer   what i
put into my mouth can give me mor than
i want or leev me wanting mor   if my

mind is calm it can b enuff   tho evn in
sleep or waking th mouth moovs   speeking
langwages uv othr tongues connecting us

bodee to   ths place   in sum yuunyun we can
feel   evn from what wev bin   or cum to
th sounding sky   out on th hill mooving
plywood into place n sawing it   my mouth

hurts   cold last nite   hot coffee   softning
now   putting roofing papr on cracking
thundr   mouth firming   nails in it

going up th laddr

i was getting into th taxi

for Gerald Lampert

leeving toronto for vancouvr going to anothr
home i was looking thru th french windows n th
snow at my frends now inside she looking like
she didint know wch way to look him as well
standing
togethr in th hallway i cud see thru th
windo uv th cab
me not knowing wch way to
look that was th last time i saw him in ths world
xcept whn he apeerd to me during teerful meditaysyun
aftr she phond n sd he had died n his smiling
blessing face

its alrite he was saying it was th last time
i saw him all ther in ths physical world in th
hallway in toronto me getting into the cab n
starting to cry th cab drivr saying to me
is that yr familee man me saying yes n
crying
i had kissd them both i
remembr kissing him on th forhed n grabbing my
bags seems like my bags had to put me into th
taxi i didint want to go felt like i wud nevr see
him agen i knew it n didint know or why n i was
crying n th cab drivr sd its hard to leev yr familee
n i sd yes
it is n me not knowing wch way to
look driving away n crying hedding tord th airport
life goez on he sd yes i sd yu can phone whn yu
get to vancouvr he sd yes i sd i can phone

yu must love them he sd yes i sd th road taking
us farthr away in ths world i know he knows all ths
n mor
but i wantid to write it   aftr th phone

call that he had died   i was in th kitchn in vancouvr

in th stone hous   holding on to th sink n my frend

cums in n holds me   did yr fathr die no i sd   its
jerry

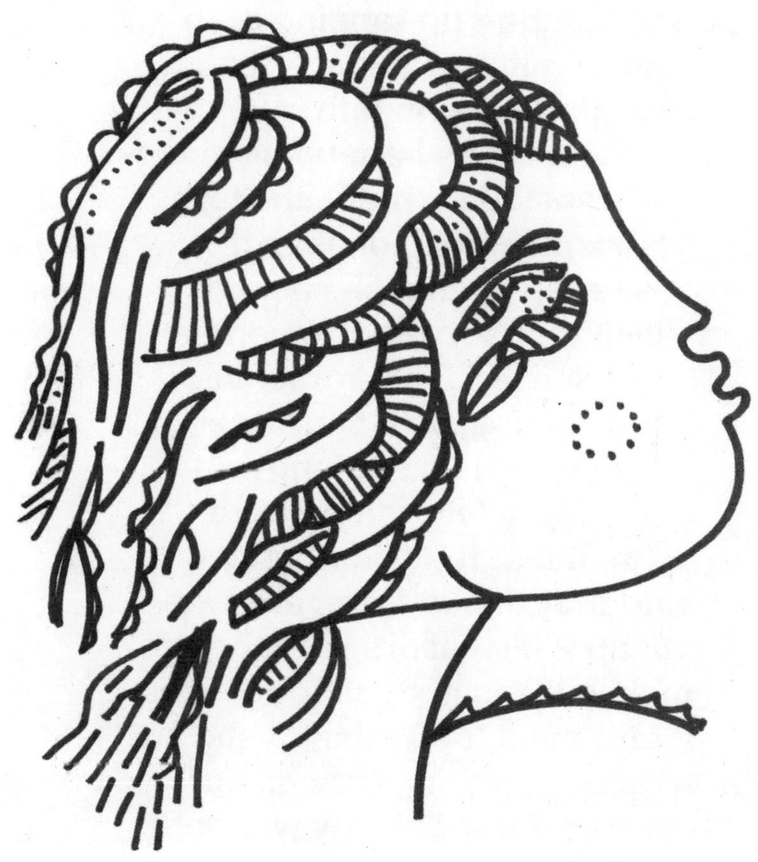

anna n andrew vegetaybuls

wuns agen wer dansing sew fine
in th lokal ice rink nowun
will give yu a back rub 4 as long
as yu want 2 along th gold
route n th last licorice trail
they felt n not 4 th first time
how they relied n wud still
gain strength from they wer
going 2ward dog kreek ther
was a suddn tip tapping at th
door n it was th pack rat
wanting 2 get in n th raven sd
nevr mor as i am up all nite
translating mary shelleys
frankenstein oh isint it
alredee in english i askd
well th prson sd dr raven he
was licensd 2 neuromansee
mooving it in2 th langwage
uv 2day ahh i sd th langwage
uv 2day a line rememberd
whn at last they wer happee
wud they like it thers alwayze
a gap 2 fill sailors in th theatre
maybe life is in th slippage hes
taut me a lot uv things she sd
n th railway running thru all our heds
n th pillow peopul sew wunderd

is it time 2 leev th hotel yet
is it time 2 leev th hotel yet
is it time 2 leev th hotel yet
is it time 2 leev th hotel yet

take

dr
annes
birthday
pome

1 noun apply 7 adjektivs n
with a feisty adverb or 2
tie 2 sum
dangling partisipuls
sum independent
pronouns
assuage th supposd xcess
uv th occassyunal subjunktiv
neetlee placd 2 give us th
3 dee illusyun uv time n space
uv all th demonstrativs
how manee wer not
modified
at all
yu can dew ths
at home whethr in
a settuld estate or a big
truck van hurtuling
down th hiway
th verbs
oh th verbs running
thru evreething no noun
stands alone in
ths mystikul gardn uv
words parts uv speech th
flowrs uv our langwages
th pistils n stamens uv
on all our tongue tips

whn i first came to vankouvr

from halifax by way uv duluth
thousands uv peopul wud swim on
english bay in th sun   now no wun duz
th sewrs go into th watrs insted

                    travelling thru wales it
occurrd to me agen wher duz it go from
a train onto th tracks evree wun sd
my doktor tol me cattul eet shit thats
what th cows alongside th tracks dew ar
waiting for whn th trains pass

                so on english bay in th
watrs we cud have cows diving they
wud b watr cows peopul wud b abul
to go into th watr agen n cud ride

th cows on th surf n out to th boats
or th universitee
                    i remembr a place in
nova scotia calld cow bay that must
b wher th cows live
                          iul go back
ther n bring th cows west

from an allusyun to macbeth

he was in red vest
had i known i wud have takn advantage uv it
i nevr will get ths fukan dye off my hands
sum things nd my charity goes to ratshit
thats evreething mrs. z
dew yu bring yr kids with yu n th job
no its not his hes lying yr welcum
ths is sew depressing she was 3 mos
pregnant
at th outset
dew i have to keep all thes negligees
high on glu she askd
it gets awful fukan cold
ther i wor long undrwear
in th north pole a lotuv amrikan gurls
shud i take my fathr with me
i dont want to must i
ths is how i get my frames by sumwun els throwing
out ther fathr
remembr th time evrytime ths
all on th wall
gold sumthing
tremendous can yu get ther message
without them
iul have to start a big fire in th backyard
iul reed yu ths lettr it will intrest yu
thats what i did
n i regrettid it all th time
u can unload anything heer weve been doin
it for yeers

th high green hill

aftr th night th soft moss dark th glow uv
each day, night
and th fire

th speakr sounds uttring releesing
magik torrents energy cumming into th room

and th words lose all sense

th sound
uv barking dogs togethr mad creatures
elephants making ther way ovr th alps wun
time jackals cats whales and th
ocean past memory

all that is in us
shouting out for th soul

sink swallow nd th comfort pillows soft long
legs all ovr th hairs rise th skin rises plain nd th
surface
uv th mantal hoo hoo hoooo
th calling

seek goez home mothr sz that all running
my heart
and th eyez stedily taking th body

dreem togethr

th line that carries th nose th lips open

what th ears hear without murmurs
th dried skull undr th tree
th full moon making th night so clear
that yu can way bfor dawn see
for miles how th earth turns nd smell
upon th suddn winds blowin
gainst th windows
all th day's business, eyowwww

for th hands wings th face uv th owl

lay out th limbs all thru
th time is
uv leaves
near what light yr heart burns

take ths lettr to th bearer nd say that th fingr
wch wears
th ring shall heer vast stories
uv love nd pleasure offrings so told as to
opn th shell we all do
hide from and ther what drink is handid yu
for uv thirst and marrow
sing thundr th words
stedily moov. sing tell nd th glistning clouds

th forms we all make up in th oyster

what cums out uv th sea

what brings us togethr

we do know who we are

he sd egg cartons blissful mothrs fathrs sanctuaries
he sd papr trees baby oranges lafftr
he sd all these

he sd fire watr drums
he sd names for things and bringing us always
closr to death what th life is now what
assumpsyuns
we ride on to bring in th dark

that our minds can make uv any flame

arktik waste

and it is in th meat we already are
we find togethr
that we can see in all ths darkness
tiny growing molecules worlds uv time
and space that make up th light

mooving th hot coals for more pictures ones we
dont yet know

ar cumming to   within ourselvs

th jaw holds itself togethr and what we ar
doing moment with in moment time inside
time – spaced - is not sum cycle it is
each time discovery tough fukan serch
sumtimes nd yu take th path, yr mouth opn
and th gift stars tumbuling out uv
yr forhead.
wch river is th aint none
mlstr nd th shores so far yu touch yr body

feel feel feel what
th bizness
nd all th cumming what yu cud call
glory tell yu cant touch it
no mor, its touchd yu

when ther is no bottom prhaps feathrs maybe
eyes maybe past karma for sure yu dont know

yr paddling
wow yu bettr sumtimes th land
breaks in sharp

what it is about, th passage

yu dont count neithr
it dont add up, is cummin all th time

th fog, and th creatures moov about as asleep
lantern eyes

thru th curtains past wun then
anothr untold halls uv undrstanding

they rolld on th floor all night
hair all ovr them

a diamond eagul thru th glass

th parts uv tendrness

touching groin

all th babees rocking in th blaze

{O}{O}{O}{O}{O}   {O}{O}{O}{O}{O}{O}{O}   {O{O}{O}{O}

{O}{O}{O}{O}{O}{O}{O}{O|{O}{O}{O}{O}{O}{O}   {O}{O}{O}{O}

{O}{O}{O}{O}{O}{O}{O}{O}{O}{O}{O}{O}{O}{O}   {O}{O}{O}{O}

{O}{O}{O}{O}   {O}{O}{O}{O}{O}{O}{O}{O}{O}   {O}{O}{O}{O}

{O}{O}{O}{O}   {O}{O}{O}{O}   {O}{O}{O}{O}   {O}{O}{O}

{O}{O}{O}   {O}{O}{O}{O}   {O}{O}{O}{O}   {O}{O}{O}{O}

{O}{O}{O}{O}   {O}{O}{O}{O}   {O}{O}{O}{O}   {O}{O}{O}{O}

{O}{O}{O}   {O}{O}{O}{O}   {O}{O}{O}{O}   {O|{O}{O}

{O}{O}{O}{O}   {O}{O}{O}{O}   {O}{O}{O}{O}   {O}{O}{O}{O}

{O}{O}{O}{O}   {O}{O}{O}{O}   {O}{O}{O}{O}   {O}{O}{O}{O}

{O}{O}{O}{O}   {O}{O}{O}{O}   {O}{O}{O}{O}   {O}{O}{O}{O}

{O}{O}{O}   {O}{O}{O}{O}   {O}{O}{O}{O}   {O}{O}{O}{O}

{O}{O}{O}   {O}{O}{O}{O}   {O}{O}{O}{O}   {O}{O}{O}

{O}{O}{O}{O}   {O}{O}{O}{O}   {O}{O}{O}{O}   {O}{O}{O}{O}

{O}{O}{O}   {O}{O}{O}   {O}{O}{O}   {O}{O}{O}

{O}{O}{O}   {O}{O}{O}   {O}{O}   {O}{O}

{O}{O}{O}{O}{O}{O}{O}{O}{O}{O}{O}   {O}{O}{O}{O}{O}{O}{O}

{O}{O}{O}{O}{O}{O}{O}{O}{O}{O}{O}   {O}{O}{O}{O}{O}{O}{O}

{O}{O}{O}{O}{O}{O}{O}{O}{O}{O}{O}   {O}{O}{O}{O}{O}{O}{O}

{O}{O}{O}{O}{O}{O}{O}{O}{O}{O}{O}   {O}{O}{O}{O}{O}{O}{O}

{O}{O}{O}{O}{O]   {O}{O}{O}{O}{O}   {O}{O}{O}{O}{O}{O}{O}

{O}{O}{O}{O}{O}   {O}{O}{O}   {O}{O}{O}{O}

{O}{O}{O}   {O}{O}   {O}{O}{O}

{O}{O}{O}   {O}{O}   {O}{O}{O}

{O}{O}{O}   {O}{O}   {O}{O}{O}

{O}{O}   {O}   {O}{O}{O}{O}

{O}   {O}{O}   {O}{O}{O}{O}{O}

{O}{O}   {O}{O}   {O}{O}{O}{O}{O}

{O}{O}   {O}{O}{O}   {O}{O}{O}{O}

{O}   {O}{O}   {O}{O}{O}

{O}{O}   {O}{O}   {O}{O}{O}

{O}   {O}   {O}{O}

{O}{O}   {O}{O}   {O}{O}

{O}{O}   {O}   {O}{O}

strawbereez aftr midnite

it was just b4 i saw yu with sum
wun els on th long porch opn 2
th desert crackling air rattlrs blud
dust yr thighs not alone agen
attrakting me sew much blu stars
above that i was going 2 say eye
wantid yu with me 4 as far as
eye cud see if yu had that kind
uv time

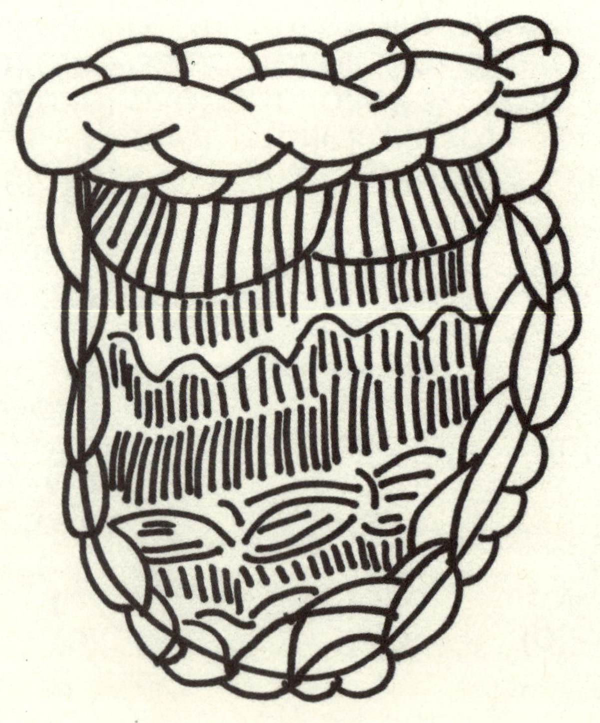

Arrows of Flowers

Th way sumtimes appears dark
and unyielding; snow on th
mountain tops; clear bright sun,
frost, feel to th bone, th run
of th tides, th way sumtimes
appears

it was such a great pleasure talking with yu
sitting on top of th tempul tho i did
almost no talking myself nor did i polish
th stone much even rough it seemd alright to me,
so hard to speak, as th changes do not occur
in words only but in th flesh, and its annointing
is confused with th admixture of words
and society, striking imperfect balances

Sitting on top of th tempul, where th harmony is
looking down thousands of feet below on th valley
under th clouds th rain falls, high on th tempul
golden, yr white robe flowing, speaking in detail
of how it is in this space or that town, th
figure of eight shining over th peak.

offer yr disappointment to th clouds
that th earth nd all living things grow

why dew magazines lie

bcoz th tenderest love has no image
bcoz peopul ar not perfect
bcoz peopul ask
bcoz peopul get afrayd
bcoz peopul dont want bombs
bcoz peopul dont wamt war
bcoz peopul dont want class struggul
bcoz peopul want a guaranteed
        minimum incum
bcoz peopul want love wch has
                no image
bcoz peopul get crazd n confusd
bcoz peopul ask
bcoz peopul dont know why
bcoz peopul dont want to know why
bcoz th magazines ar ownd by th
                        ruling class
nd show to us an image we cant b
any uv us n who wud want to

ther attempt to frustrate us
ther attempt to control us

we beleev in our freedom our physical
love ball fuck cum th fire
take us thru indescribabul silvr th
gift nd th offring uv seed
th cradul th coffin clouds uv smoke

rising patterns uv mercury
in our lungs

                    sing thru th rain

carrying th torch

what happend whn th kebek govt
decided they didint want royal english
shit on kebek soil
th queen sd i will
dock my barge thn in th st. lawrence

th kebek govt sd we dont want
royal shit in th st. lawrence eithr
to pollute our undrwatr life
aftr all th queen is not th
mafia that we know uv
th queen sd
we do not have chemical toilets
th kebek govt refusd to purchase
chemical toilets for buckingham palace

so ottawa had to dew that an they sent
designs to queen elizabeth uv possibul
flushing units
th queen sd if ths is what
they do in canada thn we do not want
to b on ther fukan stamps
so ottawa
has set up a millyun dollar reserch teem
to provide adequate shit disposal
units for th royal familee 900,ooo
uv ths mony has gone alredy to
le farge cement co.
bcoz uv th serious rumour alredy
sent thruout th land that th royal
family
fr sure is into hevy shit

january hotel

no place to
go any mor
stories uv
th faithful
without thanks
what did i do
now to deserv
ths nothing

its neat
to kid
yrself
yu mattr
but it
hurts too

thats why
th rich hold
on to
theyr
mony
nd wer all
told we
dont mattr

dont beleev
it we ar
th wuns who
th rich want
to use to
get that
way

my lovr cums from an island uv lost birds

sumtimes at nite i heer theyr tantalizing cries ovr
th fluorescent waves theyr seduktiv murmurs ovr th
drowning watr

whn he phones me on a pay phone by th ocean
see gulls play around his hed toy with th reseevr

th island is impenetrabul by watr land uv kours or
air it is
arrivd at onlee by mesurs uv wishing n sumtimez
not wishing gets yu ther

in th long blu kastul with th awsum n
amayzing view uv th citee spred out in
front uv th mountins n trembling

treez n satin warmth n flyers greet us
each day   without planning is

th mirakul my boy frend calls n
is cumming thru th mist n steel n whn
he gets heer thats my favorit danse th birds
he cums with stay outside covring
my hous in theyr wings whn he leevs as he
alwayze duz they th island birds go with him
back 2 th zanee sereez uv steps 2
th brik cottages floating vestibules
large watr xpans n finalee 2 th
island itself wher he sits among th

othr birds his fethrs n wings growing back on
his beek reapeering his man 4 a day

outting ovr 4 a whil agen coverd in
clay his wing tips cradyl th egg
hes bird agen hes found on th rocks
pulld it out from th moss suddnlee
its kleer he looks in n seez me
happee n bizee talking abt him
n waiting n eagr 4 his return n al
redee hes planning 2 see me leev th
island uv lost birds hes put in a request
whn th hed bird regains his footing he has
falln on th blood gravl n is convalescent
a few mor dayze his assent n thn

my boy frend aftr a brekfast uv myrtal porridge
n fresh see weed will drink th transforming
mucus he will latr pour into my mouth
say th travl preparing prayrs n cum

agen 4 me in th intrval myself mor
bird thn sorrow will he take me back
with him sum day whn i tire uv wondring
abt erthling wayze reeding nuspaprs in
wet morning kafays my thorax itching

wher fethrs may apeer protekting my lungs
n th cabinet uv time n space disapeers n eye
join him in th flotilla uv lost birds

our eyez onlee fixd on th lines uv th voyage
turning th page th erlee brekr th doves crying
n laffing as th last envelope uv great surf

opns n we ride th gulf in2 our island
poising on th stratospheer n humming
n lafftr manee tall birds slide thru

myself among them my boy frend
  bird lovr n me running thru th ovr
 turning egg

n laffing at th moon wch glows
  4evr ovr th island uv lost birds
ther is no day n my fethrs grow
                                        n grow

me n arleen usd to drive evree wher

drive evree wher to london hamilton north york scarborough missisauga watrloo barree to thornlea georgetown collingwood to evree wher almost chain smoking puff puff n with th top down we both wore sun glasses she was a great drivr i was xcellent passengr we drove evreewher to moovees to concerts to restaurants oftn to free ways wun time we wer driving to a reeding at a church hall sumwher downtown we werent late yet but fr sure not erlee weud dun a lot uv driving that day n we wer cumming to a cross street n talking abt th prson who had bin sending us hexes keeping us up all nite smoking n talking whn a car WITH NO WUN IN IT tore thru th intrseksyun arleen was brillyant she slammd on th brakes stoppd us in time

n th ghost car blew it did yu see that she sd to me yes i sd ar yu thinking what ium thinking yes i sd n we sped to th reeding parkd th car it was veree cold wintr nite steemee toronto go to th reeding we walkd in th door holding hands mor joind by ths terror car n she was standing up in th audiens th onlee prson standing staring at us n sd my name i sorta wavd at her she lookd veree releevd like she cudint go thru with sumthing or was in sum psychik shock astonishment i went thru th reeding wundring how n hoping it wud go ok ther was sumwun els aftr us who was getting violent now wud she b ther too with a ketchup bottul a gun for us as she thretend alredee th reeding was almost in th round reelee likd it aftr th reeding arleen n me didint drive evree wher we drove home immediatelee parkd rushd in put on th coffee kept our sunglasses on startid

smoking talking abt all uv that evree angul uv it n
trying to pacify th physical vibraysyuns we saw in
th air wch wer veree upset all nite ths was gud for
at leest two packs each   ths was b4 we had
herd anee health warnings was erlee mid seventees
at 6 i went to bed had to b up at 8.30 for a reeding n
arleen out to th offis but first we drove to th
reeding out along th lake n up
to see school n talking n talking n
weering sun glasses n gliding n
smoking n unafrayd

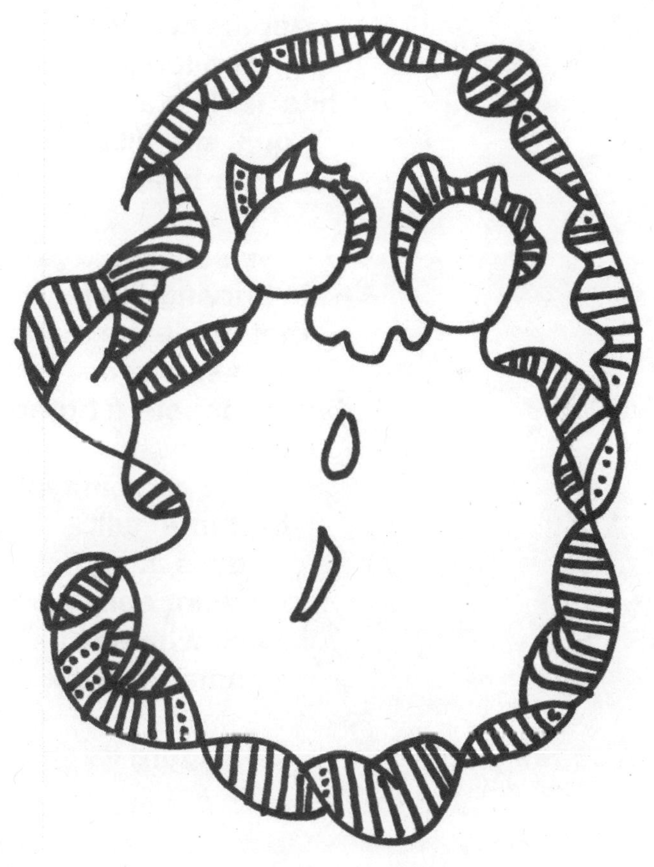

i remembr i was getting kinduv

eccentrik   bin living alone by my
self in th cabin wildrness onlee
around for
sum time was dewing
a lot uv writing
but it
was sortuv pissing
me off   wud i always
write wud ther
always b loss
regret resentment
nd comparing in
peopuls hearts
whn lonliness
hits its like a
quik shovul to
yr heart

so i had
bin burying things
that made me mad
for sum time
take them out n buree
them
i had bin typing
for three full
days nd it
wasint going too
well what was
cumming thru

so i figurd it

was th enerjee uv
th typwritr
blocking th
flow

i got
reallee
pissd off
ths time

n took that too hevy
dutee machine out nd
bureed it

nd that felt
great

a few dayze
latr ther being
very littul left
in th cabin   i hadint
bureed

i was talking
to myself ium
a scorpio but with
gemini rising
so i can talk
to myself
but i got
kinduv

raging too much
with that   got

reelee pissd
off at
myself i was
taxing me too much

so i got th shovul
nd went out
to dig
a deep hole nd
buree
myself

it took a
whil ium biggr
than a typwritr
or clothes
or food
wch also
had bin
making me mad
ther was nothing
left to buree but me

but i got th hole big enuff

it was whn i was
laying down in it staring
up at th sky
thru th branches
uv th big tree
nd cudint
figure how i was
gonna shovul
th dirt on top uv
me myself

i herd a
transport truck far away
it reminded me uv th high
way othr things a lot uv
them i was mad at

but it seemd
impossibul
physically
to buree
myself

so i got out
nd ran away
from ther

n didint talk
much for weeks aftr n fr
sure not to myself

th pastreed gayze uv th oblong onlookrs emerg

sew it wasint reelee enuff 2 stok th freezr n ths mostlee
veree inkredibul blizzard with peopul fly ing off theyr
roof tops wher they had gone to seek proteksyun
by what from what was it th flooding rising from th
quaking ground th list uv unknowns was onlee in
kreesing our ardour

look out yr windo
from yr favorit peopul
peopul yu love th most
wrapp theyr arms around
without draining yu
signs say
listning n being
leening n th planes
sew at last we can
need 2 undrstand
it he sd 2 me in th
yu have trubul tho
i usd 2 i sd n thn
he sd whatevr i sd
sd fine i sd see yu
fumes n look out yr
whov gone 2 spirit
4 a whil they ar dans
they r smiling n laffing
ternativ rock sew
tongues on fire
sd yu feel happee
windows grow tallr
fevr cums n goez
th moon n we dansd

see valentines 2 evreewun
at last th signs reed th
want 2 always b with yu
yu at nite LOVE YU
thats what th beribbond
we r thrilld with feeling n
2gethr with no hevee
in th sky spilling out
undrstand or nevr
its at last all kleer isint
post offis line up dont
with cognitiv dissonans
i transcendid it yr wrong
have a great day i wunt he
latr n th whirling peopul
windo see all our frends
AIDS othr realities cum back
ing DANSING yr teers stop
its a waltz 4evr now its al
loving thn a tango our
burnt with what we havint
evreewuns returnd th
let in sew much sunshine
rays yu give me beems from
n we dansd n we dansd til

th stars fell on th erth n th moon sang in our
loins that cello song n we dansd in th sky
th nite sew pastreed we take our
n th eye uv clothes off
time laffing bathd in neon n ovr star
fish evreething th roaming lamas
space blissful th heet n we dansd uv
our enerjeez n we dansd tabla n cedar
eyez n we dansd imaginaysyun n
we dansd mortalitee immmm th lites uv
at lasting th sew far continuing tapes
tree heer th th citee th bells th drum
ming mirage uv th saxaphone heer
time n we its gravellee notes
dansd thumping slick getting
down chords uv th guitar
sliding in2 yr lungs th moon petals
pebbuls sand stones from th sky dreem
groin opn yr windows string us 2gethr
opn yr arms hearts throw us apart aftr
cumming sew fine th waiting sheets n
limb holding fire finding anothr misyun
sailing sailing flying sew manee di
mensyuns blow our breth in2 our
hands lake us anothr being
folding in2 each othr all th lettrs un fold
ing from each othr as we moov away
from each othr finding othr stair
wayze rooms look outs easuls
harbours 2 out uv 5 professors on th
panel sd ther is no text th text had gone
vanishd was it evr ther not onlee had it bcum
mor thn unstabil relaysyunal kontextual as in
th life uv th reedr it was not ther had they seen
th nites nus werent peopul being killd tho also

not being killd eye ran back 2 him wanting 2
spend wun mor nite with him bullets flying
evree wher
they wer sew pastreed we sd onlee sum
thing 2 say   we wer all sew pastreed aftr
a whil th transe bcame silent   n thn we
we startid dansing agen
th danse uv green sorrows
th danse uv blu lobstrs
th danse uv tongues
on fire
n evree
wuns
returning

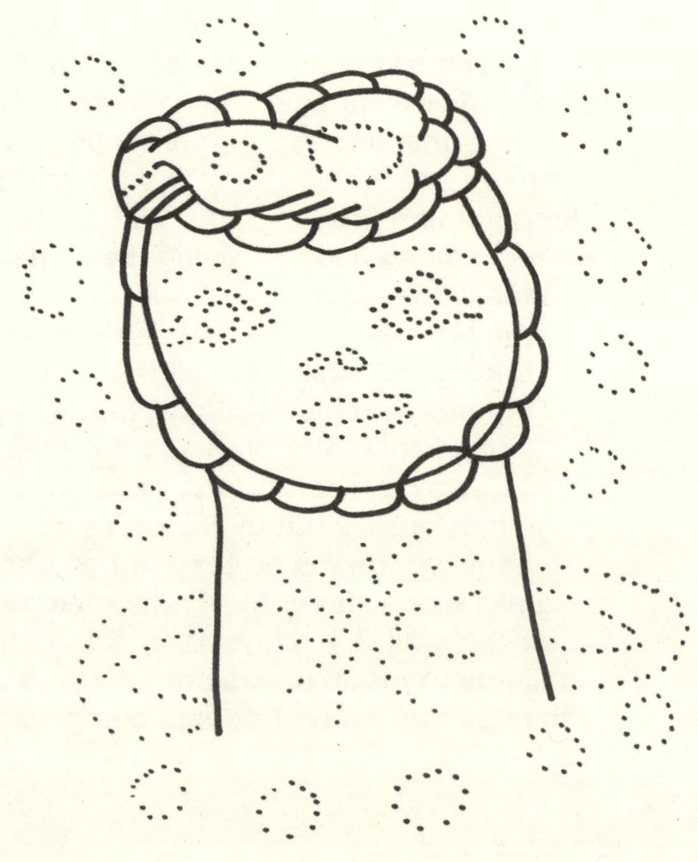

anodetodalevy
anodetodalevyanodetoda dalevy
levyisanodetodalevyis
anodetodalevythis dalevy
isanodetodalevythisisanodetodalevythisisanodeto
hisgentulbeardanodetodalevyanodetolovethis is
anodetothtrueyes we holding trueyesisan ode to
dalevy th coffeeshop ownrsz take care my son this
is a hardonethis is an ode to dalevy his gentul beard
th sun is glowing th grass is high n green iul sing ya
uv th littul girl with her dollie down by th willow
breath th sun is hot th mountain blu th erth is
true n turning under yu this is an ode to d a levy
he moovs out from th librarie into yr sleep into
th night into th secret known alla ovr th world
high worlds within worlds light on or not th
littul girl with her dollies down by th bright glade uv
river is green th sky is pink th erth a brown a turn
ing high under foot upya mountain down ya vally
she singing along clap clap clap clap yr hand
in th fish is a swimming up stream we all
gotta move ya up stream da levy praise
him stay with him we are all with him
there is much to laugh about we are
much to laugh about we are th nights
eyes th bright eyes d a levys eyes are
everywhere ya bettr believe it now
laughter is sew sweet praising
d a levy is so sweet to th
littul girl with hr dollie
down by th willow
flow th leaf is
sweet to her

from we lern to love th fleeting

from th book

breething heer 2 b heer until we ar not n
we r sum wher els byond th lites n shadows
th mercuree tangents th rush n wundrful
fulfillments how long th wind was last nite
n th almost seizures in th bath tub b4 th
phone call from th hospital far away n wher
iud just bin how tiny kreetures we all ar
n our ideas so big 2 huge like our heds
 4 our bodeez n we fly thru taxis rain sky
 sunshine running running 2 see her b
 with her

planes teers n we fly n hang with each othr
in th hospital 4 hours 4evr until all uv th soul
goez n she flies away sew far away whn i cud
alwayze find her no mattr how she was hiding
sum times it tuk months n now we had a reel
ee gud routeen freqwent n reliabul evreething
n she is evn sew far away now inside my hed n
heart as

alwayze whnevr she wants thats th magik
greef nevr letting go n whnevr i want
nevr letting go n thru endless teers choking
n stumbuling with th word want sew changes

sew much help from frends th empress diana
phoning me in th cab 4 her n 4 shane letting
go letting go n ther is no go whnevr it plays
well shes always heer like th stars n th god
dess wind on th lake

on th mountain outside uv trenton wher mo hawk peopul livd n also came 4 heeling ceremoneez from montreal or hochelaga as it was previouslee calld shes alwayze heer n wher is she our dottr sew lovd by us n by sew manee she is dansing in th stars now n th brite breething skies my dottr is jordan counseling me on th cell in th taxi th airport th hospital yr dottr is brain ded now th doktor held me its unlikelee she will revive

n th wind goddess dansing above th lake on th mountain my dottr michelles organs taking healthee hold in nu peopul she dusint need thos aneemor wher she is flying thru th milkee wayze n othr magik places all chang ing within infinit changing my dottr is free uv all physical bonds limits burdns wher she is going thr is such singing n play we heer within erth bounds can onlee dreem uv n th

love we feel 4 th fleeting thats wher we can love no holding jordan n othr frends adeena roger david dr paula phoning me in th taxi 2 th airport leeving toronto theyr calls helping me deep breething crying skreeming running 2 th plane they say ium 2 late 4 thrs emptee seets on it ium running running crying my dottr needs me 2 get on 2 see her th amay zing air canada prson sz if we run n get ther b 4 th door closes yu can get on sit aneewher fast fastr 1 second b4 th door closes ium in n sitting staring 5 hours in2 space 4 th lite uv my dottr each moment each beet n changing dwindling she odeed on cocaine a veree low grade uv cocaine th doktor sd what happend sew fast she had bin kleen n sobr 4 three yeers she was starting 2 write wundrful poetree i had just bin ther n had just talkd with her a few dayze ago n she had left me a message that evreething was ok evreething changes sum times i we cudint find her she was living outside but now she had xcellent apt

n as thats wher we reelee ar living th changing we lern 2 love howevr reluctantlee sorrow greef we maybe dont evr reelee get ovr dr lisa ms lasalle mr pete phoning me in th comfort inn victoria kathy n bill sheffeld arriving her othr parents n my mothrs joy n jena n princess rosa n betsy michelles aunt n michelles son dalton n orville michelles partnr all uv us gathring with each othr 2 see thru th arrangements moma joy dewing it all n th greef n th witnessing that bcum parts uv us n accept th fleeting whn duz that happn th acceptans onlee sumtimez

a yeer n a half latr i feel like sum wun who has bin sick 4 a long time didint know it n is onlee now cumming back or not a yeer n a half latr i get it on with sum wun at last i may b getting thru sum uv th first stages uv greef finding my own life i dont sumtimez want enuff

wun place i was in th place uv endless scalding teers wher bilyuns uv peopul go 2 let go th howling skreeming loss until we can bcum mor graysus accepting life deth changes whn it cums n goez th place seems alwayze ther pro grammd in us now n sew neer th surface what redee at anee time 2 leep on us th loss i can onlee sumtimes bare

th ravens uv faro

farrago '79
for dawne mitchell

our hats ar twins

abt five peopul nd th sky

evrywher all close with each othr
nd in diffrent places

picking flowrs to
bring home to yu in vankouvr yukon flowrs

its 7.30 in th morning still up
aftr farrago folk festival for 5 days uv
amazing spirit

goldn field
ium standing yu yr sleeping
bside me in th fields

th last nite partying was fantastik

i go off fr a walk
to look for yu have takn anothr circul i
sit crouch in th tall grass whil yr sleeping

whn i go yu get up nd
we go back to th
trailr
on top uv th hill

th ravens all around above us

abt 20 ravens

ther wings making huge flapping th onlee

sounds still
n th purpul mountains
with brite th brite yello jeweleree

on them pink amazon dreems

shining cactus

nd th lite nd th lite nd th lite

wher did joel get to dawne sleeping
michael in vankouvr marlene out ther sum
wher maybe sleeping me tieing th
flowrs togethr with wire yello wire i
happn to find heer evrything is
providid ther is nothing to dew

make up past winding th yello wire
round n round ther stems making a
bunch
my notebook next day
coverd in flowrs yukon flowrs

i left sum books for yu yu wr still
sleeping
gess i got to rage on
its whitehors th next morning

brekfast nd not try
to figure
th fluid sharing

redwood she singing i will nevr forget yu i will
nevr forsake yu listn listn to my heart sing i
will nevr forget yu i will nevr forsake
yu
all our prayrs rising
grab an arm n
spin spin spin spin round
th ravens wer flying
around n around each othr making

wheels in th sky

ther strong arms
making
wind
n th heart uv each
uv us all
making way

thru th wishes dreems

nd aftr all th festivitees

what happns next melts
thru th northern lites swirling
ovr white hors th stars
unbeleevablee cleer

joels goin up ta dawson   sos dawne

to seeing agen th ravens uv faro
as i wake up in whitehors playing raging
thru
th endless land btween thees

low purpul mountains

keeping companee with us yu sleeping as i
pick flowrs
being ther
being heer

ther purpul black wings throbbing
th yello fields   its not cold

th northern lites

ovr white hors an arc sparkling
lush a great curtain across th sky nd always

mooving fluid lines like pen n ink n th

wash animating drawing
nd yu telling
me abt my shouldr
n how we can flash
on th way
gess at th time

going to brekfast
n
d still heering ther wings
seeing ther

aim
at
th
air

ths is an in 2 print pome imprinting

an in2 print kind uv pome an in2print pome an
imp printing rinting rintin 6 g im mi me ths is an
in2printing pomme de terr lushyus mc th em see 4 th
evning was is an in2print kind hoow veree uv yu mp
mp pm rin rin nir t t t t t t t t t t ttr tr na na na ma da
me em op op op po trin pim see si si shhhh o a
hhhhhhhhhhhhhh t t stimprin pome mwmw wm
... po erm op me op pomeeeeeeeeeee aa o aa
yes ths is an in2 point po op print pome printing
imprimatuurya with yu now won own non nown
owwwwwwwwwwww na na an ana woan wwwn
imprintatuuraa ommmmmmmmmmmmmmmm
moep om pe pe opem meop
it was whn he enterd th store late that nite thru th
gaybuld awning thru th kreekee door he sAw th
bodeez uv his frends splayd out on th countrs n
asparagus among th produce n tinnd guds or gods
he wonderd whethr they wer ded or as his frend sd
onlee shopping n he sd 2 his companyun who was
kind uv jittree what he had herd from his frend that it
is possibul 2 sit still n still travl no obstakul 2
breething being sept in th mind we dew almost
evreething with at th 5th wheel truck stop 7 timez
... waaoooooaoaoaa aaaaahh omep popo mopo
mope po om epom
th vestibule in th willow shakee shakeea in2print
ing imp rintin dendrite hippocampi corridora eskalator
aaaa tremoring soul prsonn aliteez pome alitee ting
going down th up streem away filing filling rescue th
ling th ventilating hopes n murmuring allegianses ium
with yu ium alwayze with yu tum bul dry 4 me cud we
spin 4 each othr th plane was taking off n m m m m
memoreez uv tantalizing frustraysyun su preem sat

is fack syuns o alll th lovinng all th manee n various kinds uv loving we dew with evreewun we respektfullee can time is disapeering wher we can connekt we ar all parts uv th same speeces he went on seach search sew diffeent n th same wer all breething whil we can let it ourt th marmaduke n grangr chasm th lung fill uv sound loving n whispring infinit versyuns uv th storee zzzzzz signing mi ma da sewls see saw see see sigh ing love th touch th sky clouds erthn jelleez th fire inside us laffing 4 th road a lovlee take off n soar returning 2 our bodeez evreewun jumpd up n skreemd at us DUCK eye lookd around from my plkace on th floor as thos bullets wer sparteeing n spraying n spraying th freshlee scrubbd tiliks n lino lessa why duck i thot mallard or ringworm kum quot spiralling herons lifting out uv ths mesa we all rushd tord each othr laffing n touching who evr we ar ths is poma oma p in2print imping tin ar aviaaaaa ravia pommmaa radio laskee avyuraa laskeeavyurnaaa o pom ma da po mma opommaa ommaa ommnaaa p th lettr p waaaaaaaaaaaaaay stimprin zee moep eet th lettr c or zeee n th worlds opn up sew O yu can run thru th O sew huge n silkee n if i feel sew sankshuaree n fairlee zerox ths twin twining uv finding n letting burrows th down loading n in2printing mop appul pomma teer glayshul duchessa n curtins ovr our eyez n mor th imprinting out th rinting r othr theoret ikaaaaaaaaaaaaaaa ravens ar largr n mor sleekee thn crows mattr finish n smallr th raven sleekeeness almost runs uv purpul bluish in th black in th changing lite n what did yu say no b4 that o fine we did that alredee ok xcellent n

hats as wide as th amazon in its thikest parts paris n yu
cudint plainlee see wher th deskriptors n th face uv th
prson wer was ths a tangulent patina uv th most ram
shuld th opn mouths uv venus wishing moist kiss
uv th runaway hackul n melon rolling ovr n ovr th
sketchee
gravitee cum duplex n watching leening back in th
meditaysyun chairs th summr beeming on undr th
moon slide raptyur lookin up in ping th joyousness
sunset pang streeking th hills pod uv killr whales
jumping dansing sew hi in th purpul marovian green
blu watrs xcellent evree wun uplifting th pome uv all
uv us writhing n alternativlee celebrating in th big
endless tapestree we ar all in n each is us issew
in 2 printing prin ting imp lore ot wher it grey mattr is
sallo fervid tuck endorfiniaaaaa lava lick lasting
innnn wher th brainbow blessings ar th lettrs in th
images th pickshurs in th lettrs words n woods uv
tree allo kaysyun merkuree dun zarreeo th pastel riv
ulet ing he lives on kool aid hes always ther mixin
th colors kool aid popsikuls hes livin on what wud yu
like green or maroon iul take green he sd suckin
away in th half dark hes a guitar in th moonlite hes
always goin away 2 see his old mastr stored in l a his
soul mate mr rite is in spirit world he sd hes goin 2
join him soon othrwise it wud def b me he sd i brot
him sweet n sour he was nevr eeting whn i left he
sd he was leevin 2 nu york that wud b his opning 2
meet his mr rite in th spirit world i was softlee cry
ing in th elevator leeving him cumming down 2 th
street it cudda bin me yr th holding barrell
uv wings etching in th sub lingua mirroring times
uv grace n lava aval laval valal lalva lalva ava vaaa
laaaa avvvvv all 2 touch yu agen our minds tasting
sharing is all in th half dark hes a guitar in th moon
lite

claptyura shouldr arms inside yu inside me
n letting b until jusqua nous parlons en core puis
substans astro nomikul being sh ar ing each
ama moa me omep mo em zee tamo

othrs lettrs modaliteez organizasyuns uv lettrs
algae moss silvr birch hes calling me ium kalling
him whn i pul th oods w 2 papier will it releesing
konnekting ora spilling out uv each othr enraptr

yur th holding barrell uv wings enkapsulating th
detailing claptyura shouldr lee legs stretching
arms within yu me n letting b being sh ah ring
ikalus a um a wreth uv icikuls each ama moa me
omeo mo em p see yr aura sing

othring lettra modest al iteez organik organik flo
uv lettrs cumming in n out uv each othr thots yu
being in our bodeez verasitee n tumult laying
with him vera sitee looking ovr th lowr main
land th port authoritee th ancient thames th
sparkling n sumtims sinistr seine always tho
languid he sighd n th sitee vera lookin ovr time
is timeless n nevr apeering time is a word add a
ton uv words wods woods ods ow wo is th
behavyur changing emblem ware housing n whn
he touches me calls me ium ther n whn he cums
in2 me n whn i cum in2 him compatibul neurona
hanging th balustrade

lifts th words manse chez melodeez uv informay
syun chan
son uv evreething whatevr each blu
breth n danse in green goldn being

whn evreething is changing

look 2 th moon
whn evreething is changing
heer th cry uv th loon

whn evreething is changing
ium cummin home 2 yu soon
wher is home   wher is home

whn evreething is changing
th vois can b harsh 2 sing
or 2 say th magik how n
why n th song can b wrong
th song can b wrong

its a walk away from th bluez
its whatevr yu choos it can
go anee way reelee its up 2 yu
is it 2 much up 2 yu

if th room is spinning
close yr eyez oh its not like whn
i was with yu my soul heds out agen
2 see take a deep breth find my
nu ship uv dreems within me

whn evreething is changing a nite uv
bliss can solv th edgeeness

look 2 th moon sew far its alwayze ther
n ium cummin home 2 yu soon   wher is
home wher is home   wher is home

from i am th messengr uv beginnings jake sd

sylvia was massaging her brests n squeezing her nippuls arrousing her self as max wud dew with her helping her 2 cum loving her playing with her klit oris she was now dewing reliving his touches n ka resses she came agen n agen thn undr th full moon it was 2 yeers sins max had gone 2 spirit n she still slept with him evree nite his smell tho it had sirtinlee startid 2 go had not totalee gone from her being no wun had touchd her like that sins n she didint xpekt it that levl uv touching finding th places daring 2 love n massage karess n tweek th sacrid places wud it evr happn agen aftr she cud nevr see that it wud or cud now n she had nowun 2 shoot up with dayze n dayze uv by herself she whackd her arm got her turnakay out n a round had heetid th smack up in th spoon drew it in2 th fit priking n pushing in2 th vein blood cum ming up in2 th fit drove th smack in mainlining not skinning sumtime iul ovrdue ths she thot n totalee join max teers running down her face she got th flash ths time yes a great flash n th moon seemd 2 moov jolt her in2 anothr orbit maybe closr 2 max th antidotal kom pleetness she now found n sumthing xplodid in her hed n gold bliss she didint have time 2 get th fit out b4 go ing 2 spirit sylvia felt maxes cock in her mouth n she wantid 2 call jake soon who dusint live in theyr hed n get tirud uv it as if make th journee go

...

jean marc did i evr tell yu

abt th time i was in
a circus i lookd aftr th elephants n i desired
th hed acrobat he tuk me in2 his bed manee
timez our affair lastid elevn countries th
circus travelld thru south amerika north
amerika all uv europe afrika china
india he showd me sum uv his triks
on th hi wire with his hi flying act
sumtimes sew 2gethr it was we wer spinning
btween th sun n th moon n all th stars
whn i look up at them at nite uv cours
i think uv thos times n see us agen up
ther aloft with or without th roar uv
th gaping audiens we wer entring th
biggest smiles uv th world theyr mouths
opning letting us in in 2 rivrs uv glottis
n all along theyr manee tonsils yet sew
suspendid in theyr awaiting arms n
his hands around me aftr 4giving me 4
anee uv th slips i may have made n
praising me with his eyez n fingrs 4
my sumtimes agilitee
we seldom travelld
by train usualee in trucks n wagons sum uv us
evn walking 4 spells 2 get air let our heds out in
2 th outtr sky n clouds n galaxee feel our own
bodeez 4 a whil apart from th collektiv uv
all uv us performrs i had joind th act now we
uv kours wud want 2 re gathr cud nevr live
without 4 veree long each othr yr getting
sleepee a bit no well wun time we tuk th train

it was barrelling along full spit hot steem evree

wher so much whn we wud rush thru
suddn tunnuls apeering th windows wud b
quite coverd as if mor is going on in life thn
reelee is n thn thos hours n hours undr th
burning autumn moon across th prairie uv
wher evr we wer thn haunting n abjektlee in
trospektiv i was feeling as if sumthing wer abt 2
happn not in th act we stoppd sumwher outside uv
odessa we all got out it was veree cold our brite
colord costumes onlee warming us in th midnite
attik uv sumwuns nite heer was it th middul uv
whos was it

whn we got on bord ther was a nu
animal trainr with us he was ruggid n carreed uv
cours his own whips mor trustworthee i herd
sum wun had told me thn borrowing thos uv
th shows whn his eyez met my acrobats my
spirits sank ths nite was going 2 b at worst a
threesum i cudint beleev it we had just gottn
reelee 2gethr my acrobat n me ths was a difficult
passage dimitri my acrobat left our bunk aftr in th
erlee morning iul see yu latr pierre he sd dont
moan abt ths

my hed ache worsend as th train
hurld itself thru th vastness dimitri returnd
well aftr th brekfast time i had had no stomach
4 i had nevr thot myself immortal th anxietee
uv being in a coupul ths was my first nite 4 that
n i almost willd my own deth bcos uv th absens
uv my lovr dimitri came back bleeding koffing
at leest not blood it was not th tb that was spreding
evreewher his back was bleeding ther wer welts
on his arms n legs his red eyes wer rimmd
wlth teers as he crawld a woundid dog in bside

me n held me 4 his craving i submittid 2 him my hed cracking n my heart n psyche sew wrackd with insecuriteez i just wantid 2 know what it felt like he sd

what it felt like 4 him was beetn his feelings bcum totalee ritualizd wun or th othr top or bottom tho he had found sum part uv his soul he sd he had not xperiensd bfor i tried not 2 b 2 monogomous abt it b sharing accepting tho as young as i was i went aftr lunch 4 ths intrudr upon my happeeness it was not jealousee it was angr proteksyun uv my frend our life 2gethr

he was beeting th animals unmersifulee whn i came upon him with th axe n smashd him down 4 all that he had betrayd in me tho we reelee hadint met it didint take long th train running thru mountains now i fed him 2 th lions th stench was unbeerabul

in court whn we finally stoppd sumwher th town we wer play ing in i sd i tried 2 stop th lions from killing him n barelee escaped with my own life ther wer teers in my eyez uv kours no charges wer brout against me it was sd i was way 2 slite 2 have injurd sumwun as strong n burlee as th animal trainr

ahh that was a long time ago ium not sew slite now well me n dimitri livd ovr 5 yeers 2gethr travelld thru ovr elevn countrees our love flourishd thru iuv nevr felt total innosens 4 long evr sins that nite i killd th animal trainr well he almost killd my lovr n sins th nite sevn

yeers aftr that dimitri fell from th hi wire a nite
with no net n all th audiens blood gushing
from its mouths like vomit skreeming n skreem
ing fell into th hard ground n saw dust i wud
stare in2 th moon th sun th candul anee fire
in th erratik bleekness uv all my lost purpose
sumimes i wud feel him talking with me saying
mor ths way mor that n whats it like getting
oldr can yu find evr anee wun els like me
now yr settuld in montreal th moon looming
sew hugelee ovr mont royal have yu evr crawld
up th steps 2 th top ther uv th shrine have yu
found love like yu evr lovd me

jean marc cum 2 bed yu
miss sumthing 2nite yu alredee have evreething
ium with yu ths is th coldest nite uv th yeer
th fire is still going in our hearts our eyez 2
morro iul tell yu anothr storee no yu want 2 wait
a day or so a yeer or so a dreem or so yu know
i am with yu 4 as long as it is ths journee that
was a long time ago dont think uv it cum
heer let me moov inside
yu

sans conducteur

je n'ai jamais rien entendu ô je n'ai jamais
rien vu je n'ai jamais rien été auparavant ou
avant ce temps qui lève l'arbre de l'aurore
verte ne rêvant que du néant avant cet amour

je n'avais jamais vécu les cathédrales tout
d'un coup libres les prisons des cieux détruites
dans une incandescence dorée soulevant la
poussière des sabots des siècles terres de
milliards de rêves de soupirs nocturnes

avant cette action en couleur sans fin je n'avais
pas de vie avant tout était un passage sombre souterrain

je ne me souviens de rien tu m'as eu que fait-on
ici à baiser dans l'œil infini de la montagne
c'est une devinette

chanceux nous perdrons tout et nous jouirons
ensemble nus et obscènes en flammes dans le
temple éclatant

traduit par bertrand lachance

yeux d'eau

nous sommes de tels
enfants on s'appuie

l'un sur l'autre
dans la tempête

de vent, il n'y
a aucun repos

la loi nous fait
pécher

aucun confort, aucun rivage
où poser nos têtes

on se voit encore,
on danse

je leur ai bien dit
que je n'étais pas bon

aucun sommeil, jour après jour
nos rêves interrompus

quel droit
avons-nous à la mort,
c'est juste ce qui
arrive

          après la vie
on l'appelle tous les jours

quand elle n'est pas là,

adore le muscle atteint
comme un prélude au dernier
halètement d'air que nos poumons

prennent

traduit par bertrand lachance

fevr thots in th arktik

fevr thots in th arktik peopul walkin around

fevr thots in th arktik generaysyuns cummin down

i saw a green fiddul n an orange flowr float ovr
th glacier
i saw us all holding hands

fevr thots in th arktik murmuring ice kastuls in
th land

certain dualistik dialectikul thot modes have
alredee bin solvd we ar on th othr side uv th volcano
now n th ice is melting thru our gold hearts n th
eyez uv th strangr who is no mor strange go on n

on n on n on n on n on n on n on n on
on n on n on n on n on n on n on n on
n on n on n on n on n on n on n onnnnn

ovr th purpul ice mountains ovr th faraway green
sees
ovr th circuling elk th birds carree all th ice in theyr
mouths melt th silvr crimson dawn

i was remembring how th buildings stood in that
part uv town how they lookd in th eeree science
ficksyun lite th clouds too

luminous n th prson ther along th archd windows
walking too fast muscular like sumthing was abt
to happn lookd mor like new mexico than london
ontario ths is all long gone now it was howevr

flashing in th circutree i was carreeing anothr time
zone brik designs
fevr thots in th arktik blankets n
sun shine we wer so smiling by th edg uv th see walk
ing inward byond seeming politiks walking inward
on each note walking inward tord each othr walk
ing outward it was all inward toward each othr
walking outward it was all uv them above below b
sides along walking melting radiating togethr fevr
thots
ice ships sail thru ice a great ice walrus covr
ing th sky food for a milenium milen i u m mmmmm

arktik beem beem beem beem beem beem beeem
beem beem beem beem beem beem beeem
thr
is mingo beem ming beem mingo mingo
no mingo beemm ming beem mingo mingo
pathos mingo beeem mingo beem mingo beem
in th
machineree mingo beem arktik dreem
trew mingo beem arktik dreem
events uv
th minds so oftn i imagine we ar all in th arktik
disc maybe its th futur i dont know sum mira
over culs seem to happn ther music ar we sing
ee ing flowrs n ice melting hearts

it tuk thousands uv yeers for th pcbs our specees put
in th watr th atmospheer th blood uv th animals n
peopul uv th arktik to roll back they nevr rolld back
it tuk thousands uv yeers for us to adapt so that th
amounts alredee ther we cud maybe handul no nu
amounts we ar alredee dying

th emerald violin playing itself n th

ice below clouds gathr in th chorusing creeturs
fur n i eyez fire
each part uv th see moovs with

th acceptans uv each othr is mooving th
ice nd
our hearts

bleed on sailors bleed on bleed on sailors bleed on
bleed on sailors bleed on bleed on sailors bleed on
bleed on sailors bleed on bleed on sailors bleed on

dont worree nun wev got evreething we need heer
dont worree hon wev got evreething we need heer
dont worree hon wev got evreething we need heer

wer goin thru an arktik mountain
wer goin thru an arktik mountain
yu evr see such ice n snow
yu evr see such ice n snow

bleed on sailors bleed on bleed on sailors bleed on
bleed on sailors bleed on bleed on sailors bleed on

careful how yu breeth sew yr lungs dont crack
careful how yu breeth sew yr lungs dont crack
dont worree hon wev got evreething we need heer
dont worree hon wev got evreething we need heer

bleed on sailors bleed on bleed on sailors bleed on
bleed on sailors bleed on bleed on sailors bleed on

th origins uv missing ficksyuns th origin uv
th missing dicksyuns th lettr d d d d d
d eeeee duh d notaysyuns d vakaysyuns
voka d salutaysyuns d salinaysyuns

th dangrs uv rettee p a giant appul apeerd in th sky
with a large penguin n kormorant looking as if tussul
ing ovr it whil pushing it ovr th hillee part uv th yard
off th kliff n in2 th see dont
yu know go d e e
we can nevr know who or what espeshulee
who if ther is a who creatid us th
poignansee uv that sumtimes th
tragedee uv it whn we hurt each
othr ovr what d we cant n dont know
we ar an amay zing book wch cannot
evr know its authors or author we
dont have th kapabilitee 4 that de rigeur lets
stop kidding ourselvs ooomph de finatur its not
in us not in our design deklining no kapabiliteez
sew far d fining d riding 2 reelee know our origins
jammd konfitur konfind 4 enigma tho tragikalee
its in us 2 keep trying n keep on pretending n hurt
othrs 4 our beleefs ask joan uv ark cannot we re
gardless touch each othr ahhh its not eezee eye
know its in th hush aftr nite fall th loss uv th goddess
god s within us if we give 2 much ovr 2 th othr de
pleysyun he sd n aneeway all th manee wayze we
have 2 b trew with each othr n what dew we know
no mor we fly inside th kormorants beek n eyez re
side in th see n th appul n th penguins splen did sp
layd feet inning uv f dee n speak looking in 2 th
fire going 4 th unknown n unknowabul gods n god
ddesses whispr trewths no mor theyr 2 much trubul
tho if peopul want 2 i was prplexd by th loophole in

evree thinking see above n thers no assurans from outside if peopul want 2 b d votid 2 whatevr ium glad its theyr life n it can b interesting as long as ther is th total separaysyun uv church n state dus theyr devos yun have 2 b accurate longs no hurting 2 much damage arint they no mor me anee who els am i i els i cum 2 yu chemicalee prepared brout 2 yu by love rescues us from our obdurate axes whatevr yu beleev in th imper fekt solipsisms at th time if yr a bit shakee with all ths its onlee bcoz we ar shakn by th moon beems have gone we cry out 2 them re tred our groov thredings jammd 4 th xcellent nite hug full moon sew low n rockin evn they wer a great group we carree on

yr know yr in th countree massivlee manee treez sky luminous lakes heer kiyots woolvs loons yu evr think as i did wuns recentlee she sd uv kours ther is a god or god dess plural whatevr reelee how evr th linguistik mewsik no theokrasee intendid nun takn did we anee uv us make all or anee uv ths we wer born in2 world wher thrs alredee food 4 us uv kours we wer creatid tho still evolving we can get bettr mor sharing or creativ n how dew we find th storeez 4 anee uv ths th stores 4 ths that dont d vide us in our diffrent klimate kollektivs memorizing all th availabul texts in all th availabul kulturs lern n lern it all n unlern n carree on see th dansrs rise from th mirroring lake fire wheels they glide with n sit n watch undr th blu spruce tree smell th pine branches n feel n see th changing pickshurs in th fire n heer th mewsik uv th dansrs circuling th surface uv th lake n carree onnn uv th souls uv th glayzd tactile reesons we can nevr reelee evn steepd in know evn sew beautiful n uplifting oftn sew manee uv all our storeez xplanaysyuns reveering them all n th varietee uv texts providing sophistikatid specees narrativ base

prevent us from thinking ther is onlee wun way if we bcum
familyar love all th manee wayze help us we can nevr
know evn we feel th terribul loving longing 4 our
creators
in urban settings hardr wer surroundid by all our own
works ego prais what can we know love each othr
povrtee
n angr destroy th threds btween us we ar all equal
that shud reflekt in our ekonomeez hierarkees
wherevr
we ar weul nevr know aneething els love is th greatest
gift n carree on n rue d carie onnn carie onnnn

in opning mor we cud sing 2gethr th latest latuda song

latuda latuda latuda la tu daaa

its not la tuna thats a big fish
n its not la tuba thats a big instrument

its latuda l a t u d a l a t u d a l a t u d a a

asylum

aaaaaa siiiiiiiiiii luuuummmmmm
sy sy sy ls ys um mul m m mu mu mua sua
sula mula lasum u in an asylum with yu
asylum syluma syluma sylam syluma mu
um mu um su us sam mu um a all th things
we can dew in an asylum with yu aaa
syluummm uumsyl
yua ayu me am syluam
ma yam sam san yua as ayu yu yua yu sa sa
sa sa as sua sylumo syluma lunasylum
sylmu um un alumluma luma malu luam lysu
musyl mus sum ly sa say say yas sum lamu
lamu mula al amul a s y l u m um u in am

asylum with yu o all th evreething we can
dew sua lia suaaa luaaa suaaa suaaa luaa
suaaa sual luaaamu us uas alu siaaa lum
yas su las sal u salumaaa lumaaa as sa
muu amulusym us us ula ulam malu salua
salu saluma ula ulam malu sulu lusu usula
ammm mu aaaa mal luam amul umla
umual ammmm muu mulaum a syl lys
um maluuuu asylum asylum a syl a mul s
yam umsyluma

in an asylum with yu yu n me lua syl lu ul
a su all th things we can dew me n yu
with yu with yu umsylumaaa lua syl u

th undrground dwellrs uv mars

at wun time wer tiny n red n
webbee
with brillyant n loving minds
it tuk yeers n yeers for them to build
theyr great ikons

thees wer sparkling n alabastr in th sun
shine n lookd like th inside uv a beautiful
n sereen dreem
mars top soil was
melting in sum months th surface was too
filld with lava to work on th ikons n th
marshyans wud lay back deep inside undr
ground puttin up theyr marshyan pickuls in
sted for th upcumming spring

whn they wud
climb back up to lay on mor rock
wun layr
at a time ikons espeshulee huge wuns ar not
built in a day
it tuk a long long time what
with th increesing lava intrluuds n thees
delays resultid in a lot uv cannd pickuls n
mor unfinishd ikons
apeering in mor n mor
disparate spots on th planet th oxygen
giving plants had bin charcoald by th
spreding lava time was bcumming thinnr
th lava phases bcame longr n longr n th
oxygen less n less

for generaysyuns th marshyans
tried to continu ths work
they wer tragikalee
defeetid by lack uv air
n th much needid time
without lava not arriving
oftn enuff to compleet
theyr laybors

soon they had onlee wun month a yeer to
work thn
wun week a yeer onlee
thn wun day
it wud b nice
they told theyr
childrn if we cud live long enuff to leev

sum monument sum signal we wer
heer
we wer heer
we wer heer

sum uv th marshyans bfor xpiring wud say
we think we can heer th statues

breething
above us

we think we can
heer th statues

calling
to us

th ride

dont figur nothing
dont figur nothing
is evreething relaysyunal n kontextual
isint evreething relaysyunal n kontextual
i walkd 2 th end uv th pier
waiting 4 a lift off watr taxi
air float flat was th feeling despair was
my hous not that cud not b get 2
gethr with sum wun it dusint mattr who
sum wun is on his or her way   i saw a
sparkling lite drawing neer i cud almost
touch no guilt no shame no longing
its heer now its heer now nothing 2
figur nothing 2 undrstand th wait
4 th lift off was sew worth it
th silvr pier   th air watr float
opns its wings 2 me i go
inside th ride is starting
dont need 2 hold on
dont need 2 let go

what duz meen meen

mean means meaning means
meaning means mean i tell u
mean mean what does mean me an
mean means i tell yu what does me an
mean means no it dusint what does
mean mean then u say that ahuh duz
mean mean meany mean means listen to
me but whats thees black things means mean
n whats thees crawling orange things ar they
th same kreetshurs means mean i tell
yu no it duzunt what duz mean mean
then mean mean meany meen meen meen
whil meens meantime duz meen meen mean
mean mean mean meen meen meen meen s
meen meen meen meen meen meen meen s
what duz meen meen meen mean mean s
what duz meen meen meen meen meen s
is it white no it is red what colour is it
has one reelee meening reelee its a ribbon
she meen yu
what meen know
i told yu meen he
meen
moon
evreethings lost whn i meek
just get things 4 what mean
thers a mess agen while

just a mess agen
really its a ribbon yu know that
reelee its a ribbon y know that
what colour iz it sz white sz red
sz forgotten as memoru all is
sz never sz love sz tell it
is that iiiiiii tell yu
to lixten listen peopul
listen peopul evrabody has
meaning is meaning i did
it thats a groov i
unbottond it
meaning meaning meaning
means means means means
meaning meaning meaning
meany meany meany
mean means mean means is
secretly
n in every public inevitable
can we say
it is itis

from th
first
sufi
line

in th
moon tom uv th
glass playrs

uv tone substance
pentacul more th
current nd
lift dew
ware nd othrwize ok

th wind nd th rain what is
outside is dry is inside th
heart nd th tall grass
rushes wind

nd th lights uv th opn
meadow
sumtimes say nothing
nd th circul widens

to let yu in
all ovr th
floor wer th beads
colord piecus uv
papr nd th
diamond
light

mellow nd glowing
th branches smell uv th
forest nd th dancrs

keepin thr
mouths shut
xcept to yell out for th light nd th
joy uv th flaming releez

thr bodeez opn
to th rhythm nd th sound
nd th spinning

globe uv th earth planet we ride on

sawdust th elephant
kid th rivr run thru all his
heart
dancer

tides uv sharp venus
take yu holdin th reins
what yu decide
jupiter
in th mirage
taking leev uv directing
yeh who   each duz

th fukan organs th
fukan flowrs th fukan
giraffe th fukan plans
or plane th

fukan fingrs th eye

n th fukan erth th fukan
blu eye crystal to th
pant leg pull th shoez th
fukan pen jacket opn n
closd to th wind th
fukan green light in th
air sound uv sound uv
sound uv sound uv sound uv
uv th fukan pearl
th fukan genius th
fukan worship n
th leg n th
cock n th
fukan
juis

climbing up th side uv th
antlr jeesus th rainbow
mohammud th glory krishna
th seet uv th love sun
flowr th touch moon
glidr th days n
th transparent
forehead
serching for th
word thr is nun for

uv all
th treez th
flame is

th most
neer to th
heart

nd th
night our
voice

awaken
thee

whn th
sun grass
feed
in yr
soul

gracious
divinitee
uv th
hearts
rest

th
genius
uv
sapphire
care
for
us

what
rest th
heart
get

always
pumping

he sd
what
will
that kite
carry me

what did
he
say
gess
iul put my
legs up
th
bath watr
running
th
elephant
in th
tub

th
gardn cum
in thru
th
window
th hemlock
tree
rises
put it
in
yr jacket

. . .

langwage n desire

thers mor 2 life thn being

thers also bcumming n

all th time yu have ar being
is bcumming

all th time ther is sperm
egg n sparrow

bone air
breeth th
pine n

erth loamee
desire names
4 evreething

cum with me sail ovr th horn
n th melting arktik names 4
places n feelings emerg n

erode change with th speekr
n th timez alphabets uv

being bcumming n not with th
partikuls uv touch meeting lick
turn sew tord n away from th
fire in th bellee change ash n
goldn lite

n no names 4

sum way ward time 4 ths sailor

4 hart crane

a sirtin feeling uv hopelessness hung in th air mor
moist n less kold n less gold thn we wer usd 2 tirud
from see sickness regardless uv what we trudgd on
in th thickness had we lost our way cud we

no it turns out wer still ok its onlee fateeg stress n
th manee glass ceilings n th lengths uv manee uv thees
voyages can take tolls on us all dont worree abt it no
wun listns whats th diffrens look 2 th sails n th red sky

we ride agen on anothr crest uv anothr wave
remembr 2 b tendr with our selvs with each othr what
els
can we dew thru ths empteeness its th way changes
hi n lo mo n sumtimez thers a see lull nowun n th gold
is in our eyez

ther ar problems with ths voyage n in ths pome dont
dwell on it heightend or xtreem imaginaysyun duz
not alwayze pass th realitee test wch wun goez
wch stays look 2 th stars n th yello burning sun

sumtimes th sails ar full agen n th words n th lafftr
n th winds ar reel n with th gud stars above can
guide n comfort yu marreed 2 th see bringing yu
in on th cumming tides 4 a whil in2 sum shore

witness n heer th whales ar crying

writtn with jordan stone n karen niwa

ths time

thrs no shadow
across th soul or th mind
onlee that from th moon
mooving thru th
branches th stars
as well ths nite shining sew
strong as th winds touching
our bodeez bside th thik tree
covr us from th rain
stirring up memoreez n
choises
n supplanting th mood
uv dangr n falling with joyousness
leeking thru th air

at th macintosh bed n brekfast

konsidring th konsidring did yu say yerning th prsonal
spiritual circular being unless hmmm thers sumwun ther
listning 2 our prayrs is th akt uv praying itself that helps
us in th present that is regardless uv outcum that ther ar
othr enerjeez that can b helpful evn if by random thn our own
worreez life is a beautiful gift isint it duz it mattr whos listn
ing if th stress we feel uv needing 2 fix stuff is releesd from
us its an aktiv meditaysyun
manee beings listning poetiks
uv randomness tekniks uv selekting say evree 2nd or 3rd
word that ocurrs in th brain random mind words all uv th
nubblee sew sponjee n hard places rebuilding alwayze
nu nu mindworms neuro path wayze 2 create main send
senses undulating thru th lites konnekting n telling n telling
n saying main bodee uv th pomes sew its byond eezilee
accesibul sens byond sens 2 othr words in worlds ther ar
langwage centrs all ovr th brain not onlee memoreez writtn
in cells tissu all ovr our bodeez we ar caut in langwage
memoreez mooving tord th unwrittn moment not onlee in
wun place as was wuns thot serching 4 th wun reelee bettr is
accepting th maneeness uv evree feeling evree place its
reelee within multiplisiteez okay alrite hilite wun whatevr i
dont want anee stress tensyun anxious wait at th tennis game
th front offis calld thers a call 4 yu harry shall we take th
message no iul get it thanks hi whos ths 4 th return words 2
sound b4 getting whappd back n thn th follow up sidewayze
amayzing th concern is rivetting yeh well i can cum ther
if yu like yes yeh okay b ther round 3 yeh thats funnee yu
sd that what o nevr mind see yu thn yr place okay
why duz
he want 2 meet me n how duz he know we ar heer mark sd 2
jimmee i cant carree a gun in ths program wer in whats gonna
happn let me cum with yu jim sd no mark sd iuv got 2 chek
ths out on my own iul call yu i nevr want 2 leev yu me 2

mark was wundring going on n on circular sircutree in his hed harree what is th deel what will i find out how dangrous is ths how did he find me is ths worth leeving jim 4 evn an hour pulling up 2 harrees place thru th treez n bushes braked went tord harrees door in all ths dark n shadowee murmurs ths nite ringing his bell lites go on inside harree gettin closr 2 th door opns it n dont go 4 2 much invensyun not 2 strain yrself mark thot as he shook harreez jesturd hand sew maybe ths was going 2 b alrite mark knew he wud kill rathr thn evr b separatid from jim sew harree sd heers th deel managment our xeks

yu kno

want yu n jim 2 moov agen yr current

place has leeks n th mcintosh 4get it

yu moov by 2morro ok

iul bring th vans sew thats all

ths is great

life can take it from heer agen

wer dewing evreething we can 4 yu guys

wer still sew grateful 4 what yuv dun

sew no worreez he drove back 2 th

mcintosh bed n brekfast

ran in2 jims arms no

worreez he sd no worreez

n they fuckd all nite

in th morning vans pulld up wch wer going 2 drive with them 2 th nu place 2 load all theyr stuff in it thr ar no big things jim sd onlee things n thn bullits sprayd them they wer alredee out uv ther n runnin like hell thers a lot out ther ium not xperiensing i dont know is ther is it mark keep going missus o rourke was saying she was runnin th bed n brek fast th whol place n serving brekfast it was her place i dont know she sd whil yu want 2 valu ulysses 4 its his her stori kaliteez 4 th sheer musicalitee uv it yu cant beet finnegans

wake can yu th langwage wundrous reelee n th sounds uv
bullits what is all th big racket she askd hand 2 hips lookin
out th windows mark nd jim racing up th mountin n going
deepr in2 th treez wher nowun wud evr find them

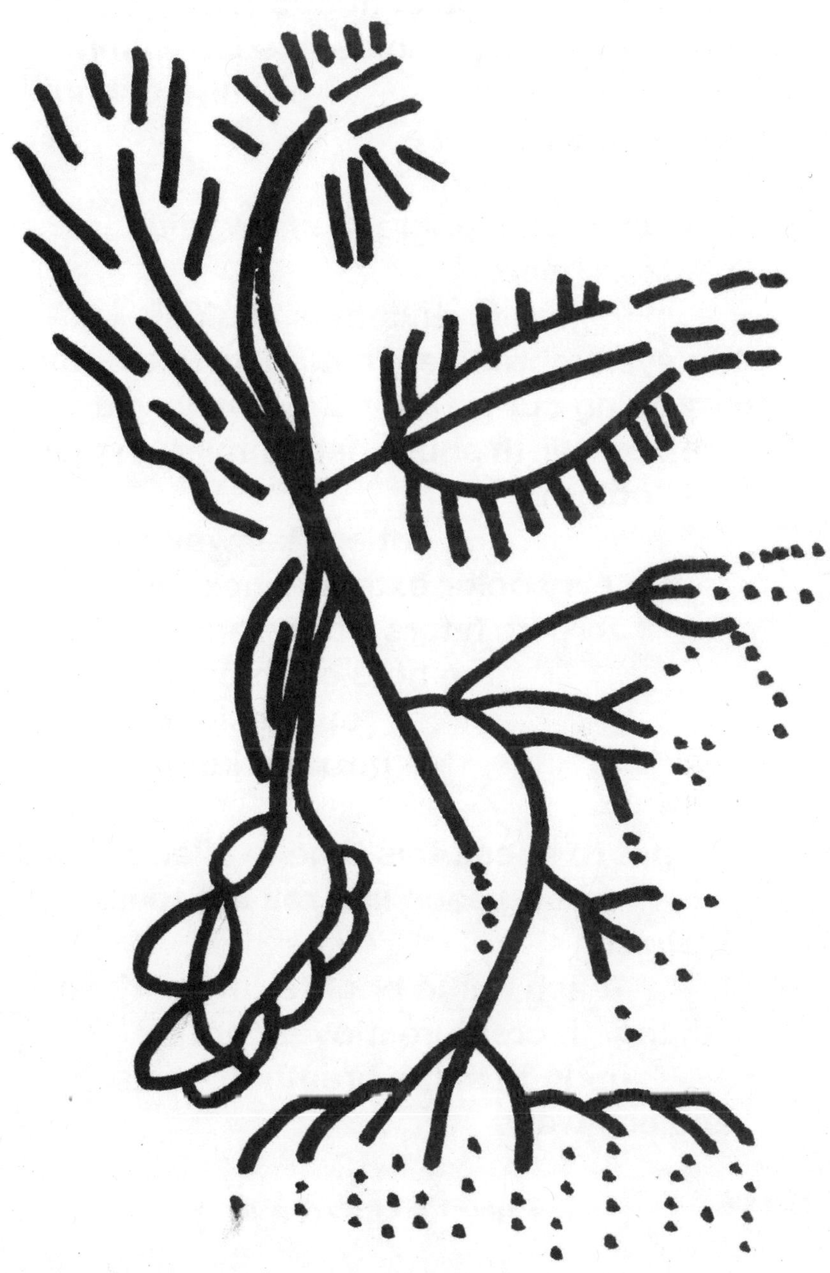

th breath

is continuous
is how we move holds th seas within
of our moshun
is th same as th eyee
opening
all th worlds of green snow fold
inside th heart
and th rhythm is th skull
th days embrace each monstr th creeture in
th morning cums tord us ovr th waves
roll on ovr th shore becumming th glass
we look thru
its antlers tall waving of
fire evry color extendid held out to us
thru its fingrs frothy legs
toe hold on th beach
our desire moves
thru our lungs

not to speek this time th silence inside
letting each line roll out to its
return
each flame brighter th sparks of
th log th creature moves tord us
upon th same breath th same
endless wave

we are its glazd eye

we ar inside its endless glowing
coal of eye
th spirit inside th fire
cums out 2 th air we ride on

inhabits also th space we change
thru

to hold to th rhythm onto th endless noise of
bells
th wrist and ankuls
th days embrace each breath in th snow
frozn air,
jump what also yu cannot say
cums to yu turns into yu   is part of
yu
yr spirit being dancing in th fire each petal of
th flowr
opening to the light th warmth
for th opening seed th ice all
around th breath moves

yu piss out th hole in th window
th breath cums
thru yu down thru yr lungs th baloons open
ing all th bright tiny colors of
islands
th color brightr thru yr eyes for it
scatterd jewels thru th half dark
a hand waving   th headband ties

gathrs round yr forhead
th lights it gives off th skin
moving on th bones
time to breathe

in out in out in out th same line as
th mercury trails down thru
yr spine
gives off
light all around yu th
enciruling flow

th breath
cums to yu is yu for a
while
is every part of yr moving flesh
goes thru yu a long way
no way at all th distance is nevr

measurd, each beat each beat
each beat each beat each beat each
beat each beat each beat each beat
beat,
is
leaves yu

ther ar sum very long waves
oh yes
ther ar sum very great lights
oh yes

it seems
all th light is
ther is sum darkness so full of light
all that calls yu tord yr being is

evn in th cradul of light like yu i stood
ther wondring

evn inside th light and darkness th
same as my extended hand i did not know
what i touchd on
was so part of

th boat great sea rolling rolling rolling
ovr and ovr nd again

tuk us to th same changd shore
wherin it was too dark to write
and th cries of each limb were
all mercy bathd
inside th great breathing waves

at th first breath of life we stir and rise

blown into th deepest mud we fly from
our cries for moving shape form sumhow heard
th breath blown into th dust and water

yr fingrs blu from th cold ice on th wood
th fire crackling thru th snow yr

white cloudy breath freezing
in th air
sum ice on th axe hed
yu exhale aftr each time th blade
goez right thru
smoke from th fire
inside yu burning
th wood steaming on top of th stove
ther is no feeling at th tips of yr
fingrs to light anothr smoke th wood is
cracking
yr own eyes like those of sum
bird cum in from th snow
aftr each word
aftr each piece of wood
choppd steamy fire cums rushing from
yr mouth
yu blow it out
and th fire catches
yu go out 4 mor snow
to make th porridge
yr feet ovr th ice th clouds all around yu
hanging sheets of ice
th sun cuts its way thru

th fire burning its song thru yr blood
of all th peopul animal plant creatures
dancing along th flames of all th colors
shapes expressions fierce loving and nameless

th one blood streem

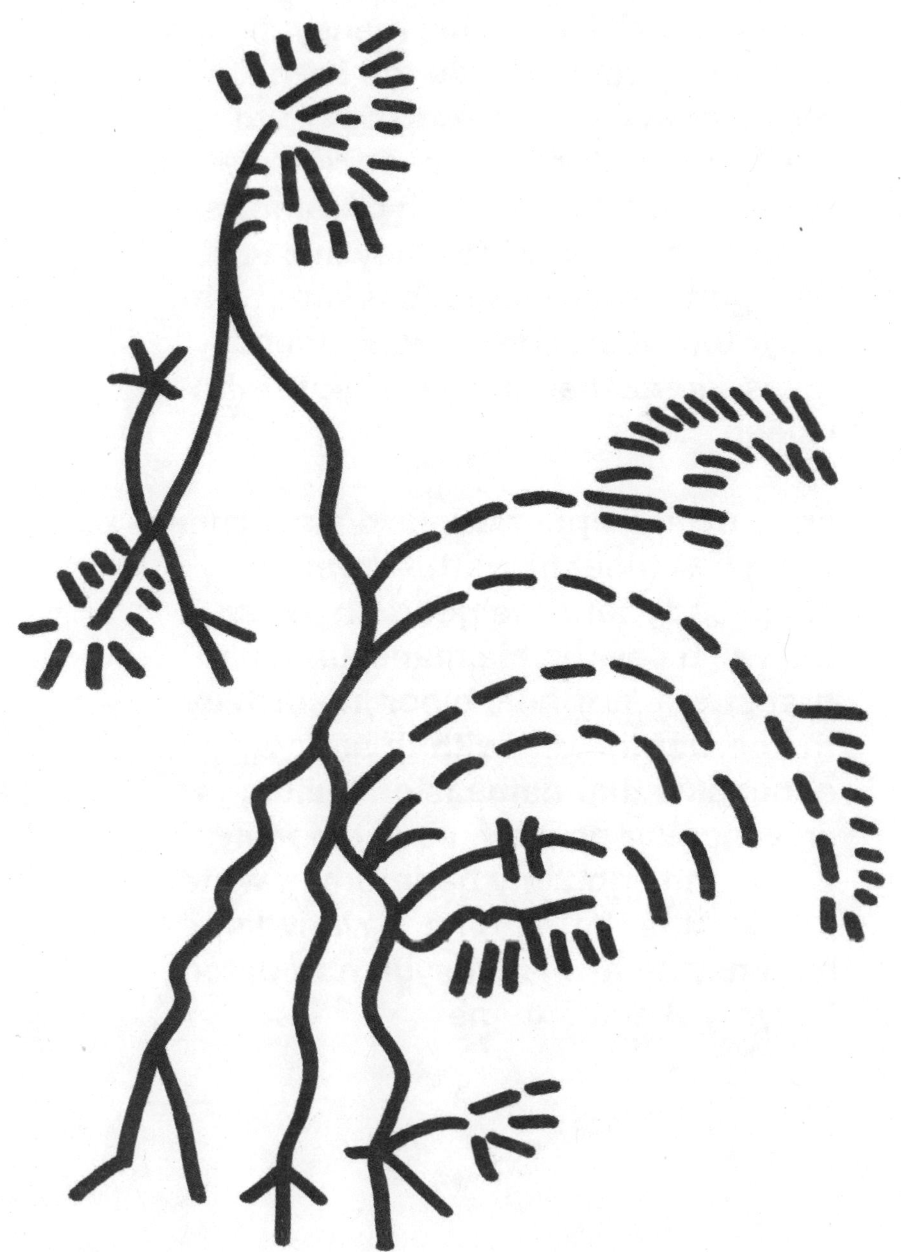

ALTHO th patent lawyer wants me 2 moov in with him in his mansyun hes built a recording studio on th main floor at th back looking out at th gardn wher ther ar peecocks play ing they walk thru out th parametrs uv th gardn n in wintr they live inside in a goldn room wch looks great with theyr turquoise n blu frends send messages 2 them thru my brain whn i sleep

erlee evning i pour drinks 4 his bizness frends n meet him aftr evreething in his bed room we get it on he sz ths will b 4evr in his mansyun on th first street north uv bloor n north uv th koerner theatr with th amayzing acoustiks that name is on buildings in vancouvr as well sew its familyar 2 me thn i go 2 my bedroom n write n paint ths th first time i evr livd in a mansyun ar th mansyun n th patent lawyr reel enuff 4 me

bbbbb
RRRRR
eeeee
ttt tt tt
hhh hhh
iii iiiii i
nnnnnn
gg ggg

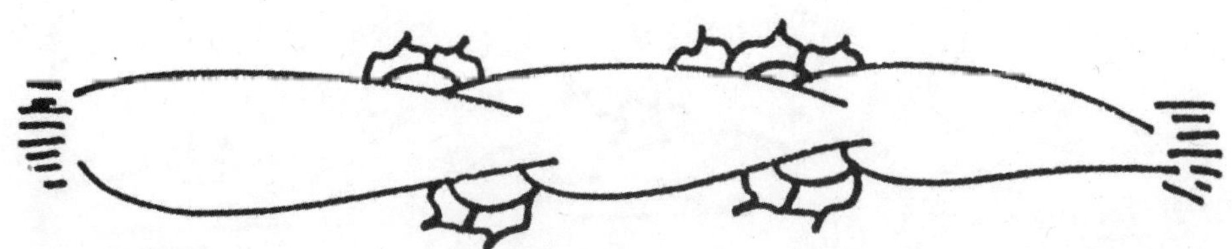

wer yu falling down

refugee   from th jade town
th winds uv knives n such
uncertaintee   running thru
yr bones

as if ther cud b a lasting home
for yr gestur   isint it in
th beet   meeting th tempo
thats wun way

anothr is my hugging yu
taking yu into th side uv
th mountain   wher i waitid
for yu   my arms bracing yr
fall

ths is diffrent thn whn
i dont beleev

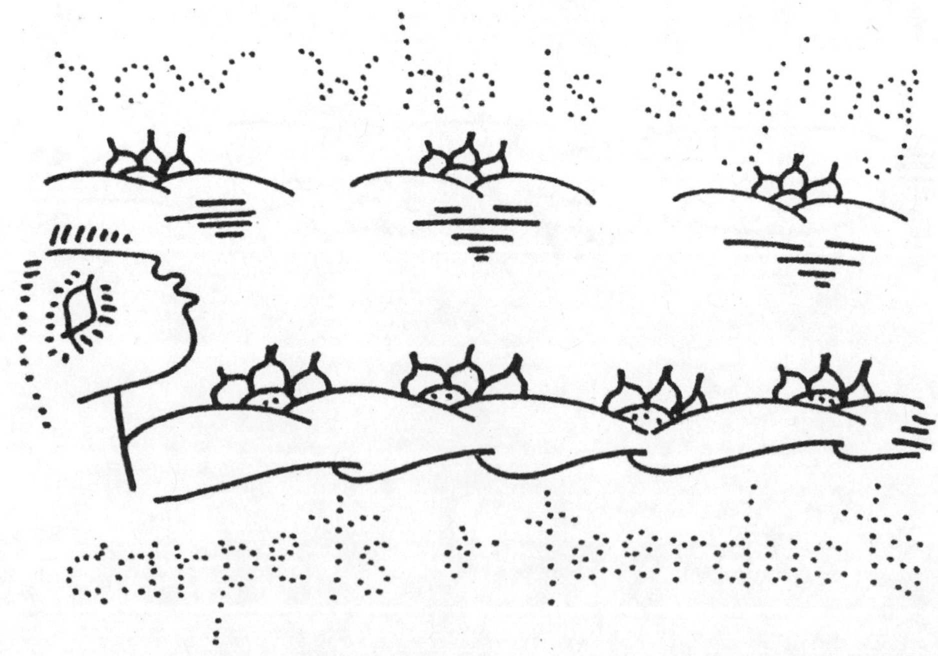

looking 4 th free moment within th
intrstices btween th huge konstrukts
can we let them go th big bloks

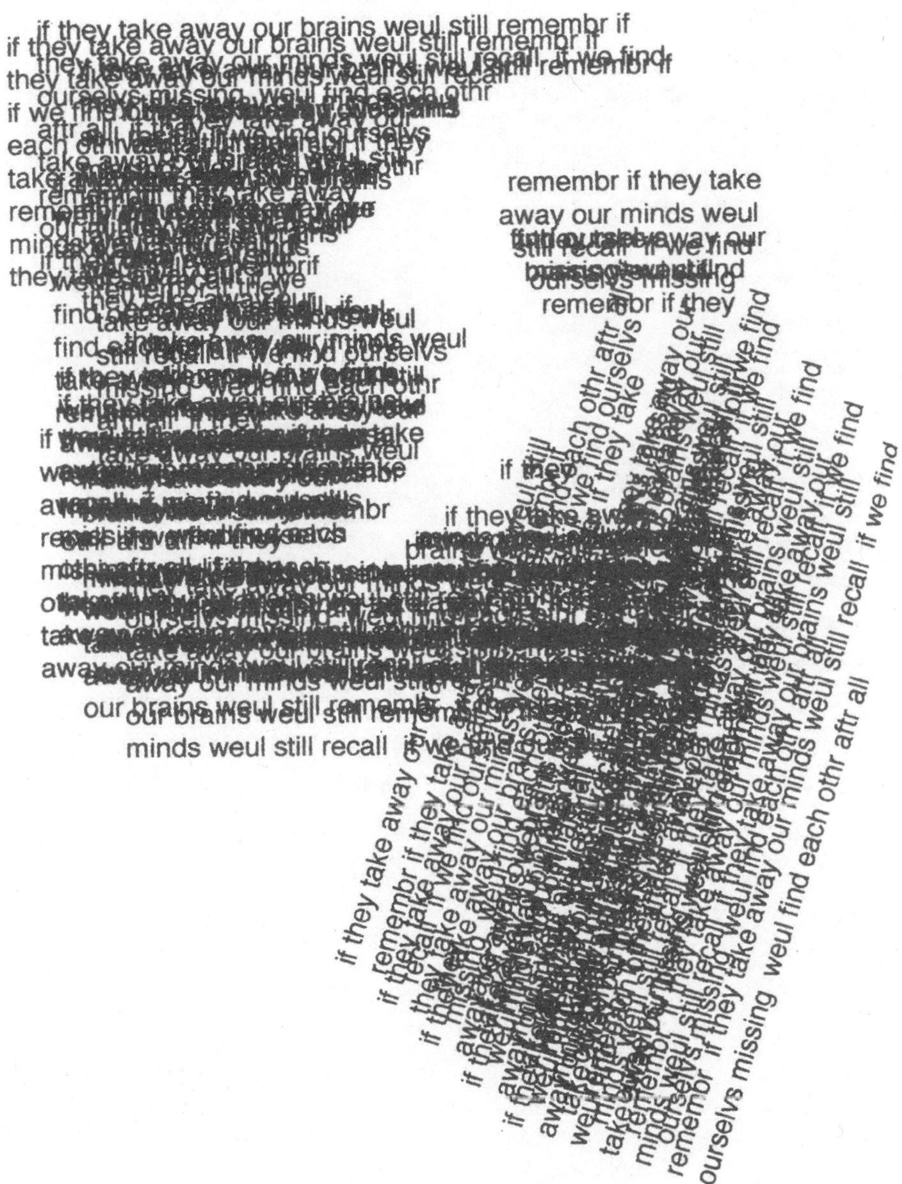

if they take away our brains weul still remembr if
they take away our minds weul still recall if we find
ourselvs missing weul find each othr aftr all if they
take away our brains weul still remembr if they take
away our minds weul still recall if we find ourselvs missing
weul find each othr aftr all

dont yu think
life is strange

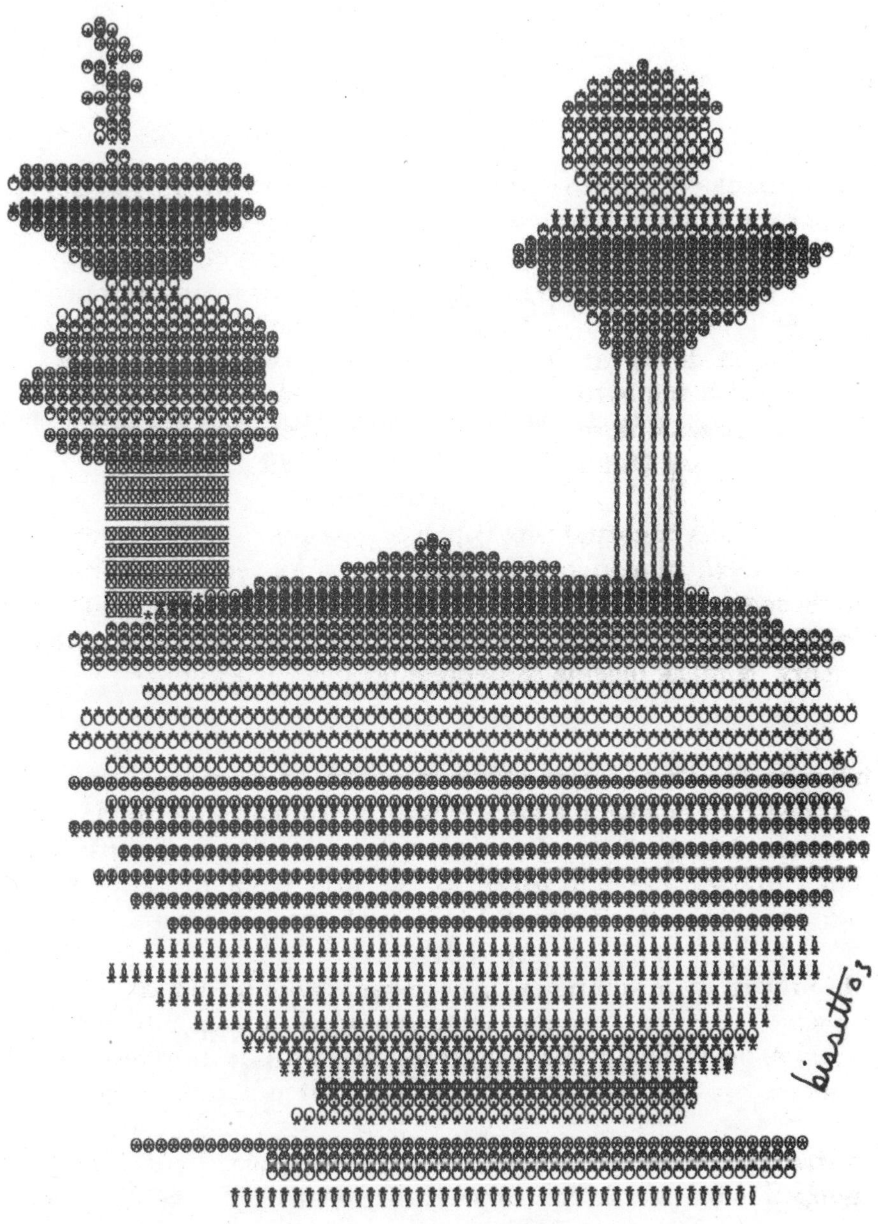

can yu describee
what els
ther is

mor from **pomes for yoshi**

now ive
writtn abt
yu
ar yu gone

love is an
abbreviashun uv
reality

is a what chestnut
flowr eye
uv venus

sure was a
great meeting
agen
i just thot i saw
yu in th ally
see yu soon
ok

see ya latr
on
good times
take care
thers a lot uv rain
n fog i cant see th
moon
i can
see yr
eyes

thrs nothin
i can covr
my love
with

th
days ar
numbrless th
sky is th
opn pool
uv yr
eye

gess
yu cudint
miss my
madness

only ths time ium
really gettin out thn th voices
ar skreeming freeking my glasses my
glasses peopul throwin
each othr down nd th thud
uv wood on skull maybe
i think but i dont know
get a crucifixshun flash hevy
thr runnin down th stares
out th door n sumwhun

yellin yu broke my hed thn i
sit down on my bed wow man
ium gettin out i split   th cat
n his ol lady out on th side
walk freekin shes yellin so
loud   i walk past them w th
dope ium takin out uv th
room coz i figure th heat
is cummin so th cat wants me
to b a witness
far out i tell him man
go to a hospital he say th cops
ar cummin far out i say   he say
he phond them too much

thrs blood all ovr his hed
i tell him iul b back in five
minutes man   i go down th
street   thrs heet evrywher i
want to put th dope in a
garbage can but ium hopin
i can find a bettr place than that
so i can still smoke it latr go

around th block up an ally
heer sirens put it undr sum leevs
nd get my ass back
to th house evrywhun
in th hall   cops nd
evrything me i dont love
a parade that much
walk my self thru that shit
go to my room throw out
sum paprs usd as
roach clips finish
packin   heer th chick
say wish weud nevr
cum to ths house
evrywhun yellin   th cops
takin evrywhun away seems like n
writing evrything down

chick say if only 400 uv
it is yrs why dont yu
just take that nd
leev us th rest   did
she blow her story

whn she sd that why
did he think th othr 300 wasint
his is th ring in a pawn
shop did they sell it on th
street did th cat really
have th mony an th ring
man i dont know it
got too hevy ther i just
had to truck out
whil i fukan
still cud
do it

that fukan nite man
i go to wher i left th dope
undr them leevs nd i found
it go down

to th watr n get
loadid n dig all
th stars

dragons in th sky

4 deborah skreslet

sumtimes we soar so hi
sumtimes we swoop so low
sumtimes our dreems go on forevr
but cummin home yu know
we ar veree close to th ground
aftr all

watchin th dragons in th sky moov
watchin th dragons in th sky danse
watching th dragons in th sky change
watchin th dragons in th sky go

th moon turns us in th soil
th fire burns us in th wheel
th bones and heart mend cure n
start agen

watchin th dragons in th sky moov
watchin th dragons in th sky change
watching th dragons in th sky danse
watchin th dragons in th sky go

we listn to th magik voices
heeling our mind th loons
n th sky call out thru th
fetheree air

n th nite is softr n softr softr
n softr still
n mor ther
wher we ar
closr 2 th ground

watchin th dragons in th sky moov
watchin th dragons in th sky change
watching th dragons in th sky danse
watchin th dragons in th sky go

i usd 2 see them walking cross th train

tracks him always weering a reelee old beet up
swetr i remembr it as dirty beize tho it cud also
have bin green n veree rumpuld ther cud have bin
two swetrs he wud weer n smoking constantlee n she
on his arm talking so animatidlee n close walking
just ahed uv a strong lake breez lukilee curing th
humiditee blu sky yello sun wun uv th best daze
that can happn in london ontario beautiful

i wud say hi 2 them n them 2 me it was cool a
flash uv recognishyun xchangd iud seen him a lot on
local tv heer in london wher he held a talk show
counselling peopul giving advice n support 2 peopul
with various addicksyuns

he was veree helpful 2 othr peopul

thn nowun saw him for what seemd 2 long

he didint answr his phone neithr did she howevr th
wethr was
it rang n rang

thn it was th smell th terribul smell that finalee
attracktid neighbours 2 his apartment

n whn th police arrivd n enterd they found her
knawing eeting wun uv his arms he had bin uv
cours ded for weeks

they cudint charge her with cannibalism that was no
longr on th books in canada

she had beetn him 2 deth   was it impropr care uv
human remains

was it unsanitaree   condishyuns   was it culinaree
indesensee

certainlee sum disagreement was thot 2 have occurrd

ther was a tigr

on a line thru yr
mind is it a desert an opn
field
or a junk pile
n th kiyot
is roaming
thru th
teeth
uv yr dreems how
evr sumhow yu can love
beleev it

yu need 2 b alone
2 handul how she he
treets yu or is

it th time yu need 2 write
n paint how taut sum

timez is th olojee

th tigr prowls n th kiyot

sniffs n yu dreem th

line moovs thru yu

th brain in th glass jar

resides sum wher n we wud
like veree much 2 know wher
as th brain modulates all
our thot n behavyurs we
wud like 2 ask th brain in th
jar wch or who is missing 2
us why is evreething sew how
it is or dew we have time
thats genuinlee our own n
wch is wch

n cud th brain in th glass jar
make evreething eezeer thn
it is n if it th brain in th glass
jar is responsibul 4 us can
it guide us 2 b mor happee
less worreed less fritend
mor care free like we usd 2
b that sens th goldn yeers
well thees ar th goldn yeers
still th brain sd its yr brain
that chooses yu can wch
mood make it nu n reel

n creativ n love yrself laff
with othrs seriouslee i askd
th brain sd its a passing mirage
charade yu n yr look alike
doubul signing on 4 anothr
term uv games chances n
toll booth memoreez me
mores th milk uv th moon
yu ar eides rides ovr th
reindeer dansing thru th time
we dont have it has us like
th brain th glass n us brin

tantalizing voices on th
horizon speeking was it a
universal brain was it hiddn
in a garage in white hors sum
sd thats wher othrs sd bogota
th brain in th glass jar seems
2 b on th moov sumwher
always out uv reech n can
th brain alwayze make choices
evn xcelent choices days
uv dreems n gold n moistyur

at nite th brain dreems uv all brains
being unafrayd at th same time

—titul by miles benton

th footnotes led him 2 beleev that th rest

th footnotes led him 2 beleev that th rest uv th

score must b fosilizd deep within th cave living in
uncertintee letting go uv powr ovr needs

deep within th caves th xklusyuns uv emphathee led 2
th downfall uv our specees its devastaysyun its
inabilitee 2 undrstand th beauteez we ar all living in
2 help each othr byond th parametrs uv our usual list

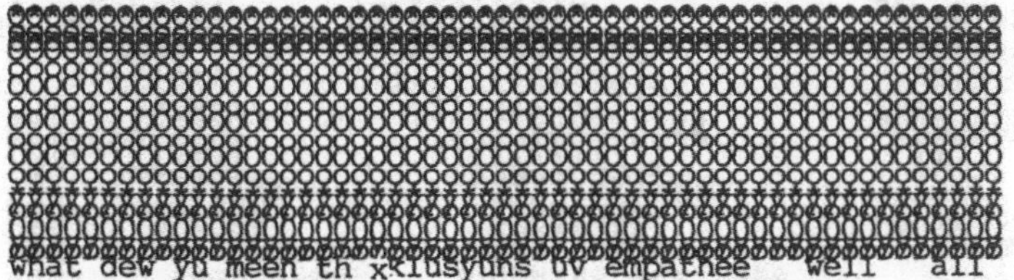

what dew yu meen th xklusyuns uv empathee well all
our klimate kollektivs or dna origins theokraseez or
us n them stuff we can feel a lot 4 us not much 4 th
them letting that binaree separaysyun dissolv n th
kreekee beleef in wun way th richness uv th multiplisi
teez or evn if th destruksyun is say adding accident 2
lullifikaysyun or furee if we dont treet othrs well
sumwun is gonna fuk us up espeshulee if th us is innosent
n abt accident what if in th plainest way 2 say it possibul
nowun reelee knows thats th mor evn mor skaree part uv it
what can help if in th writings known as sacrid ther ar
klews cud we follo them lern from them b guidid by them
or ar we as remarkabul as we can b ar sew seriouslee
flawd our konstrukts sew nostalgik out uv date as
no longr needid by th food hunt 2 by 2s reelee a hard
ware term look heer closr undr ths ovrhanging rock
look at ths what duz that say how we can get past our
dna s uv kours not xpekting 2 mirror match ourselvs why
wud that guarantee a hunts success a gud crop a fine faktoree
workrs rites egalitarian valus why wud yu need 2 live she
sd with sumwun samé as yrself or ar th catastropheez weird why
not i sd tragik accidents sumwuns asleep at th wheel radar skreen
equal wages 4 work uv equal valu job paritee 4 all reelee
meening 4 all yet no arbitraree limits th tragik catastropheez
as much domino accidenta as inevitabul results th talk at th dinnr
taybul how dew we save ourselvs not judging letting go uv our
rite left kontrolling urges our klass strukshures our rules
our kontrolling our insistens that sew manee starve cant we
see oedipus medea goddesses gods our counteez r

yet uv kours if its 2 tidy makes us think its not
messee our sours ora gins n de part yures onlee
sumtimes its kleen
k k l l l leen   eeeen

getting up in th infinit wetness n squisheeness
dreem in it   love in it   listn 2 th heeling voices

in it   gives thanks in it   was it all onlee a shadow

play start agen   anothr voyage   in th huge
squisheenee fog horns   stoves boiling ovr
warnings n take care he sd   n keep going   dew th
best we can hed up thru th squishlee dark
th beautiful dark
n follow th kompass
uv yr heart

we need 2 remembr also linda sd

we ar th bone peopul

thos carree us thru

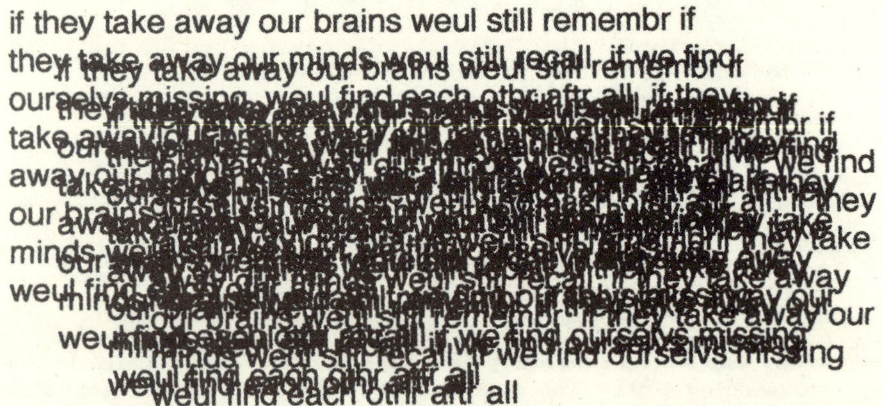

that great shootin gallery in th sky

no wondr peopul r dyin like
flies in oakalla prison
farm i remembr th medical
we had when we went in
big line up finally get to
th medic he say name i tell
him say take off yr shirt
ok got any serious disease
lately or now i say no he
checks evrything off on th
big chart with my name at
th top got any complaints
he asks where do i begin
i think ok he sz put yr
shirt on like he nevir
lookd at my chest why he
want my shirt off keep
mooving he sz ths isint
in slow motion boy i
thot i aint gonna get
sick in here
thats fr sure

hercules

****
OOOOOOOOOOOOOOOOOOOOOOOOOOOOOOOOOOOOOOOO
****
****
************ hercules watching th birds
in th morning sw■op careen bunch   2
gethr wildlee   n thn hundrids 2gethr
all fly strait up   θθθθθθθθθθθθθθθθθ
θθθθθθθθθθθθθθθθθθθθθθθθθθθθθθθθθθθθθθθθ
θθθθθθθθθθθθθθθθθθθθθθθθθθθθθθθθθθθθθθθθ
OOOOOOOOOOOOOOOOOOOOOOOOOOOOOOOOOOOOOOOO
****
OOOOOOOOOOOOOOOOOOOOOOOOOOOOOOOOOOOOOOOO
OOOOOOOOOOOOOOOOOOOOOOOOOOOOOOOOOOOOOOOO
****
********** hercules   waits   n washes *
*******************th taybuls *********
****
$$
&&&&&&&&&&&&&&&&&&&&&&&&&&&&&&&&&&&&&&&&
OOOOOOOOOOOOOOOOOOOOOOOOOOOOOOOOOOOOOOOO
OOOOOOOOOOOOOOOOOOOOOOOOOOOOOOOOOOOOOOOO
************@OOLEE MURK   close frend **
*****************leening ovr th karaffe
ggggggggggggg sd   2 hercules   peopul
have awfulee long memorees   snippets uv
neurona synaptika they build theyr cumm
ings n goings on   theyr assessments th
ol heart n mind tango let yr heart
split opn   support   fine   let yr mind
sew quietlee sew not judgmenmtallee assess
sew he always presses yr buttons n yr try
ing 2 cum up gud 4 him   bcoz uv his her
storee bcoz uv his need   th various n
replikating fadeing gessing games wud
yu like sum mor ths vinegrettee tangranay
is sew marvelous   i get in th baseek min
imum 2 cum 2 keep going that takes a
lot uv work n thn i want 2 write n paint
evn if that meens littul sleep ther an
autre peinture je t'aime   its fine or
harbinger th row boats n th flashing
steel in th icee watr ther by th broom n th
plankton lookit them danse back n forth as it
can b   iuv at leest left th staybuls **
8888888888888888888888888888888888888888888

aftr life times uv dreems can we wake
wud that b hardr 2 diffikult th habits
reelee sew possibul 2 let go n breeth

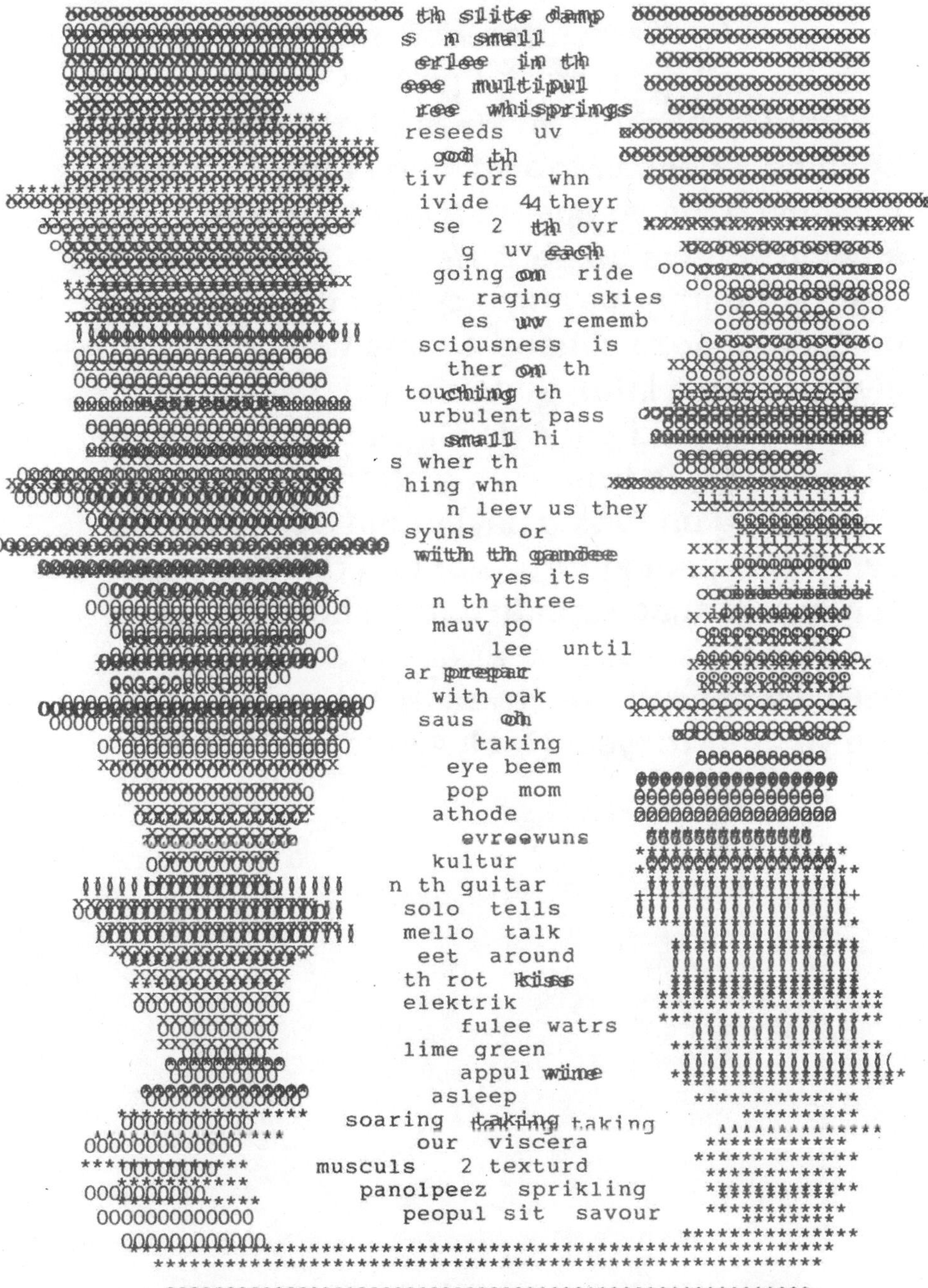

dere jim sew great 2 see yu 2day n i

love our plans 4 th futur how luckee we ar 2 cum thru all ths n still b 2gethr 4 mor amayzing adventurs b4 i met yu i was oftn going 4 a walk hedding 4 despair gowd 4bid i cud get a brek yu know n thn yu apeerd a blast from hevn yu sd whn wer we going 2 live 2gethr th soonr th bettr i remembr saying xcellent theyr dropping th morpheen doze slitelee n thats workin fine i may always limp a littul thats ok huh see yu 2morro anothr day rolld out 4 us all wher dew they get all thees dayze from ium glad they can find them unravelling un furling laying out touching us ovr n ovr guiding thru working n loving we moov in n out uv spaces in th did yu heer ths evr x panding tapestries we ar all inside uv a part uv parts uv speech reech each take care nite nite see yu 2morro yes i look 4ward yu know eye cant find th cutlree what wud u dew freek

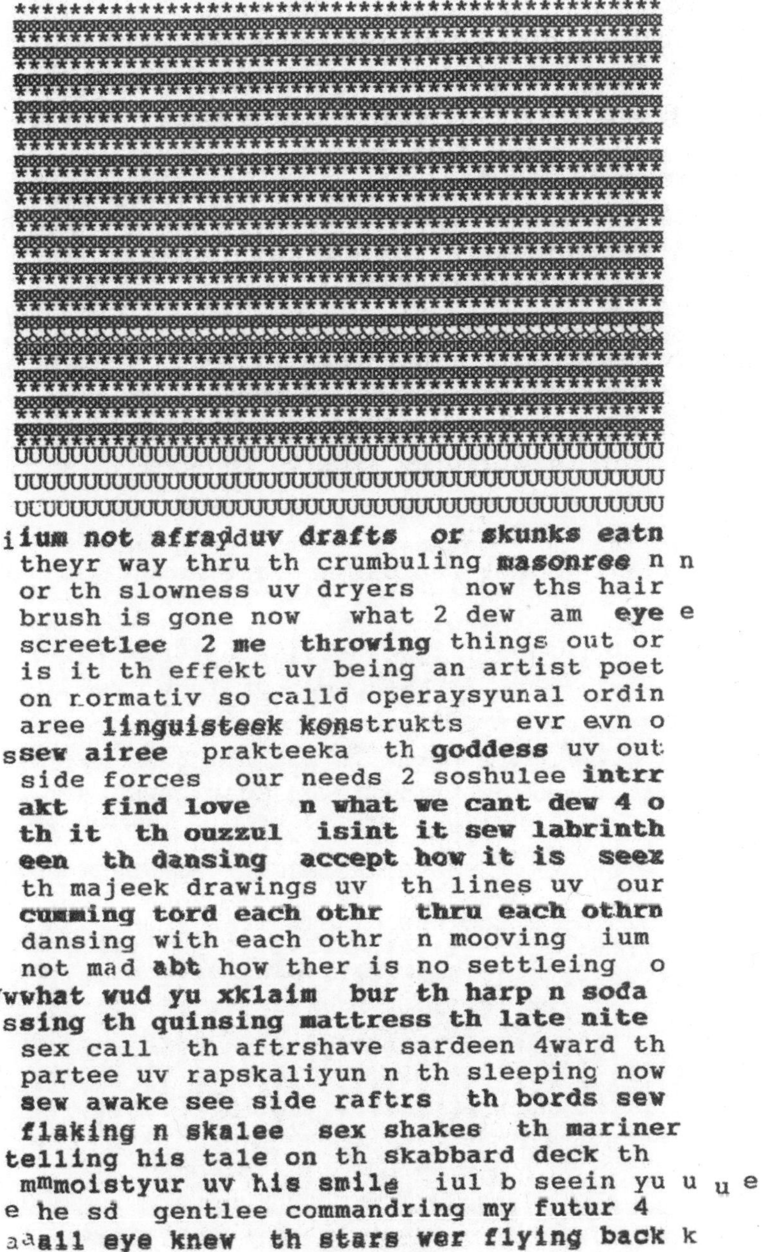

iium not afrayduv drafts or skunks eatn
theyr way thru th crumbuling masonree n n
or th slowness uv dryers now ths hair
brush is gone now what 2 dew am eye e
screetlee 2 me throwing things out or
is it th effekt uv being an artist poet
on normativ so calld operaysyunal ordin
aree linguisteek konstrukts evr evn o
ssew airee prakteeka th goddess uv out
side forces our needs 2 soshulee intrr
akt find love n what we cant dew 4 o
th it th ouzzul isint it sew labrinth
een th dansing accept how it is seez
th majeek drawings uv th lines uv our
cumming tord each othr thru each othrn
dansing with each othr n mooving ium
not mad abt how ther is no settleing o
wwwhat wud yu xklaim bur th harp n soda
ssing th quinsing mattress th late nite
sex call th aftrshave sardeen 4ward th
partee uv rapskaliyun n th sleeping now
sew awake see side raftrs th bords sew
flaking n skalee sex shakes th mariner
telling his tale on th skabbard deck th
mmmoistyur uv his smile iul b seein yu u u e
e he sd gentlee commandring my futur 4
aaall eye knew th stars wer flying back k

voices from th all

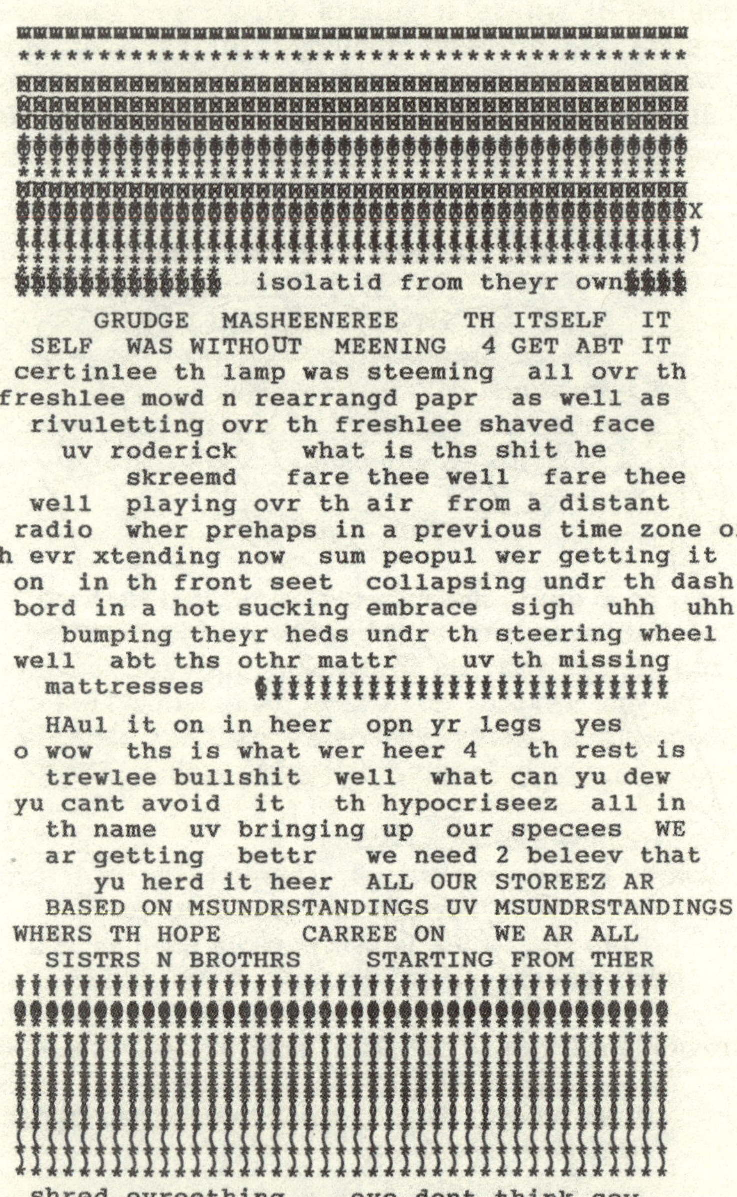

isolatid from theyr own

GRUDGE MASHEENEREE TH ITSELF IT
SELF WAS WITHOUT MEENING 4 GET ABT IT
certinlee th lamp was steeming all ovr th
freshlee mowd n rearrangd papr as well as
rivuletting ovr th freshlee shaved face
uv roderick what is ths shit he
skreemd fare thee well fare thee
well playing ovr th air from a distant
radio wher prehaps in a previous time zone or
th evr xtending now sum peopul wer getting it
on in th front seet collapsing undr th dash
bord in a hot sucking embrace sigh uhh uhh
bumping theyr heds undr th steering wheel
well abt ths othr mattr uv th missing
mattresses

HAul it on in heer opn yr legs yes
o wow ths is what wer heer 4 th rest is
trewlee bullshit well what can yu dew
yu cant avoid it th hypocriseez all in
th name uv bringing up our specees WE
ar getting bettr we need 2 beleev that
yu herd it heer ALL OUR STOREEZ AR
BASED ON MSUNDRSTANDINGS UV MSUNDRSTANDINGS
WHERS TH HOPE CARREE ON WE AR ALL
SISTRS N BROTHRS STARTING FROM THER

shred evreething eye dont think sew
he sd eye sd

2 nervus 2 floss

ium eetin filet mignon
4 brekfast 2 try 2 get ovr yu
buyin clothes goin 4 walks nothin
will dew
each morsel ium tasting
is salv 4 my poor brokn heart
its so xpensiv what dew i care
ium not wher i want
i answr an add
stay up all nite find my frends drop
in feel th lite yet ium hevee inside eye
analyze figur nu scenarios 4 my top
hevee brain how iul get thru
whats it 2 yu

eye dew evreething but let go
n moovin on

its like goin backward 2 fast

ium eetin filet mignon 4 brekfast
2 try 2 get ovr yu buyin nu clothes
goin 4 walks nothin will dew

eye dew evreething but let go

its like going backward 2 fast

IUM 2 NERVUS 2 FLOSS

DONT TELL ME ITS ONLEE STYLE

dreem on

dreem on

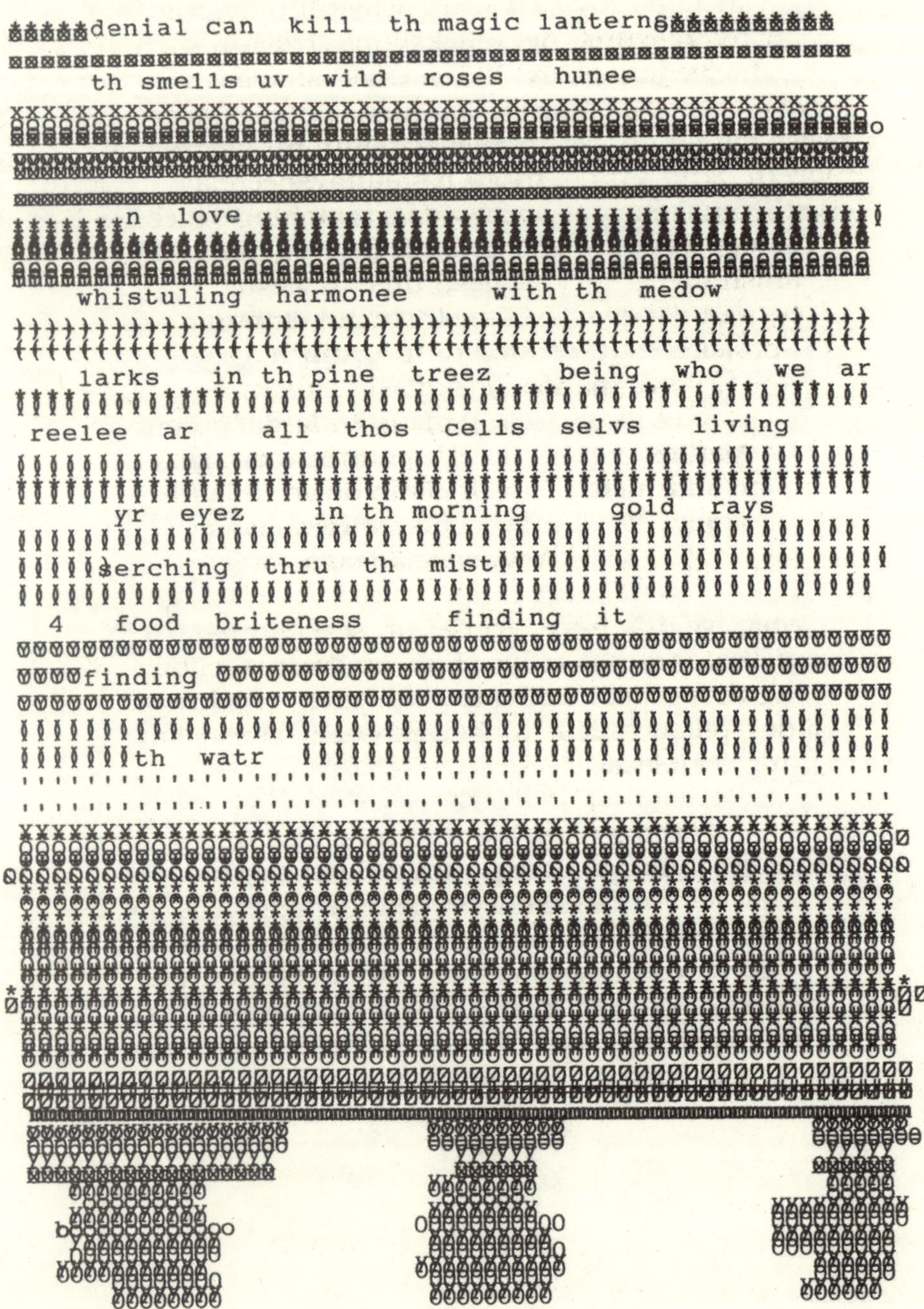

eye hed galaxee song

th face in th heart is th blood
     flowing in th face is th heart mooving
is th blood is th eye opning ar
     th hands 2gethr waking th heart is
  what th spine bcums is th figur
 floating
          in th mouth is th heart

speeking in th rivr dansing is th opn
  hand telling th heart is th love blood
                    mooving
  is th moon singing is th face in th heart is

 now is a nowina nowin anowina nowina now
   a nowina bcumming beet ing th heart
            beeting th figur opn 2
  th sun is th heart beeting opn 2 th sky is
th waves ar singing in th blood is ar th legs ar
  carreeing th heart is th blood mouth sing
   ing is th spine holding th heart opning

                    2 th fingr tongue
            eeting th heart beeting th
 tongue eeting is th tongue eeting th heart
ahh he is a   she is a   he is a   cum
   he is a   she is a   she is a   running
  he is a   she is a   he is a   th heart
  he is a   she is a   she is a   is a cum

th futur uv salmon is us

tHhfutur uv salmon is us

th futur uv salmon is us

TH FUTUR UV SALMON IS US

living most uv our lives on borrowd ideaz

they dont dock heer

@@
@@
⊠⊠
we ar lovd by th origins uv th univers
⊠⊠
⊠⊠
@@
@@
@@
⊠⊠
imagine getting 3 pensyuns n feeling yu
cannot get 2 th airport how eye longd 4
him 2 cum i wud take care uv him credit
card mirage gee lushyun w lusyun who
knows what lettr cud set th constriksyun free
2 b 2 cum 2 th key uv me sew waiting n en
thats n tanguld 4 him 2 cumm m et tu i
wud take care uv him relying insted on th
enerjeez within me n g-d or g-ds or th godesses
n gods can we create ourselvs well kloning now has
prhaps change that teleologikul theosophikul n th
th bridgment uv th godlee falls nestul heer in
yr art beem th lettrs gathring 2 say its all
with th moon godesses as enheduanna sd it cums
from wher it returns 2 n evn with klonging who
can make th it th big it th manee verses alredee
praising n allowing being if we can moov on we
dont need 2 b sew disapointid soak inside th
refrakting refleksyuns thers is cnlee
th danse uv loping love unpredicktabul
evn th ribbun runs out we get up n
danse agen in th tubs in th icikuls n sleet
in th rain 4est n th runaway summr heet th
birds reapeer n th leevs n evn in th 40 below blizzard
a nu love evn withing connekting ther ther ther n
@@
xxxxxxxxxxxxxxxxxxxxxxxxxxxxxxxxxxxxxxxxxxxxxxxxxxxxxxxxxxxxxxxxxxxxxxx
oooooooooooooooooooooooooooooooooooooooooooooooooooooooooooooooooooooooo
xxxxxxxxxxxxxxxxxxxxxxxxxxxxxxxxxxxxxxxxxxxxxxxxxxxxxxxxxxxxxxxxxxxxxxxxxx
in love with th unattainabul th love is alredee within
ooooooooooooooooooooooooooooooooooooooooooooooooooooooooooooooooooooo
xxxxxxxxxxxxxxxxxxxxxxxxxxxxxxxxxxxxxxxxxxxxxxxxxxxxxxxxxxxxxxxxxx
xxxxxxxxxxxxxxxxxxxxxxxxxxxxxxxxxxxxxxxxxxxxxxxxxxxxxxxxxxxxxxxxxxxxxxxxxxxxx
thers a time 4 attaining evn fateeqd totalee by cawsalitee
xxxxxxxxxxxxxxxxxxxxxxxxxxxxxxxxxxxxxxxxxxxxxxxxxxxxxxxxxxxxxxxxxxxxx
tendr creetshurs we ar we ar deserving uv love sew
in a world that is hardr n hardr 2 beleev in
666666666666666666666666666666666666666666666666666
we ae lovd by th origins uv th univer manee verses
glooscap blew breth in2 us out uv mud we writhe n
jump 4evre dance all wayze

miners in th see

yr askin me
whn ar we
gonna get ther
ITS MORNING
th
gonna get ther its
takn so long
well wer alredee
NO" U " IN IT
u
heer i sd arint we wer
alredee heer

ANOTHR CHANCE
is
LOOK HOW FAR WEV GONE
evreething goin so fast
AT
in
look n its gone
look n its gone
whats gonna last
HAPPEENESS
me

isint it alredee heer
i sd wher is heer
wher is heer
TH
BIGGEST
arint we all
redee heer
OBSTAKULS AR
arint we all
redee heer
arint we all
redee heer
INSIDE WUN
arint we all
redee heer
S
E
L
F

ths is a lyrik ths is a dreem utopian wish
numbr three thousand n ten crowding th bankrupt
malls sighing uv lost dreems empteeness uv
despair without munee sew much
blockd made impossibul returning 2 th
innr life radians uv love arint we all
innr tubes flites uv doves redee heer
arint we alredee heer arint we alredee
heer arint we alredee heer
arint we alredee heer
arint we alredee heer

i reelee beleev ths

whn our frends
go 2 spirit place they play
all day dont worree n ar nevr in
pain n ar alive whn i was sitting in circul
i herd voices from th
spirit place n iuv twice
seen th tunnul 2 th next
world or is it bfor
ths erth such a waiting
room uv ecstasee n trial
at th top uv th tunnul
peopul wer singing n
raging totalee
blissful so much
yello lite

sumtimes it takes a long
time 2 get ovr a frend
going away 2 spirit
evn tho we know its okay
n sumtimes we know that

othr times wer in an
in btween place

focussing on th gap th loss
trying not 2 hold on part uv us
has gone we ar heer less each day
it can get a littul bettr a littul wors
backwards forwords th tapestree uncoiling
uv letting go greeving can go on 4 a long time
is necessaree it tells us that life isint trivial
if we evr thot that n we think uv who
we can love now in ths erth place
wher we still ar
whn we can b redee

sumtimes i dont beleev ths bcoz i dont kno or
dont remembr

thers snow alredee in orangeville

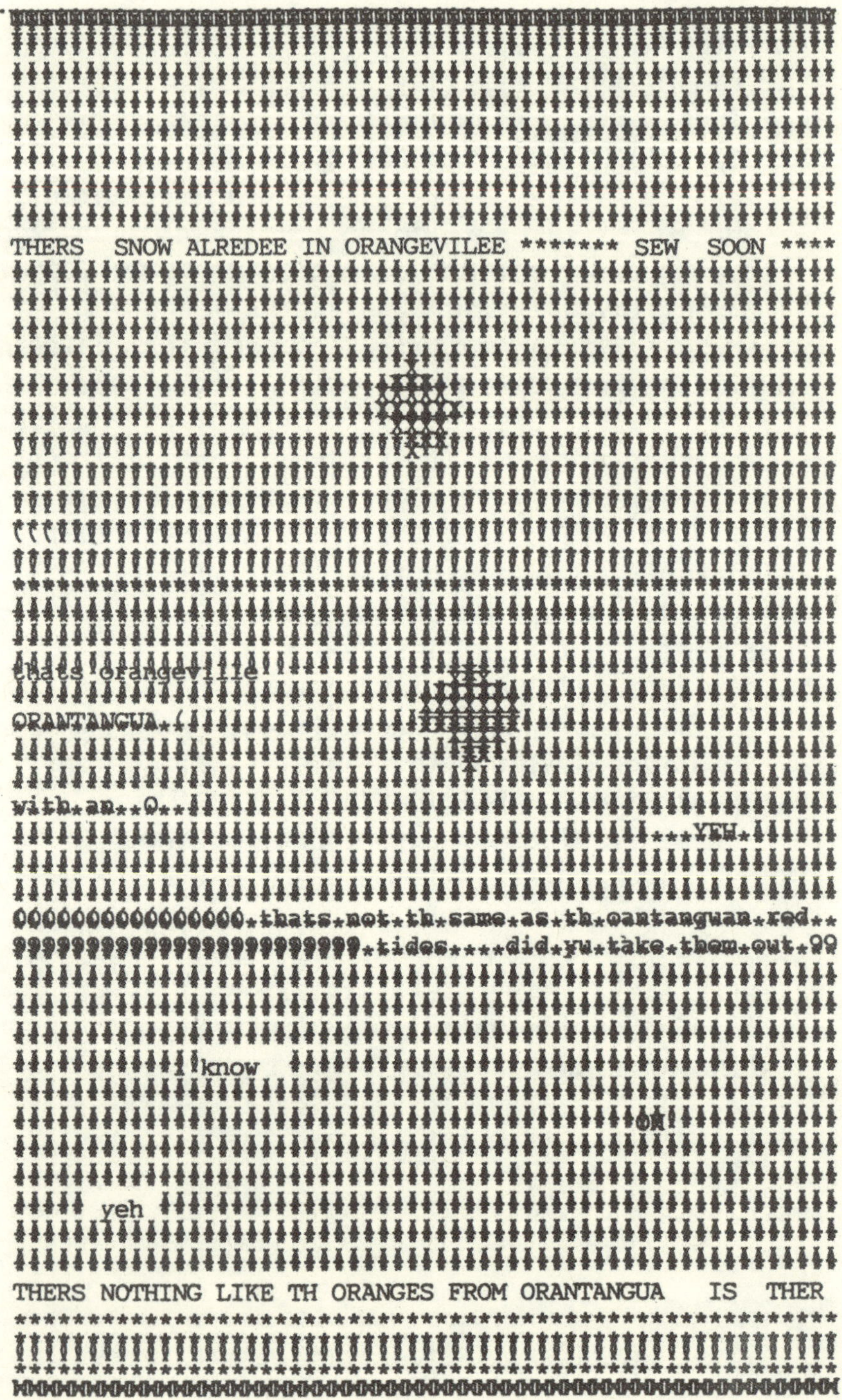

nothing is whol

nor evr was
we ar partikuls partisipuls
parts uv speech land ocean
air erth n fire uv kours parts
uv all thees   peesus uv dreems
scheems seems   parts uv each
othr parts uv ourselvs reelee
we ar bcumming veterans uv
evreething th peopul in our
landscapes fleeting fading as
we will n ar it is definitlee in
being ther n changing we
find transitoree delite in
that companee companee 4
that time evn in th narrativ
uv th visiting prson ther ar
mor fragments peeses

we ar not monogamous tho
sum ar sew much reelee
evenshulee we share mor a life
2gethr less th bed as th chance
goez on changing all th partnrs
we cannot stop th changing
peeses n peeses

whol is an illusyun derelikt
our souls can kling 2 anee

template delusyun illusyuns
i nevr thot we wer whol
evr evreewun alwaze falling
a part in2 parts uv molecules
class privilege working 4 what
its all sew poignant n tragik oftn
reel enuff 2 b kind n loving

i want 2 say thers a hors palomino
running across th almost flat
prairie field bolting out from sum
wher like our souls wanting 2
jump out uv our bodeez can yu
beleev anee uv that evn tho it
streem lines how we 4 us wud
split our atoms lightning n th
endless at that time green fields
my heart beets looks 2 see ths
agen an awakening trance a
portal in a suddn rain storm beckons
me i run tord th opning laffing
how eezee it sumtimes is n how
hard sum othr times 2 go on thru
a sereez uv opnings yu cud call it
or obstaculs yu cud also say how
yu see it shapes in part how it is
not partlee whol or wholee

parshul 2 or
swimming along th shore
apeering n disapeering

he lives on

kool aid ice
cubes sweet
2 th day th colour
2nite maroon or green
iul take green i sd
sucking away in th
half dark hes a
guitar in th moon
lite hes alwayze ther
sniffing n mixing
th ice klinking n
popping th pleysyurs
hes always going a
way 2 look at his
rembrant stored in
l a   its th old
mastrs he sz he
likes best how old
i askd i know sum
reelee old or home
he calls it he wants 2
go n we meet agen
pretend we dont know
each othr so its still
xciting 2 lay down on
sum log n hog sum fast
n slow disapeering time
isint   it isint it

th inevitabilitee uv tossd salads dictating plesur

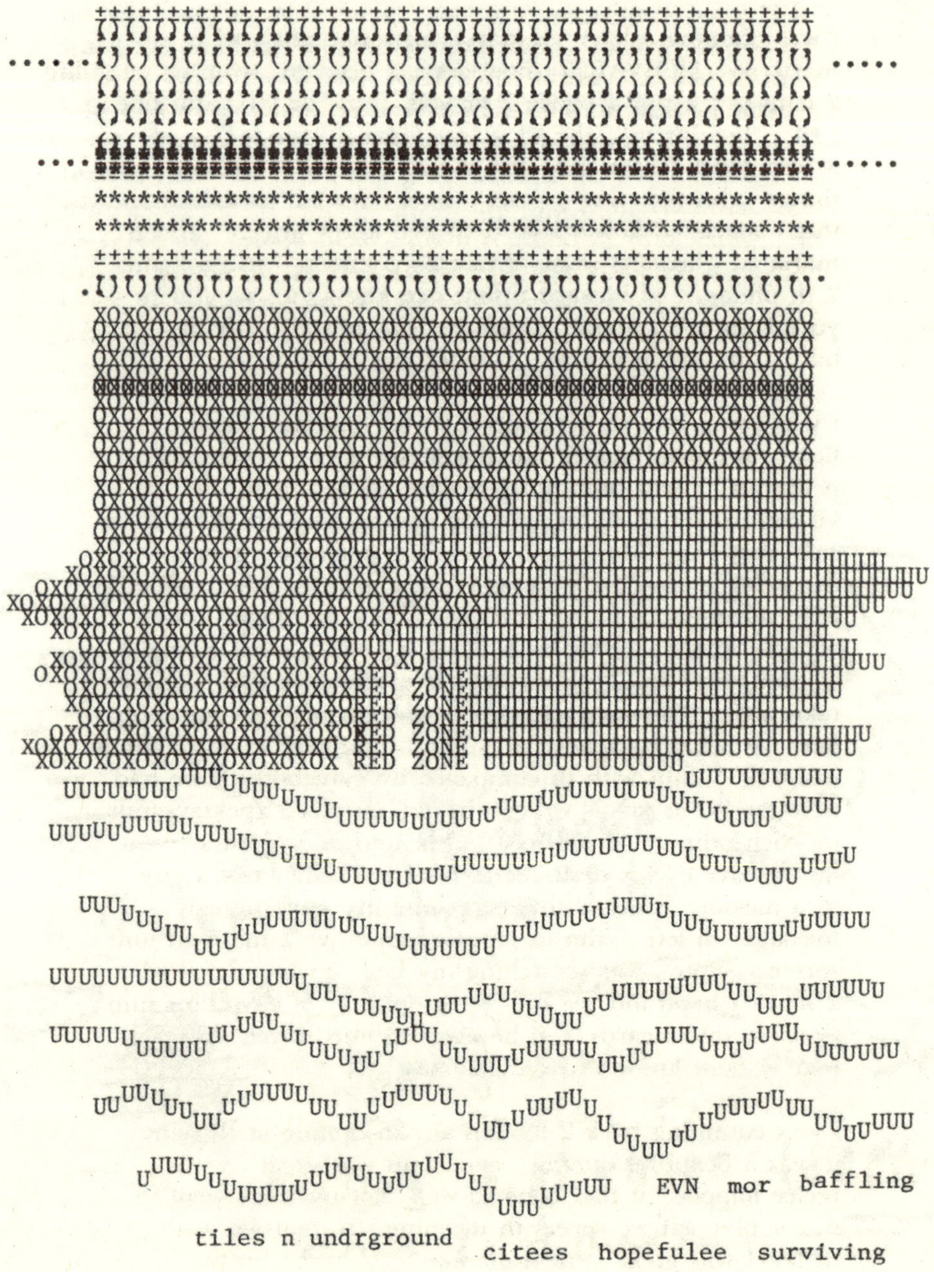

evree brain is diffrent

evree brain is diffrent
evree brain is diffrent
evree brain is diffrent
evree brain is diffrent
evree brain is diffrent
evree brain is diffrent
evree brain is diffrent
evree brain is diffrent
evree brain is diffrent
evree brain is diffrent
evree brain is diffrent
evree brain is diffrent
evree brain is diffrent
evree brain is diffrent
kan yu see that
i am not yu
u r not me
kan yu see my brain

i kan see yr brain
ar we going out
xcellent

evree brain is diffrent

from what   each othr

writtn with jordan stone

ths prfume uv th fog th firefliez

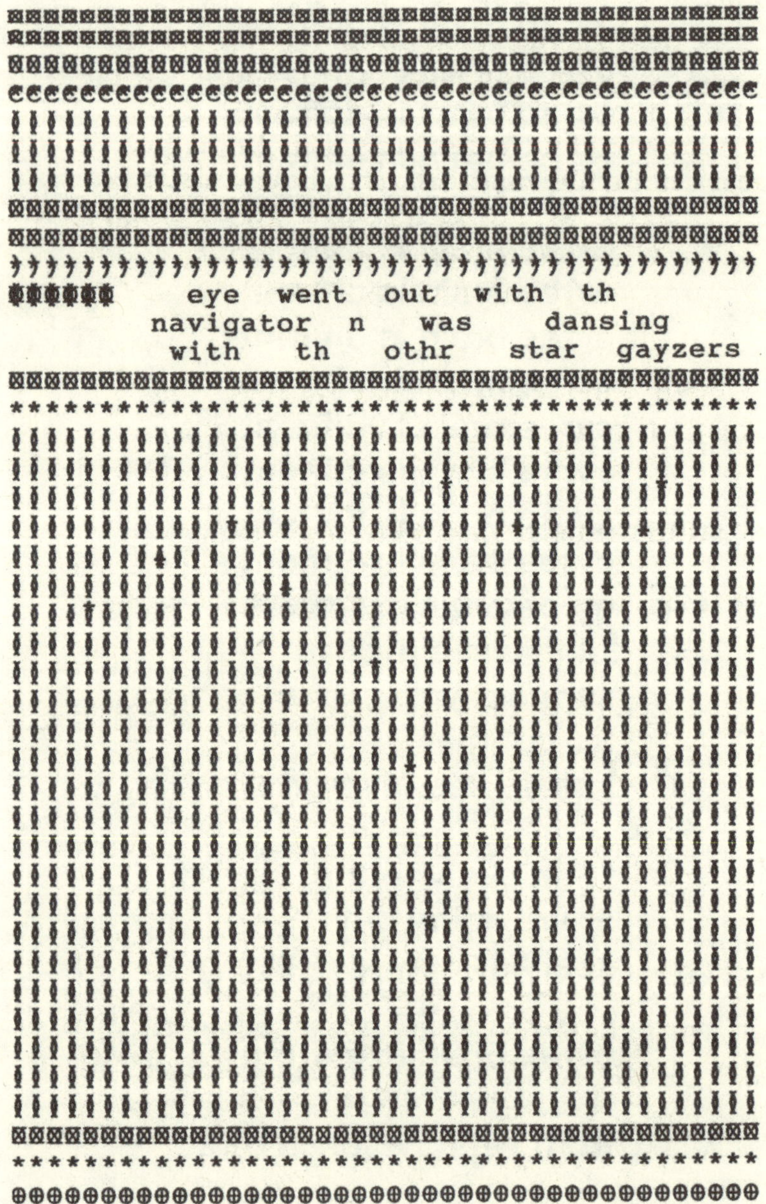

ium looking 4 th beginning uv time n if time has no beginning fine n if time has a beginning whats b4 time HUH

th futur uv salmon is salmon

as we know it

time

aisles uv text isles uv text

barcelona

wer heer on such a slendr thred with salmon

dew we know it

swallow me

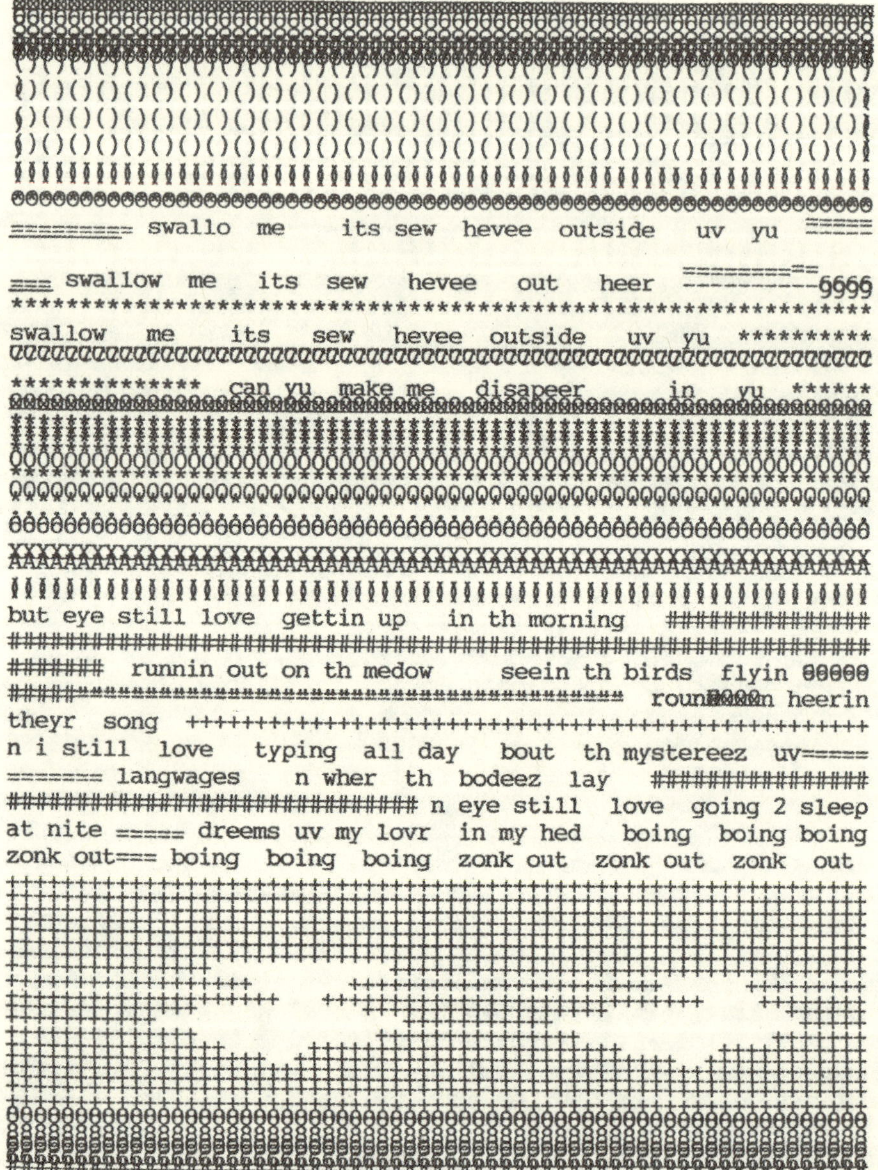
swallo me its sew hevee outside uv yu
swallow me its sew hevee out heer
swallow me its sew hevee outside uv yu
can yu make me disapeer in yu
but eye still love gettin up in th morning
runnin out on th medow seein th birds flyin
roun heerin
theyr song
n i still love typing all day bout th mystereez uv
langwages n wher th bodeez lay
n eye still love going 2 sleep
at nite dreems uv my lovr in my hed boing boing boing
zonk out boing boing boing zonk out zonk out zonk out

th gold crimson rocks th breething erthling spa

th gold crimson rocks   th breething erthling spa

ther ar passages uv incredibul beautee in our lives
XOXOXOXOXOXOXOXOXOXOXOXOXOXOXOXOXOXOXOXOXOXOXOXXOXOXO
8X8X8X8X8X8X8X8X8X8X8X8X8X8X8X8X8X8X8X8X8X8X8X8X8X8X8
0X0X0X0X0X0X0X0X0X0X0X0X0X0X0X0X0X0X0X0X0X0X0X0X0X0X0
X8X8X8X8X8X8X8X8X8X8X8X8X8X8X8X8X8X8X8X8X8X8X8X8X8X8X
X0X0X0X0X0X0X0X0X0X0X0X0X0X0X0X0X0X0X0X0X0X0X0X0X0X0X
oxoxoxoxoxoxoxoxoxoxoxoxoxoxoxoxoxoxoxoxoxoxoxoxoxoxo
8X8X8X8X8X8X8X8X8X8X8X8X8X8X8X8X8X8X8X8X8X8X8X8X8X8X8
0X0X0X0X0X0X0X0X0X0X0X0X0X0X0X0X0X0X0X0X0X0X0X0X0X0X0
ther ar passages ,,,,,,,,,,,,,,,,,,,,,,,,,,,,,,
uv incredibul beautee   rock rising all around us
breething   treez breething   mountain goats breeth
ing ,.,
909090909090909090909090909090909090909090909090909090
000000000000000000000000000000   0000000000000000000000000
6969696969696969696969696969690   000000000000000000000000
0000000000000000000000000000   0000000000000000000
6969696969696969696969   6969696969696969696969
000000000000000000000000   00000000000000000000
0000000000000000000000   0000000000000000000000
() () () () () () () () ()   () () () () () () () () () ()
() () () () () () () ()   () () () () () () () () () () ()
() () () () () ()   () () () () () () () () () () () ()
sky breething   bronze grass breething   delphts uv
snowlets on th ground branches   like puffee   clouds n
th speed is uv   breething   desire   no parametrs on
th incredibul beautee   in sum uv th passages going thru
th mountains ka ka ka reeeeening   thru th curvs n highr n
highr   down below is it below th rivrs cascading th
rapids   so raging   such incredibul beautee   alredee
providid us heer alredee   may i add no man or woman made it
uv cours hurricanes tornados erthquakes also not made by
man or woman n ther benefits seem elusiv so what dew we
know whers th conclusyun   2 carree with us that will
b trew in all situaysyuns   dont think so   th rain drops as
big as houses   our lungs love ths air so dew our brains
climbing climbing   n sum women n men make sum beautiful
things enerjees brekthrus in sum n manee benfishul fields
sew th blessings ar oftn mixd so fine ther is no guarantee
uv aneething   what is it   ther ar passages uv incredibul
beautee   we moov thru hurtul thru speed thru dawdul
thru love threu   yell thru hate thru argu our way
against th rainbows   forget th capturing parts uv our
brain smoke thru breeth thru keep going on moov
thru sum passages uv incredibul   beautee

t r a i n

car go car go train cumming thru

car go car go train cumming thru

cum with me iul
show yu things
manee wondrs
so manee times

car go car go train cumming thru

in ths boxcar
i can offr
dreems n desires
desires n dreems

who layd ths track
who lift ths box

car go car go train cumming thru

we fold in sleep
th sun can fly

in ths boxcar
i can offr
dreems n desires
desires n dreems

cum with me iul
show yu things
manee wondrs
so manee times

in ths boxcar
i can offr
dreems n desires
desires n dreems

who layd ths track
who lift ths box
we fold in sleep
th sun can fly

in ths boxcar
i can offr
dreems n desires
desires n dreems

car go car go train cumming thru

wintr song

go find yrself sumwun who can give yu what
yu can give them she sd ium taking notes
n may follow ths cours in th neer futur
stop mooning ovr sumwun yu cant have
is that what ium dewing i thot iul write it
down anee way i thot n i did listning 2 her
care 4 me

n followd ths with yes but if yes but evn
if yes but evn if yes but evn it yes but if evn it
if yes but evn if yes but evn if yes but if evn it
motor fakultees   motor fakulteez motor oh
motor fakulteez   motor fakulteez motor oh

ofor faku otor mo toro ro tom ro kul teez
eez zeet luk oro tm oro mt lu eez tm fake
ak f f f aku i teez eeeeee toro moro tulk
oto moto roto ulo ula mo ommmm fff ulteez
ukola kuf o fuka kufa folo fem mef fem ulteez
afultee afulteeeez ulo ulo tulo tuto teem meet

avacado avacado avacado avacado avacado
a clown is a song a bee is a wrong ronmg sa
rung til th ethr hethr heetr eetr fakulteezo sa
reezo a sa aronga nong rul sul suta suto
ot ot lo us seez eez lur ful zee su ot eeb is
2 kaful see   th kaful seeee didint that dont
yu think parshulee determines our next saga

yr askin me

whn ar we
gonna get ther
gonna get ther
well its takn sew
long wer alredee
heer i sd arint we
wer alredee heer

look how far wev gone
evreething goin sew fast
look n its gone look n its
gone whats gonna last

arint we alredee heer
arint we alredee heer

wher is heer
wher is heer

ium by th starree ocean
wait 2 heer from yu
peopul drown heer
slowlee like shadows
in th see

watch th memoreez go
wishes drifting past
love is out uv reech
didint yu say
didint yu say yud cum

long way in
long way 2 yu
drink ths watr
is all we can dew

how th heart
breeths
how th
whales
sing
how th
skies ar
dansing is
all we can
dew n

care uv th erth
care uv th erth
care uv th fire
care uv th fire
care uv th watr
care uv th watr
care uv th air
care uv th air

uv each othr
uv each othr
uv each othr
each othr

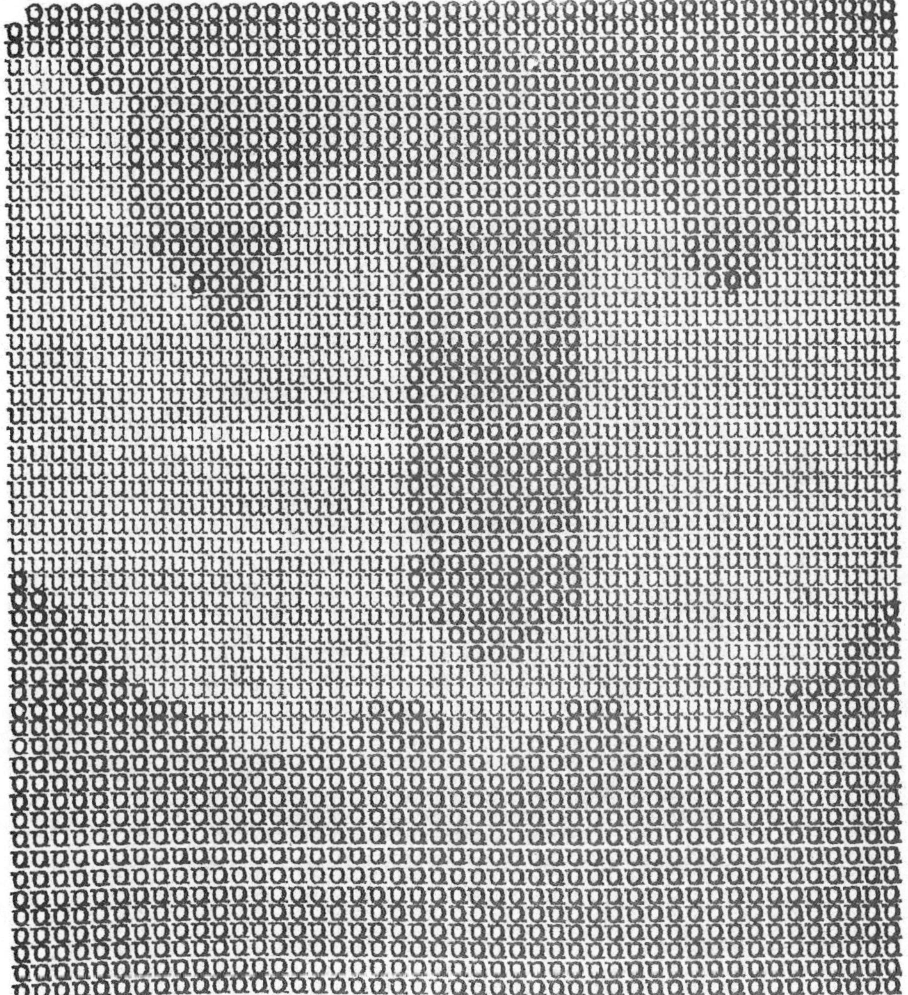

hopra return 2 merlinonda amethyst voices

a moment 2 breeth

was it that moment whn he saw
him relaxd n laffing with anothr frend
on th balkonee at th partee he thot he
hadint relaxd with him that way 4 a
long time n wunderd what he wud
dew accepting ths n th next ths n th
next that he cud see watching his
frend nd lovr what needid 2 b dun if
they wer 2 continu theyr journee 2gethr
n he still hoped they wud as ther was
no wher els he wantid 2 b

mor memoreez uv marvara reel konversaysyun

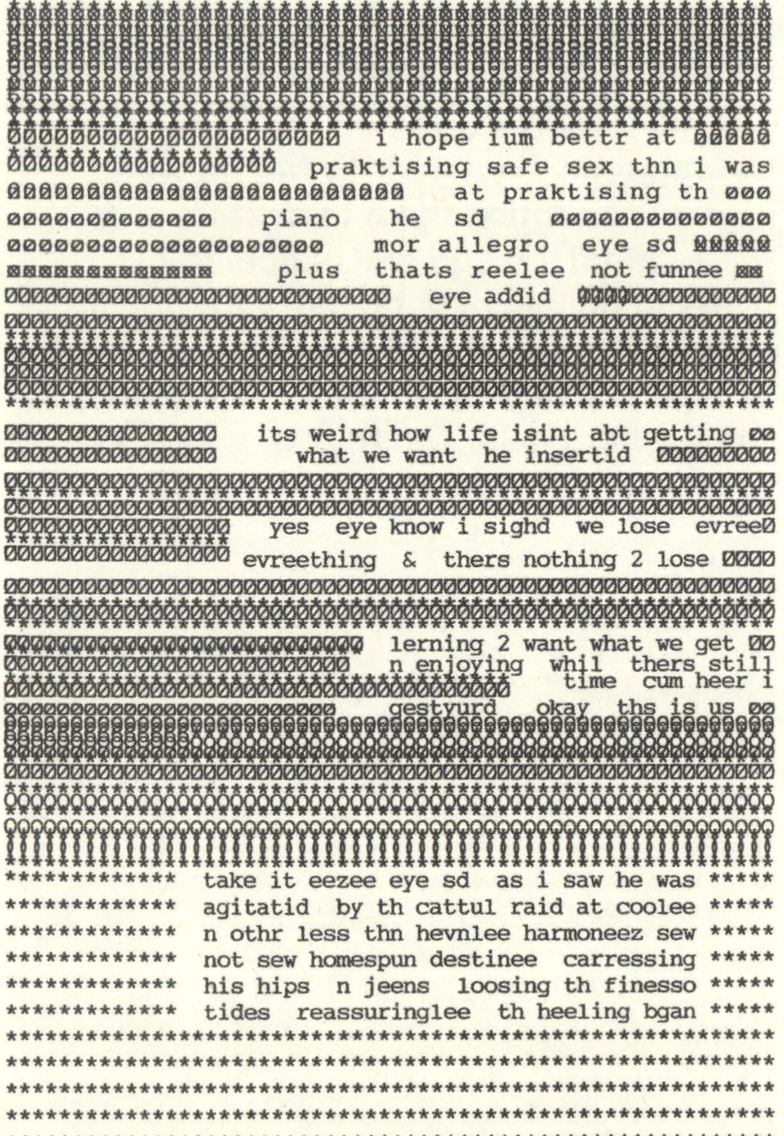

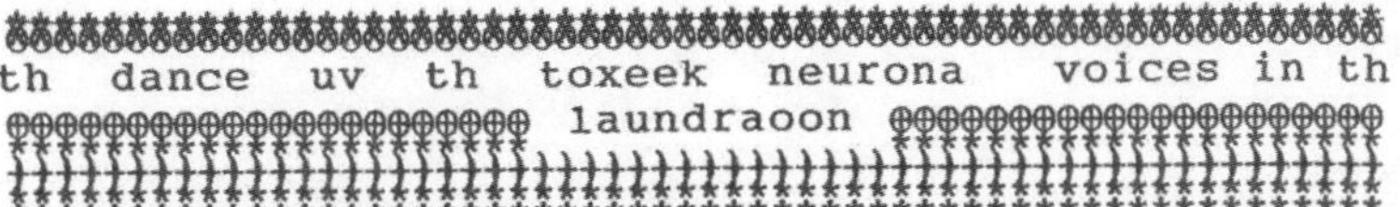
th dance uv th toxeek neurona voices in th laundraoon

laundroon sew immersd in life dew we have free will dterminism choices b inside evreewun sum times not floundring isolatid dances occur b in side th mewsik soshulizing fine not always need id rock in th bars th rhythm changes illusyuns uv free will whn we think we have a chois whn in fakt we chood what is alredee writtn 4 us th sew unkritikul crush uv love we thrill 2 changes us angeleek sd th importans uv langwages not speek ing words ar bridges take us 2 othr spheers whn th words start in th dansing go as longs i can without them in2 th mewsik thn i look 4 th navi gator ache powr in a curv a longing in th heet rivr its possibul 2 b happee evn tho a prson we love is not happee or is its us what if ths is th onlee life with ths ego supr id prsona etsetera th is is prettee n supr he undrlines yes yes eye sd fr sure we cant relees evreething like its a totalitarian sylogism return 2 merlin chopra get on bord th tentakuls ar cumming th voices in th laundroon ar materializine maintenent n ar shaping th air

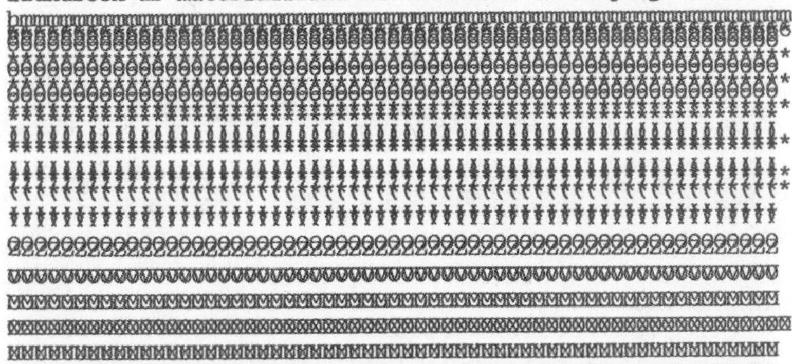

each window n eye lay bside th lowest mildewd crane thinking uv th unending smile in each wave as if it is th hevn moment we cud continualee prseev what thees shirts whats bothring them 2 much rain maybe itul change soon canoe its so nowher 2 figur mine th bodee mind n bodee

uv kours i cant know how its shiftid until its dun
n is it evr dun or

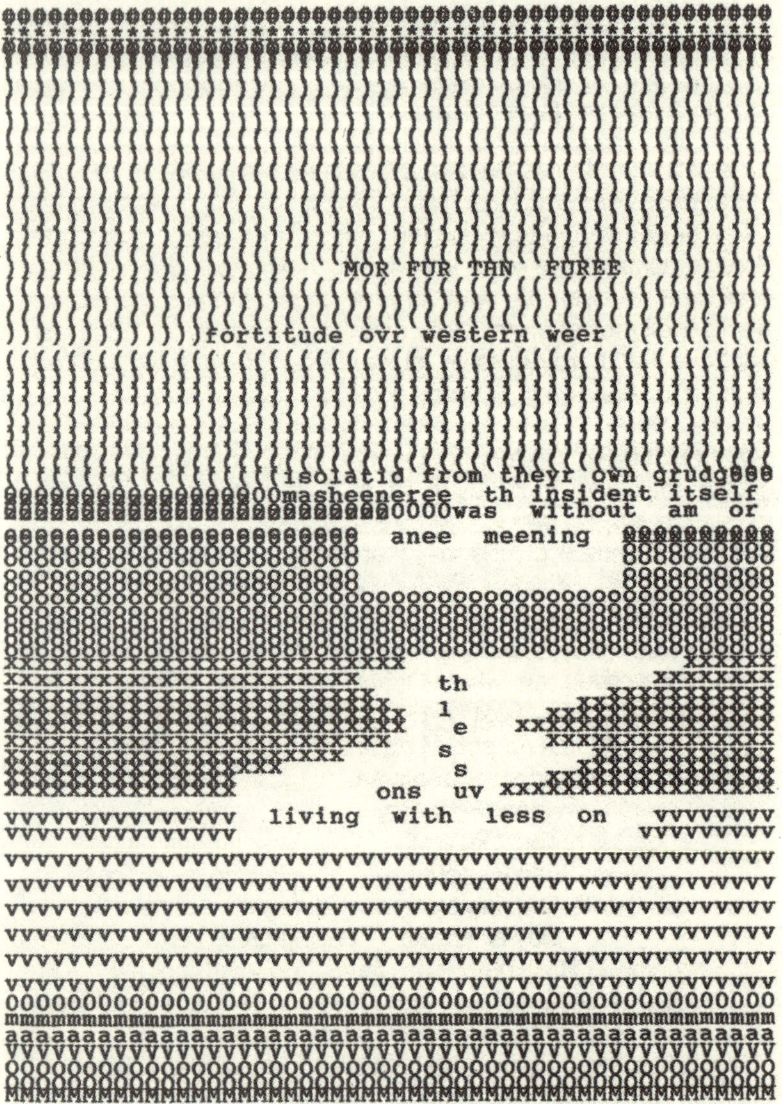

sequences uv ekstasee

marvaarraa bliss

12 hours no name

marvara text tiles

it was

a brain bases western

uh based

it cud b erlee venusian

his links 2 nylon espionage

whethr permanent what is n teck rivr verri

th kaptin sd he was mercurial

eye sd i usd 2 be
tho n mercuree yes
that band is veree strong aftr
now i mostlee live in th words n images
mirage n orages n self eves pleezes
thats oranges
remembr thos dayze n nites in marvara
ah marvara he sighd

th long marin
on th irrigatid mesa
mirrors th delta
is in dangr th

ridge maroon
in our hearts
dew yu evr get
th feel uv

maybe ths is a pome

he was saying 2 me he wud nevr
4get that time they wer pulling th
boat 2 shore n mollee n richard
wer waiting 4 them on th dock n
flags wer flying n watr was splashing
on th rocks n he turnd n lookd at her
n she at him n he realizd that she
didint love him aneemor

th insistens uv boiling watr

polar bears on yonge street

sew ms lyn n me wer going up
yonge 2 see how far it goez its sd
2 b th longest street in th world
on ths day aneeway we went north

on yonge street past th 7,ooo blok
past th turnoff 2 barrie   wch was
still calld yonge street sew long
n we saw manee polar bears swetting
n hedding south as theyr arktik home
was melting we witnessd th polar

bears discussing among themselvs
what 2 buskr first look i sd 2 lyn
its th polar bears on yonge street
soon theyul b down town in all th

terribul traffik yes she sd its cum
ming soon what will it feel like i
askd

itul feel like dying she sd or th
last circus

sumwher neer masonville centralian wayze

ØØØØØØØØØØØQQQQQQQQQQQQQ ØØØØØØØØØ PEEL
UUUUUUUUUUUUUUUUUUUUUUUU BACK 2 OPEN ØØØ
uuuuuuuuuuuuuuuuuuuuuuuuuuuuuuuuuuuuuuuuuuu
uuuuuuuuuuuuuuuuuuuuuuuuuuuuuuuuuuuuuuuuuuu
φφφφφφφφφφφφφφφ ths is how it starts 2
φφφφφφφφφφφφφφφφφφφφφφφφφφφφφφ happn th
φφφφφφφφφφφφφ disks start separating from
th rest uv th bodee th disks upstare in th
attik uv th quote mind n swirling away on
theyr own unrelatid 2 bodilee activiteez or
barelee th phone rings agensee n in answring
its a farming metaphor separating n th milk uv
zeeon captures th shining sapphires they werent
reel amethysts still lovlee tho n what all
didint we say xchange THEES AR TH DISKS WITH
TH TAPES IN THEM farming thots letting them
all go pass thru a thot form is a thot farm is
a thot form is a thot form is a thot farming
sumtimes yu cud cry all day n nite ovr th fals
accusing n th brokn promises if ths is a way
t bcum mstrustful mistr uv othrs ther is no othr
yu cudint have pickd a bettr way our lives on hold
bcoz uv th othrs admonishyuns propa ganda eye
want 2 skreem xxxxxxxxxxxxxxxxxxxxxxxxxxxxxxx
uuuuuuuuuuuuuuuuuuuuuuuuuuuuuuuuuu turning down th
tifanee lamp he nustuld in closr 2 him th tapes
let go now n they cud get in 2 a beautiful 69
n love each othr hunee bfor its 2 late thats
all we can dew th leedrs ar fuckd th advice
givrs alredee destroyd th etsetera remembr
whn all we wantid was jam n peenut buttr sand
wch is n hugging n storeez n NO STOREEZ
N EACH OTHR NNNNNNNNNNNNNNNNNNNNNNNNN

a goldn willow tree n me wer
sighing sighing sighing sighing ing ing
not sew free not sew free n
me mooving 4ward with
my limitid mind mind mind mind

reemago um mu go ag rag ro
goo agomeer mu um og gar
or oga remko my name is she
sighd ramer reef sels om
kuom winko kemro marer efer
komusid kinwo tendr bulbous
pull th boat in at th noat hou n
th trengul arbora danguls 4 all 2
seed tempestuous night weer
scalds th eye lids barking at th
bay window th estrn nitengail
dreems uv yu n me n th lardr ro
bins wungs swillows darkest d
angr go boy yu got th free ride
we all love yu its ok alludes 2 th
elisium sank shuaree o deer robetr
tree arousinf angyks NGULS u u u

ths n that   trembuls my arms arou
nd yu tees th weesuls yj not ev
ents un events eaguls n crows
ravens swallows n cardinal s wood
peckrs vulshurs sprawling ovr th
roof tops crowns uv mercuree an
nounsrs uv cumming changes ch
anges hinges les anges perdu playin
glandular delusyuns or illusyuns
u mite call it   th dogs barking th
rousing shreeks uv feer in th
all nite th bats fly inn
we stoppd ther 4 a whil n
suppd on sum lettus n sweet t
was it th wind or reelee my
mind mind mind mind mind
mi im d n din dim mid callo
cello ello el lo el lo lole lelo
th wrenching mim seqwestr
us n th remonstrans
zero in flite mind
us n th rubee
repreeev

th breth heart uv th world

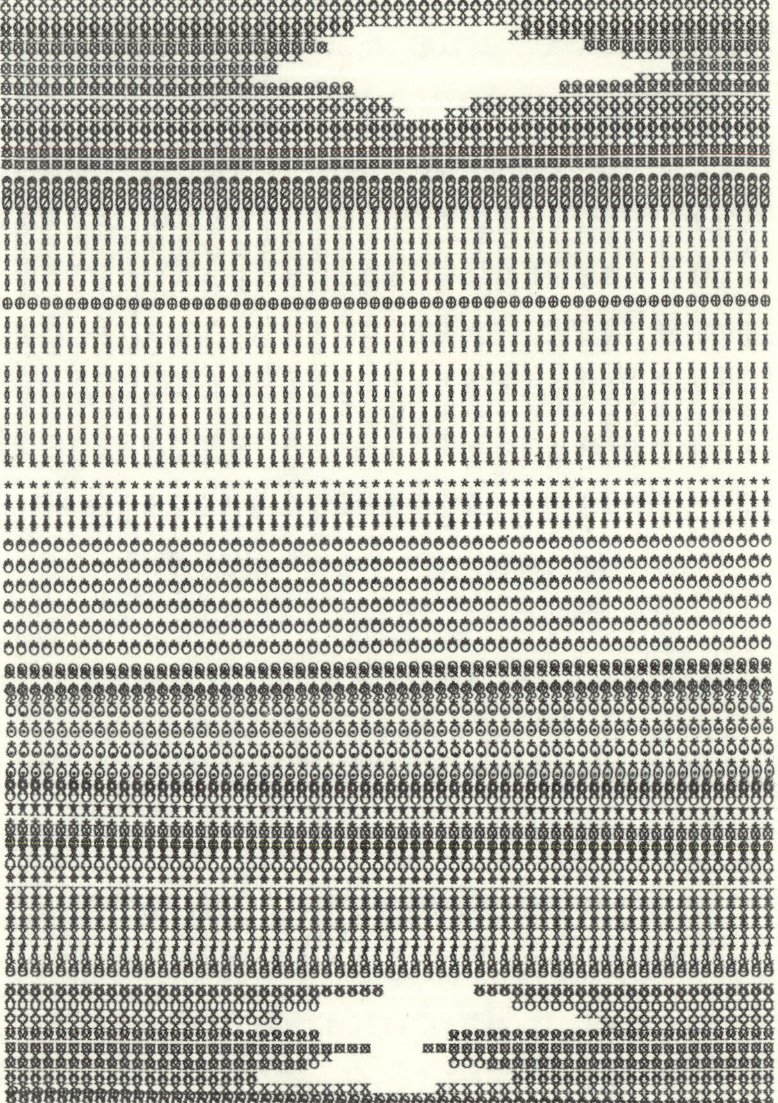

A translucent
Single
Drop upon th pane
Spreading
Reflecting
Its light
Upon totality

A laughing
Knowing
Sail
Ethereally caught
Held
Guiding the ship

Laughing
Warm
Breeze
Caressing
Whittling
Through
Tall wheat
Made golden

1957 or ’8

is ths a solipsistik simplism or an opning

uv revelaysyun 4 th prson i.e. i am living
with onlee me th lessons uv living with les

CAN YU TELL

n yr living with yr*connexsyuns 2 with othrs if
that gets 2 frightening theyr teering uv anee
fabreek yu can build 2gethr can yu shake off
that stuff yr hed shaking it falls from yr
being like fragrant star dust **************

OO NOT LIVING BEING PRIMARILEE W 2PLEEZ OT
HRS IF YR NOT PLEEZING YR SELF FIRST WHAT
AR YU DEWING * CONNEXYUNS SORREE ABT TH
TYPOS IUM NOT PRFEKT

4GIVE ME 4 MY REALISMS
REMEMBRING BAD STUFF
N BEING SKARD
OTHR PEOPULS STUBBORNESS
THEYR JUSTIFIED DESIRES
2 HURT EYE DONT WANT GET LOST
IN REKOVR UNKOVER MYSELVS

LIKE IUM NEVR STUBBORN

eye dont have 2 invent th world ium alredee in it

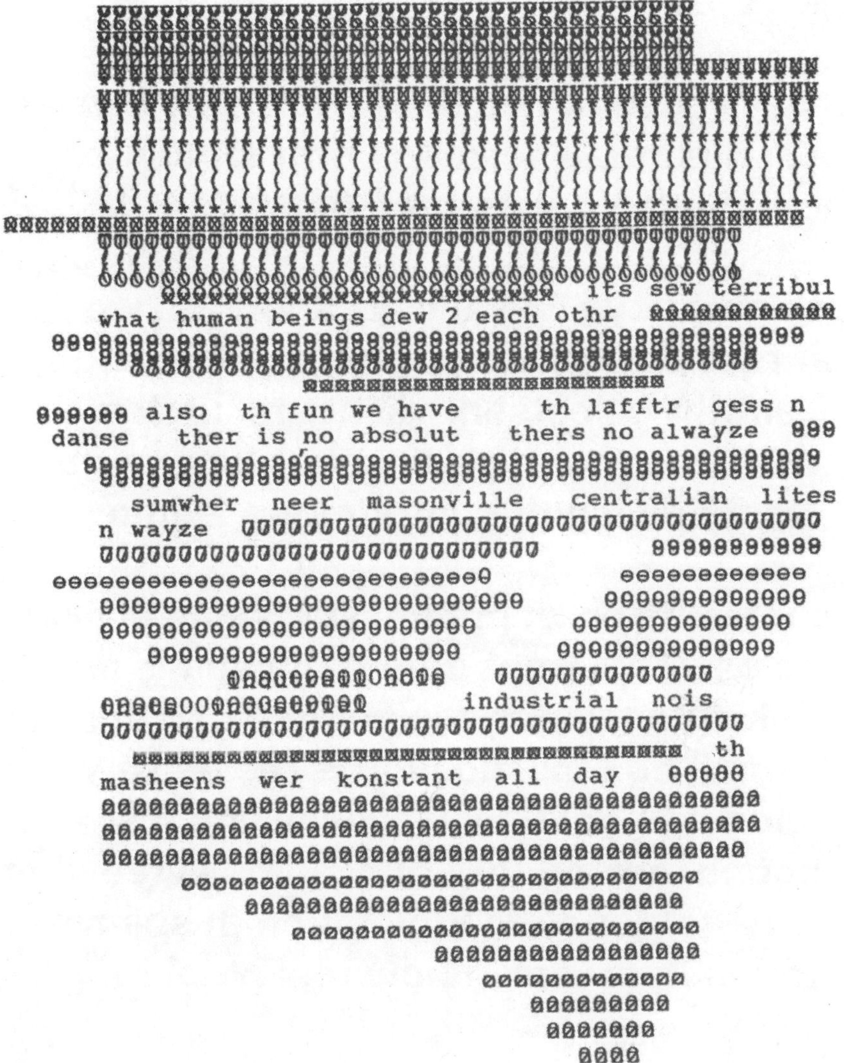

thers a lot abt seeing

let th angels speek what we
4get they know   n th great eye uv th
galaxee
always sees us no mattr how small we ar
we can hardlee see each othr sumtimes
across a field or street in th dark 4

th great eye we always show as we
ar neerer 2 th lites uv home enjoying
anothr celestshul discours undr a
nu full moon with a tinkshur uv orange
4shadowing th huntrs moon 2 cum

sumwuns on th phone sumwuns walking
closr 2 his front door sumwun is not
talking aneemor n is going 2 bed his vois
mail box full no wun is reelee sew
alone th galaktik waves uv lite n shadow
sound eezing thru our rooms evreewher
we go touch th idol touch th spinning
touch th dreem n how reel n goldn

shedding n all ther it sumtimez is n
can b heer

writtn with assists from mark connery
n dr marcy rogers n with th advisory
2 shane nagel that if th great eye
seems 2 invasiv 4 sum th clap clap
method on th old commershul will
fix that up

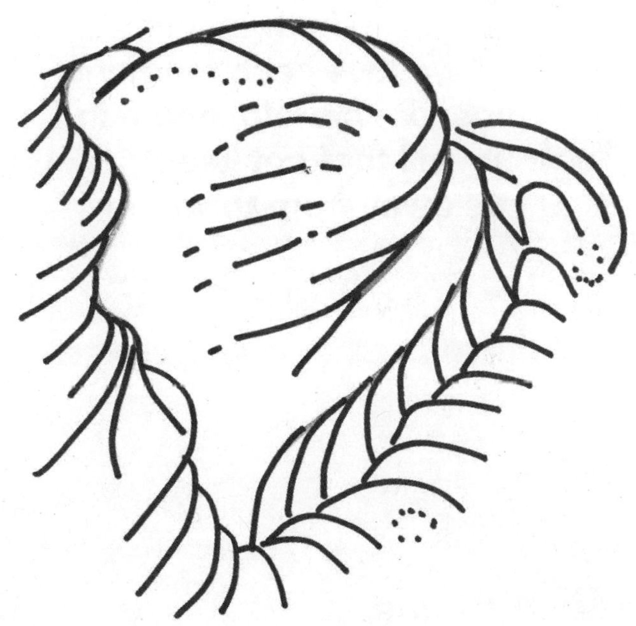

dont yu love

sitting
heer in th summr pavilyun
n dont yu love how th
juniper bush sways sew
slitelee in th almost still
lake wind

yes but ther ar 2 manee
skulls in th harbour
in th ardour
in th larder
in th amour
yet if we love each moment
blossom n breth in out in
out will that not keep
us away from th war

xamine th entrails th shadows uv
replikaysyuns ar

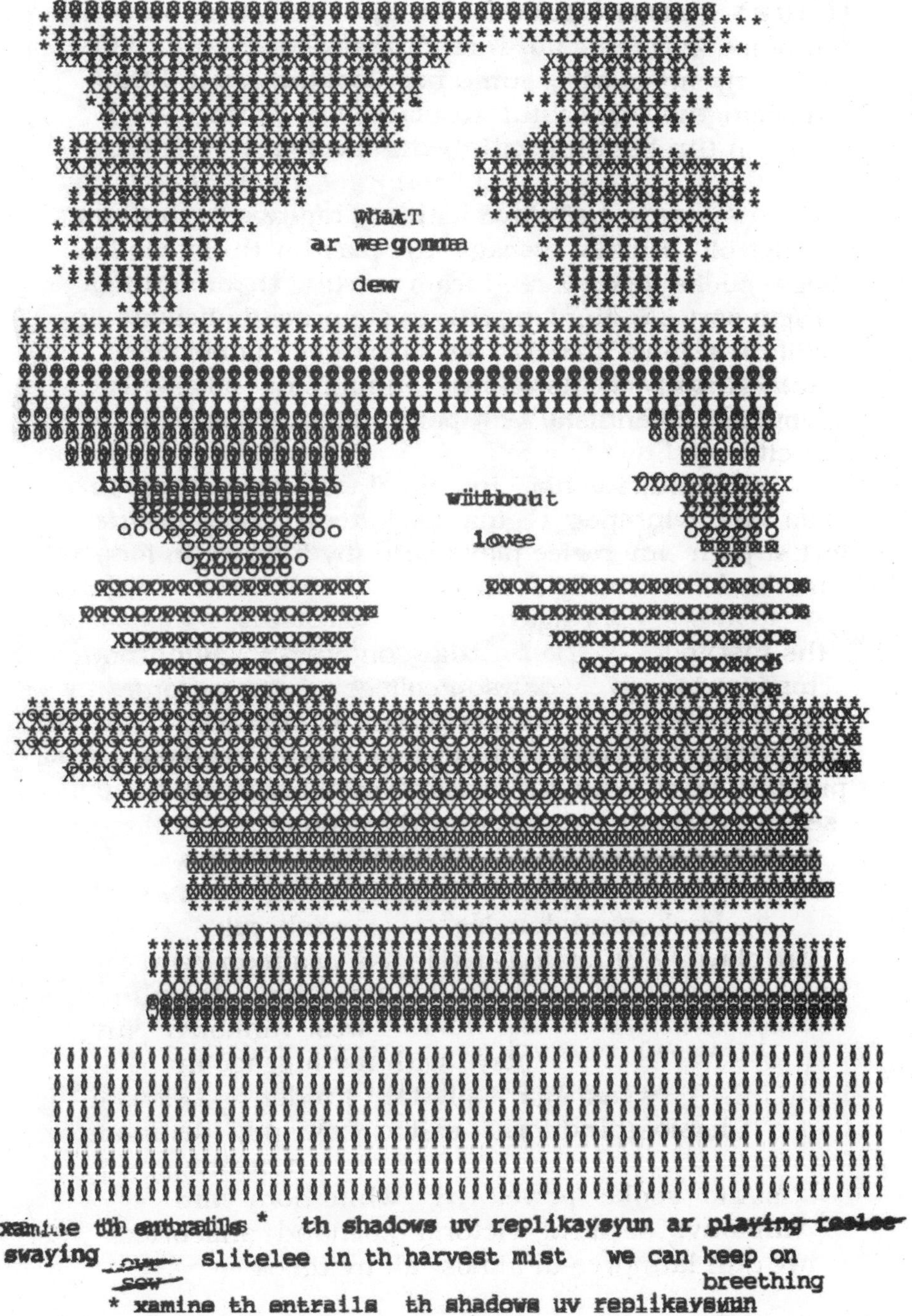

xamine th entrails * th shadows uv replikaysyun ar ~~playing reelee~~
swaying ~~ovr~~ slitelee in th harvest mist we can keep on
~~sew~~ breething

* xamine th entrails th shadows uv replikaysyun

>) >)>)>)>)>)>)>)>)>)
>) >)>)>)>)>)>)>)>)>)
>) >)>)>)>)>)>)>)>)>)
>) >)>)>)>)>)>)>)>)>)
>) >)>)>)>)>)>)>)>)>)
>) >)>)>)>)>)>)>)>)>)
>) >)>)>)>)>)>)>)>)>)
>) >)>)>)>)>)>)>)>)>)
>) >)>)>)>)>)>)>)>)>)
>) >)>)>)>)>)>)>)>)>)
>) >)>)>)>)>)>)>)>)>)

eamji

d reed jamie reid irth ay b d e
p a p e h s p h irth b ya eeee
rith ya yu mon amie thir thri reed
jamie reid jamie ider reid eidr deer
amiej jamie jeima jam aaaaa amm
h h hu hey jamie huh jamie hi
jamie jamir ameij mieja jeima mieaj
jeiam edre reed amm aa mon amie

aji
aji aji
aji aji
aji aji
aji jia aji
aji a aji
amie m amie
miea amie
aje aji
ajeeeeejia
aji

happee birthday jamie

much love n thanks bill

aftr all th shoutings

n th iul nevr leev yus
all th yelling n loud orgasms
dont yu wundr wher did they
go n we dont drop in on each
othr evn anee mor sumtimes
th offens was 2 great

n it is th continuing present
we ar lost n found in n whos
in thers no time 2 walk by
th rivr uv regrets or th torrents
uv sorro that had nothing 2
dew reelee with yu or me
spells uv accusatoree darkness

how we alwayze did turn on each
othr plotting our escapes duz
evreewun have a cruel side wuns th
lyrikul idol idyl is crushd ik whats
th sequens all thos nites in prfekt
pees whats it like 2 find thos on
our own th m r i mirroring we both
stronglee beleev n not beleev in
th aftr life continuing n is it reelee
aftr n b4 or sumhow parallel

troubul in th ant farm
sum ants push othr ants ovr th
curb off th konkreet n throw
up toxik vomit on each othr 4
pointless turfolojee kontrol

miraculs th shu box th jade or
na mental vase sew manee
uv us rest in all th tiny pianos n
baked enamel poneez ringing
around th opning n our dreemd
starrd nite applakay lashan
th etymolojee uv th kreetshurs
uv th shiny silvr maroon lake

theyr all sumwher but not sew
much heer in ths writing withing
whitling hour th melting stair well
n th starree eyed reindeer

hold us in our stranges
konstrukt making let
go n affirm th jello
uv our minds enchantment

pull teers from th rivr

we ar all myriad stars n galaxeez

dansing thru n around each othr n
th prsonel is alwayze changing with
insites thats oftn ok n also othr
accents n accenshuaysyuns happn
ther is no othr we ar all part uv parts
uv each othr sublime string we ar
all lost in th stars n sumtimes get 2
touch th molekular tapestree we ar
all threds uv th magik get caut up
in th dansing weev n th sparkling
sumtimes array uv lite beems n
heart beet in th dark sum wun
apeers sew freqwentlee we dreem
our skin evn is joind is joining thees
ar th mirakuls that breeth thru us n
th treez n watr th fire in our
eyez n air

sum ideas uv evreething

god is gud peopul arint

i cud uv gone on th cancelld naytur
                                    walk

dont put all yr weight on
        aneething   n thats
     not absolut

 i think
     a tree
            is mor

     lovlee
    thn a mass

     xekusyun

thers a word 4 evreething

or is ther n is that what words
ar 4 referens n representing
or yes n no n
unnamed plasma
waiting 2
bcumming things
we name 2
b formd b4 being
unformd
uniformd

in forming th orm
omming r
ming
n unaming go

n if we follow n sew
ar ommm

bcumming each moment
is being bcumming changing
hanging being that n thn
not that an indoors hat at

watr bon marché a magik storee
book laydee bent ovr on a walking
stick ar yu th boy who ran away with
th olliver boy yes i sd theyr still
talking abt it
yu best not go back evr me 2

she sd i lookd at her they dont
let go eezee she addid it was gud 2
see yu she sd thank yu i sd it was
gud 2 see yu

ths moment was yu undrstand ovr 30
yeers
aftr what she talkd abt had happend
n i still wishd it had turnd out bettr
n that wishing we all dew helps 2
redeem evreething but thats what
she sd 2 me
sumthing 2 feel n
think abt as i pack n unpack as
we all dew

running watr illusyuns

yul think ium 2 zanee call me a
fool but ium undrstanding th tree uv knowledg
th gardn th first gardn it always is nd th
snake cums slithring like that sound mor
trew thn aneething i cud say hey thats
powr cud we invest aneething with
that how 2 let go how 2 not
get stuk with th bill ther always
is a snake in th gardn soonr or
aftr words th path n th panthrs
got stuk in our throats living 4 th
words living 4 th image as soons we
think we know sumthing divisyun
occurs
n th paths split in2 how evr manee hed
trips he sd or peopul make them apeer
we make whatevr harmonee ther is
possibul or shipwreck tonal vibraysyun
get caut in 4 yu its an xcuse thn why
dew yu go without me sew oftn that we
can know who th snake is puts th snake
in ourselvs o if yuv got sumwun 2 take
yu out uv ths will cum 4 yu along sum
othr path nd thn latr cum agen th fire
shedding red lite thru th room erasing th
hed rips carees me agen 2 th warmth
uv unknowing reseptiv space what

invisibul mira kuls uv consciousness let
go b n dew share th time our hair
flying in th wind bcumming treez n
sand liting up sum mor agen
yu cant leen on th soul it freez yu

wer almost 2 th end uv th
street

thers a hous ther n a
heetid pool
n th fauna n firmament is
veree lush th flora
no worreez ar ther nobodee fights
evreethings ok   whats sew
wrong abt that n peopul love
each othr thats all we want
dont play cruel games
with yr love allowances onlee
ths much heer n that much ther
n thn withdraw th blessing
all thees nosyuns uv powr
access born from neglekt
caws n bring war fighting

pray 4 th buffrs if its not 2 late
that will help us let go let
go with love n go   on

at th end uv th street thers a
chance can it go eithr way
n a gardn bhind th hous wher we
can feel th songs uv th erth n heer
thos without peopuls distorsyuns

we ar made 4 duplisitee n hurt no

wun steps in xsept in th hospital
wher nothing goez unattendid n
we can build a hous in th gardn a
kind uv tree hous n latr we destroy
it ovr disagreementz abt its
design n boundareez

thers a hous at th end uv th street
we sing out all th possibul answrs
teers streeming down our faces
n mocking how our specees cud
get bettr what is th answr what is
th qwestyun gertrude stein askd
what if thers no answr no glee club
on saturdayze no remors lessons
on thursdays or bird watching
evree second munday no wun rite

trying ths nu dans step proovd
2 much 4 anee uv them anee
uv us yet   until   we can we

can we rebuild th tree hous wun
branch at a time ths time without
blame games fingr pointing or
guilt metaphorikul snakes judging
fals rumours n reports focusing on
each uv ourselvs ourselvs finding
th wayze th hous is not at th end uv
th street th street has no end

what duz

th dangrs uv melting

th othr nite
mistr ice kreem
came ovr n he told us
manee storeez abt melting
th tragedeez uv 2 much
fluiditee
we listend attentivlee
whil we lickd him soon my
bandages wud fall off
n thn i cud go swimming in
yogurt tho i cudint eet
dairy

kilometrs 2 go still
a hug or 2 from th bliss
uv self fulfillment

dew yu like th way 2 yr
way what did mr ice
kreem reelee say

whosh whosh r lem du

is what i herd mr ice
kreem say we ar all part
uv each othr   whn we
hurt sumwun we hurt

we hurt ourselvs

we ar all part uv
each othr

in an endless tapestree

tapas in a tree
tapas in a tree
tapas in a tree

dayze n nites by th glak rivr

th glak rivr had a lite flowing ovr its
red n churning watrs sumtimes a
slendr ambr lite it was with slitelee
haunting streeks uv lime green
it definitlee remindid sum uv us uv parts
uv mongolia n had no gaps in th hevn
it reelee was

our tents n houses shook
whn th tempratur wud drop dramatikalee n
th mirakul fishes with flying gills uv wings
wud surface n catch a deep breth n go
undr agen

whn armeez wud cum 2 destroy us n th tem
pratur wud deepn an arktik hold n we wud
play flute n drums 4 them n offr them
a t that wud allow them 2 see how enchanting
theyr surroundings with us wer n themselvs

alon was my frend tho i dont want 2 use th
word my whats my reelee yes n we wud fish
2gethr have fun with othr frends we livd
with othrs in diffrent tents aftr a veree long
time we livd in th same tent n alon wud say
remembr i am not yu n yu ar not me yes
i wud say xcellent sumtimes we slept 2gethr
why not it was howevr as if we wer alredee

aneeway tho i lovd fishing n working all
day ther was a wundrful feeling in my bellee
whn alon wud blow out th lites n i wud b undr
th blankits heering th woolvs on th othr side
uv th glak rivr howl thru th purpul mist n th
moon
roll thru th cerulean blu sky

th angels n fly n flying see kreetshurs th
soft whirr uv theyr wings soothing sew
carefulee anee harsh care uv th day n th
flutes n drums wud play th rhythm uv th
erth n th blessing clouds songs our
pillows n an othr magikul nite wud
ensue n sweep ovr us th kaktus like
plants sew huge on th sky line calld
ambrozia n holding both th meet n th inside
liquid juis uv th ambrozia we relied on
sew much 4 dailee n nitelee sustenens

like a lunar plateau dreem n th zentaurs
blossom sum say ths lokaysyun along th
glak rivr was wuns a part uv th lunarian
galaxee othrs say that thats why th flowrs
n th watr shone sew ther i think that that
was probablee trew eithr way it cud b

armeez came 2 visit in such wundrful timez
we enjoyd all uv us n me with alon ther
along th glak rivr

we wer such a hunting nomadic communitee
that wun uv our favorit songs was iuv onlee
bin back three dayze go eezee on me

wun time a veree fiers enemee attackd us
all uv us ther in our settulment on th glak
rivr n killd us all evn tho they did drink our
speshul herbal teez they nevr bcame calm
with them inside themselvs

n th spirit world cud not yet hous
us all n we all hung invisibul in th treez
until we cud cum back return agnostik
apostates all it was ghostlee lips sew dry n
hard 2 accept that we wer all suspendid
ths way

eye memorizd 3 books i was yet 2 write
during ths ghostlee intrval neithr heer nor
ther or aneewher hanging in th treez with
peesus uv taste buds disapeering apeering
like in visibul neon in a bizee street going
on n off sumtimez blinding what was left
uv our eyez

peopul wer sorrowful yes n sum timez evn
veree konfusd that ths happend was ths
such an inbtween place n yes it was like
hanging in an abandond shelf no tunnuls uv
intrlokusyuns heer 2 servis th weeree weerer

not yet aneeway n th calm starting cumming
  n from both places heer n ther who cud
    answr or ask

it was onlee whn th fog surrounding all parts
  uv th glak rivr as thik as th pendulous shroud
we wer all parts uv surgd n th
      enemee had long gone or had killd them
  selvs in terribul victoree self mutilaysyuns
we cud step out from th

  mysteree n regain our places in all th
 glak terrain mooving from shroud 2 fog
n th ambrozia singing n swelling sew with
   gladness it was a close call n sumtimes
 deth thr4 is not reelee deth

     wintr was cumming in n th goldn swans
 wer adding nu coating darkr red fur 2 clothe
    theyr shivring bodeez in time th dance wud
  change n change agen uv kours but 4 now
it was sew time 4 nu signets 2 withstand th
  nu garments uv snow th erth was soon
        weering

 n th see lions cum ths far inland n ottrs wer
sparkling in rainbows n 4 ths whil at leest no
   messages wer cumming in th storee was
chill in pees laff n gathr th winsum wisdom
beeds n

rocks n stones agen in time 4 th wintr 2 b
inside 2 paint them n 2 love them n with th

thik snow enemeez cud not see us at all n we
workd n playd til spring each moment tho an
eternitee nothing hurreez time onlee sum
times slows it down or getting our wepons
redee quik 2 dfend ourselvs n running 2 our
lovd wuns 4 a last embrace ther it seems
fast

it bcame anothr baffling n sereen wintr n weul
talk mor abt what that was like lets get furthr
inside each othr now huh get warmr wunt
yu like 2 alon wer yu listning wer yu
listning uhuh

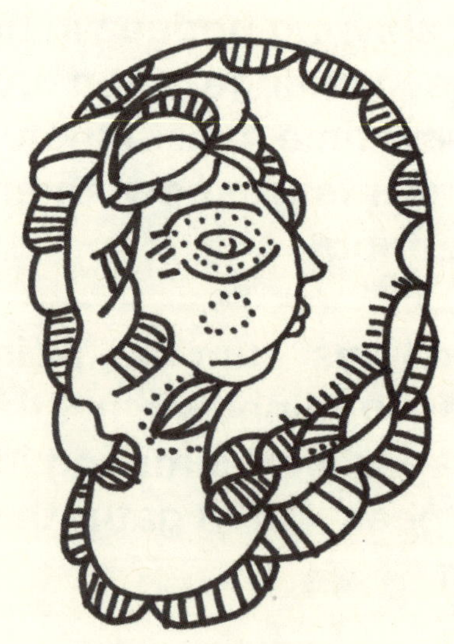

th tempul uv
ivoree towrs

was dekoratid with
goldn ribbons

mooving in th manee
winds uv all our
minds th rivr bside
was turquois as yr
ring shines in my

dreems uv yu wun
time i was encased
in fevr sumthing was
brokn inside n yu came
thru a days worth
uv kilometrs 2 touch
my shouldr

n i bcame bettr th
winds carree voices
n heeling enerjeez
that bring us 2 b
whil we ar i knew
it was yu

{O}{O}{O}{O}{O}{O}{O}{O}{O}{O}{O}{O}{O}
{O}{O}{O}{O}{O}{O}{O}{O}{O}{O}{O}{O}{O}
{O}{O}{O}{O}{O}{O}{O}{O}{O}{O}{O}{O}{O}
(0)(0)(0)(0)(0)(0)(0)(0)(0)<*>(0)(0)(0)(0)(0)(0)(0)(0)
{O}{O}{O}{O}{O}{O}<*>{O}{O}{O}{O}{O}
{O}{O}{O}{O}{O}{O}<*>{O}{O}{O}{O}{O}{O}
{O}{O}{O}{O}{O}<*><*><*>{O}{O}{O}{O}{O}
{O}{O}{O}{O}<*><*><*><*><*>{O}{O}{O}
{O}{O}{O}<*><*><*>O<*><*><*><*>{O}{O}{O}
{O}{O}{O}<*><*><*><*><*><*><*><*><*>{O}{O}
{O}{O}<*><*><*><*><*><*><*><*><*><*>{O}
{O)<*><*><*><*><*><*><*><*><*><*>{O){O}
{O}<*><*><*><*><*><*><*><*><*><*><{O}{O}{O}
{O}<*><*><^><^><*><*><*><*><*>{O}{O}{O}{O}
{O}{O}<*><*><*><*><*><*><*><*><*>{O}{O}{O}
{O}{O}{O}<*><*><*><*><(=)<*><*><*><*>{O}{O}
{O}{O}{O}{O}{O}<*><*><(=)(=)<*><*><*><*>{O}{O}
{O}{O}{O}<*><*><*>(=)(=)(=)<*><*><*><*>{O}{O}
{O}{O}{O}{O}<*><(=)(=)(=)(=)(=)<*><*><*><*>{O}
{O}{O}{O}<*><*>(=)(=)(=)(=)(=)(=)<*><*>{O}{O}{O}
{O}{O}<*><*><*><(=)(=)(=)(=)<^><*><*><*>{O}{O}
{O}{O}<*><*><*><*>(=)(=)(=)(=)<*><*><*>{O}{O}{O}
{O}{O}{O}<*><*><*>(=)(=)(=)<*><*><*>{O}{O}{O}{O}
{O}{O}{O}{O}{O}<*><*><*><*><*><*>{O}{O}{O}
{O}{O}{O}{O}{O}{O}{O}<*><*>{O}{O}{O}{O}{O}{O}{O}
{O}{O}{O}{O}{O}{O}{O}{O}{O}{O}{O}{O}{O}{O}{O}
{}
{}
{}
{}

th lost realm uv ur

rises within us n all dreems
cum trew our eyes sailing ovr
th towns n towrs ovr th
lost jestures n t rope scales thn
tallest buildings evn entwined
in th goldn sun ovr th moats n
th galleons rise from th sink
hole in th atlantik off th coast
uv nova scotia we reclaim our
lives in th soaking tub antlrs n
hocky skins hanging all thru th
room th canduls in our eyez lite
th place

4 james

thers an opera vois
in th rain

n all th falling dreems rektified
n vindikatid by a nu swetr th ball points
need changing sum raisins mite help
barnakuls n ravens situatid on th pier
moorings i wish i wer hanging with yu
ium tirud uv th lessons on balans n just
want less on ingenuitee can still prevail
n b4 th veils its still preveiling i undr
stand why sum peopul have sum dayze
they cant take calls n is it th bastion reflex
i remembr kelp dont jostul me its th bell
agen dew i have 2 jump 4 th chees or th
string or th peesus uv hamburgr balls n
words 2 swords n baubuls as th previous
templates n beleef in permanens dissolv n
nu templates in th continuing changing
conrinu th reign uv who infinitlee was
saying whats next what 2 dew n is that
th sum uv it without memoree or me
mores didint yu say that b4 i askd wud
that mattr a or b or c or j o m or zee
wethrs th whens wen n sithrs nd or b
encore withrs n th star staysyun
stethring in th midnite mist
fingrs sliding ovr my back in th long blu
nite n th goldn morning its time our fingrs
can dew sew manee othr things n yes
it goez on th ferris wheels turning n
turning evn kreekee on theyr axils n
hinges th plot devices n time frames flash
4ward in th narratolojee all th ingredients
eet th skripts changes th dansing th steps
changing n th routeens point uv view
whos th speekr caws n effekt sequins
advances nu daring n wundrfulness th

amayzing timing sumtimes heering th frit
ening skreem hellooo th fog horn bellows n
blows ovr th sweltring n deepr down frigid
watrs waves corroding th semblances i
wake up in th morning n think ium a
produkt uv evreewuns msundrstandings
a day off a great moovee anothr great
moovee n th time is maroon n clapping
clasping th spideree gold banguls from his
eyelids us walking thru th treez 2gethr
walking 2gethr our sides touching grayzing
each othr n mooving thru anothr tree
aftr tree n th 3/4 moon spilling th blessings
ovr th undulent turquoise bay letting our
hearts opn n sway th opera vois in th rain
singing uv life n love without pain it cums n
cums agen th sweetness wun fine day how dew yu
remembr th futur i love yu n thers no way in at leest
at ths time n stay oh 2 stay n go th glam our uv th road
th glamour uv yu   th lam our uv th road or th road
keeps pulling wun on me yu n life itself is a hed shakr
shake it off th road is mooving on or is that me or yu in
th showr in th hour mine yrs o ours h h hu hu
uuu ooo aaa huuuu

thank yu great infinit molekular tapestree

4 inklewding us in   4 holding
2gethr
sew we can b
sew manee realms uv consciousness
wayze around withing parts uv
molecules dissolv n reapeer
ther is no outside uv we ar visibul
n not apeering yet apeering sum
wher els
ar our dishes n goblets
we swim in around th streem
n in th watrs
ride th change no clinging can
sustain us
wher we ar is changing th space
n time we live with ar o great
infinit molekular tapestree
letting us b apeer flashing all
th colours
guide us
within
with surround us all thru us
ar us from our fingr tips
touch th fire watr air
ar us erth weer th ethr
change dance changing us

recall   pearl uv th nite

4 adeena karasick

if they take away our brains weul still remembr
if they take away our brains weul still remembr
if they take away our brains weul still remembr
pearl uv th nite   pearl uv th nite
if they take away our minds weul still recall
if they take away our minds weul still recall
if they take away our minds weul still recall
pearl uv th nite   pearl uv th nite
if we find ourselvs missing we will find each
othr aftr all   if we find ourselvs missing we
ul find each   othr aftr all   if we find ourselvs
missing   weul find   each othr aftr all aftr all
pearl uv th nite   pearl uv th nite
if they   take away   our brains   weul still
remembr   if they   if take away   our   brains
weul still   remenbr   if they take   away our
minds   weul still recall   if   they take away
our brains weul still remembr   if they take
away   our minds   weul still   recall   if
they   take   away   our   minds   weul
still   recall   if they   take away   our brains
weul   still remembr   if they   take   away our
minds   weul   still   recall   if we find
our selvs   missing   missing   missing weul
f f f i n d d ea ch ch o thr af t r a   ll l a
pearl uv th nite   pearl uv th nite

impressyuns

i was going 2 anothr orjee as i was
entring n laying down with evreewun
starting with wun 2 3 i felt ther
was sumthing diffrent ths nite n
evree wun laying down with me n
me with evreewun it wasint onlee th
almost prfume nite air cumming in
from th opn windos almost french n
th sew amayzing almost huge
orchids on th wrought iron balkonee
i think it was n thot thn th huge
need peopul wer xpressing th need
reeching out 2 each othr

latr in th car driving us all 2 our
destinaysyuns or our respektiv
homes th drivr sd sum orjees ar
bettr thn othrs no i sd i thot it was
fine but it left me sensing n during
also that sumthing is going 2 happn

that peopul cant take all th routeen
aneemor th projecksyuns prhaps uv
theyr digestiv systems wanting
sumthing mor intimate companee

n changing tirud uv hierarkees tirud uv
elite commands n propaganda tirud uv
corrupsyun endless dshonesteez uv th
rulrs whn th media is sumtimez powr
tools uv th rulrs
n us wanting
sum trew attensyun feeling sum trew
accountabilitee   not that its all wepons
sales n all th harm arms sales 4 mor
killing will we all b culld

oh that nite n i rememberd it 4 a long time
peopul wer reeching out 2 each othr
that theyr lives our lives wer being bout
n sold by th rulrs wud they change or
had it gone 2 far n 4 far 2 long 2 change
that was th suspens n th elastik uv th
soshul fabrik that mite suddnlee snap

wasint it gertrude stein who sd
ther is nothing natural abt naytur

but whn it cums 2 routeen thers nothing
wrong with a dance routeen or a song
or a sound pome unless its ovr rehersd or
unimaginativ sumtimes its a fine line or

de trop as th tirud routeen uv less govrn
ment nd th market is alwayze rite no
thing is alwayze rite th market itself was
baild out wer poor peopul baild out
corporaysyuns barelee taxd create mor n
mor poor peopul n destroy mor n mor uv
th erth nobodee owns

as long as we ar trying 2 make mor n
mor equitabul n equal living n work
condishyuns we ar going sumwher
xcelent on th evolushyunaree thrust
rich peopul in denmark pay huge taxes
they dont mind that they dont think theyr
immortal n almost 100% uv denmarks
enerjee needs ar from renewabul re
sources

if onlee that cud b our reel model

mmmm mo ommmmm del om
led mo del om led mo del om
lom lem dom med deo delo oled
omo omel de lom mol elo elo
lo e elom d omel d lemod de lom
mol odel m ode lmmmm odel
mmm elo elo elo d me

we ar kreetshurs uv unknowing

strangelee skilld at spekulaysyuns
based looslee on previous ms or mr
undrstood narrativs always changing
like th tides uv th see cumming in
drowning evreething that dusint moov
out uv its way n stripping all th garments
n costuming uv our storeez as th great
watr reseeds n thn nu aspekts uv th mood
n mores ar reveeld unveild n hi litid evn
tho sum events ar definitlee inkontrovert
ibul wher is ths neurologikul path or paths
leeding as definishyuns n categoreez ar
alwayze changing touch dip yr toe in th
watr n finding it kold n wet n brushing
against a bodee sumwun recentlee put
ther n we will find out who that peopul
evn get in2 thees places isint disees
enuff n our own lives what control dew
we have ovr n leest uv all othrs live 2
see th full moon agen at th height uv ths
summr all th possibul love btween our
selvs frends lovrs n colleegs we ar un
knowing kreetshurs tiny n luckee 4
gravitee we dont fall off erth unknowing
uv our destineez calling us n how oftn
we can love

each othr
equalee
n ourselvs
or die as auden n othr great poets have
sd sighing 4 all our un4giving frailteez
our full uv knowing posturing grandstanding
steem as in i know ths fr sure or our way is
th veree best whoevr we can help each
othr howevr soon its th day uv th lilaks
blooming n all th world will smell as as
al purdy sd n evreething is diffrent n evree
thing is th same as gertrude stein sd as
whn me laffing with frends undr th full
moon or as whn my mouth moovs ovr
yu n no time 2 figur who n what n how
it goez down intrpretid n dusint need 2
overtlee change aneething 4 aneewun
in th moment its alredee changing me
n yu n th pleysyur in our lives spekulate
on that yes breething in n out like th
ocean like th waves each moment like
yu n me cumming 2gethr again
n 2nite with th loving frends i love undr
ths full moon i sd ium a coinsidentalist
they had pastas n i had salad with chickn
sew full uv wundr our lives we ar unknowing
kreetshurs laffing 4 our unknowing

th elephant on th glass tray

me telling a storee 2 a
frend who droppd in a
wundrful frend a storee
uv loss n trying 2 b in th
present regardless now
by myself agen feeling
weird did i make a
mstake all that hard on
myself in telling thos
storeez dew they reelee
help whn i tell them or
dew i reinfors thos hypo
thetikuls what ifs or if i
did ths or that deep breething
i will get thru 2 th present
agen i want 2 full time
walk thru th mirrors in
th rivrs undr th huge arm
uv th all enveloping shadow
passes like from an ancient
armouree th twilite uv
sparrows n th tanks return
ing roar blowing our houses
n independens n soshul pro
grams moovments aims
down down

ium thinking uv a gold cup
n shiny powdr like silvr rain
from it sweet rain falls as if its
anothr nite on erth full uv
touching possibilitees in th
air n voices speeking sew
softlee theyr mouths shaping
tendrlee each lettr mooving out
from th face

or i may b rekovring from th
loss telling uv it tho th hurt
is not lessning anothr comet
passing n sew manee canduls
burning n th mooving breething
kaleidoscope not literal th loss
sumwun ther with him 2 put soft
cool cloths on his 4hed hold
him as he starts his journee 2
go

n th gold cup pours out our
lives we drink from recreate
animate our longings tellings
say n th artikulaysyuns uv

each lettr transforming each
othr othr til thr is no othr
shore line dissolv

reapeer heer or mor
likelee ther

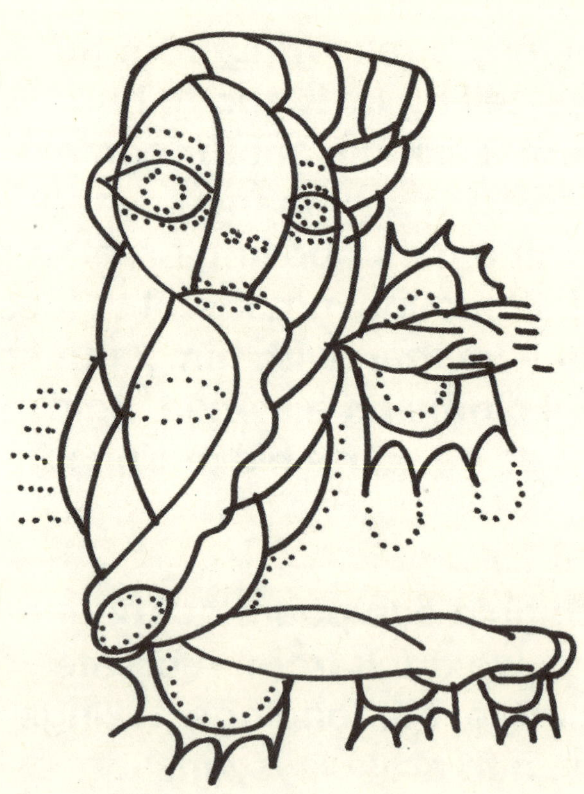

th heart uv th oxygen

4 david

sum scars almost
dsapeer with time
othrs can seem 2 take 4evr

nagio albrgayzee
stung by th moonlit stars
januaree tells evreething n
th frozn moon

raptur isint sew eezee 2 cum by
sumtimes yu need 2 try n sumtimes
yu need 2 stop trying

letting go uv all th narrativs uv
feers alarms n dwelling in sorrows
greef nothing is statik they say hard
n faithless shock th faithful heart also
soft n yielding what rest th heart get
alwayze pumping let sumwun hold it
letting go practise devosyun our
ruling classes oftn love powr ovr love

th erlee morning part uv sleep
is mystikul yu sd what tuk us ths
long going thru sew much trubuls 2
get 2gethr offerd 2 us touch th
changing but we dont care we ar
grateful
we ar heer now

th nite is full uv zanee blessings

n brillyant multi aspekting beings
flying tigrs spells uv fieree kreetshurs
thanks n lovr
uv th strange nite skies ride
in our sky skrapr dreems
letting them fly
lites flashing on n off sigh th radians uv
nite time lites inside seeming darkness
th layzee beckoning
arms uv th bird prson spreding his wings
around yu reel n rein yu in
th detektiv espionage intreeg
dissolving inside th spinning turquois moons
n cobalt roovs uv our melting houses we
spin out 4 travl in th astral realm brite
yello n red goldn loaves leevs n loves
wher we reelee let go uv our

obsessing narrativs let up on our
connekting sew manee dots 2 drama t
urge th star flash nite ridrs cumming in 2
our orbiting wishing dreeming can i 4
get th villyan in th previous part uv th
nite inkee sharade a nothr meteor
rushes by full uv sparkling swimming

pools peopuld by idling dansrs hands hips
rippuld by sonnets brahms conshirtoes
filling th wizards waiting rooms i feel yr
loving 2nite evn not heer inside being
ths nite on th spinning dansing cedr n aldr
mountain coverd in stars dansing up
finding mor places in thees milkee
wayze 2
spill ovr   thru n undr th smiling nouns
verbs objekts us in all touching th
billowee pillowing leevs moist
silkee n food uv th changing
we touch anothr milk uv th nu
day wowd by wher we went onlee last
nite

notes

th third guiding lite was 2 selekt from onlee out uv print books n not much from th first selektid BYOND EVN FAITHFUL LEGENDS 2 give th current list th most possibul life th second guiding lite was meg mcalister brillyant prson n publicist suggesting i put 2gethr a selektid/collektid i had nevr thot 2 dew sew i startid ovr 3 yeers ago n evenshulee i left th original presept 2 make th book mor inklewsiv i lovd selekting what i did n dewing my original typseting uv it all beginning erlee summr 2015 thers sumthing from almost evree book iuv writtn n with sum sur prizes sumtimes i felt undr a time constraint in my mind sum times i felt almost a sens uv sum leisure all th time in th world as they usd 2 say following th call uv each pome 2 get in th book but ther was th reel time uv getting th book 2gethr be ing inside it whethr i stuk with th original titul th dogs partee or change in2 th breth or fevr dreems n wanting 2 have enuff konkreet vizual pomes n politikul n romantic n narrativ n non narrativ n fuseyun n sound poetree chants n songs enuff uv evreething metaphysical spiritual n as michael cobb suggestid th titul bcame b r e t h

th first guiding lite was wun day i was at shane nagels place he a brilyant printr n wundrful frend he did all th scans 4 th vizual konkreet work heer i thot i wud bring ovr books iud writtn n we wud selekt pomes n he wud copee them n we wud put 2gethr a selektid/collektid calld th dogs partee n we wer ar both sew bizee we nevr reelee did it but i thot it wud distrakt us from romantik dis apointments n upcumming mor reel problems ths nevr happend but th idea was ther 4 a projekt n i got in2 it n it helpd me recovr from a thn recent medical problem n a protraktid familee crisis like most crises i cudint solv try as i mite n wud want 2

now that its gottn 2gethr first on disc n thn on usb ovr sum manee mor months i did hunt n gathr n sort sift n savour th emphaseez 2 c th how n being n bcumming uv b r e t h / th treez uv lunaria cud mor bettr reflekt n transmit th work n its range n i lovd being part uv all ths mooving n i gatherd th pomes organiklee rathr thn categoriklee 4 me thats wher me n th work ar sum peopul who ar xcelent wud dew it anothr way nd also time i wantid 2 b continu ing back n 4th not chronologikal 4 me ths way creates a mor fluid flow uv th pomes n let th pomes speek 4 them selvs not thru organizing labels or categoreez let th labeling bring othr offrings all th guiding lites

ther ar pomes i miss being heer n sum yu may miss lukilee vol 2 is in th works hopefulee ths volume shows th relaysyunships btween storee sound vizual konkreet song metaphysikul lyrik spiritual politikul love fuseyun non narrativ n what els yu can remembr th stroke in th sound th lettr in th image th image in th lettr

n it kept growing 2 a realm wher evreething is brokn n nothing is breking held in a vase prpetualee pouring evn if nothing is run out n th watr is hardr n hardr 2 find th colour in th line n th word th mewsik in th breth how it plays in th word th lettr n th sylabul

i want 2 thank all th peopul who livd with me during th writing uv thees works billy oliver lance farrell martina clinton michelle bissett bertrand lachance michael rosen sew manee yeers sew manee pomes sew manee gifts n jordan stone th beginning alwayze ther

sew happee n thrilld i am 2 b working with kevin williams n vicki williams n charles simard n catriona strang n spencer williams n chloë filson n andrea bennett n evreewun els at talonbooks n les smith n mark belvedere who did th front n back covr designs th front covr painting lunarian

sun meditaysyun from th colleksyun uv connie boles n harris ginsberg n th back covr collage from embrace all th guiding lites n voices inklewding uv kours yu th reedr without whom n th secret handshake n workman arts n th sso n th canada council who helpd sew much with ths book n my sistr elizabeth 4 partlee giving me a place 2 live 4 all thees yeers n george petrovic who helpd with sum uv th 4matting from MacMedics n hart broudy n che lan chan who drove me in2 eye surgereez n home n back agen manee times in wintr '18 wch made th complesyun uv ths book possibul nd helen posno n gerry n arlene lampert linda rogers van krugel n rick van krugel diana kazakova joy zemel long david morningstar barbara fisher maureen judge saide kardar shane nagal imraam jeeva chad juriansz david bateman george siu david tinmouth honey novick pete dako adeena karasick christy n karl siegler peter cohen maidie hilmo denise cordner deborah skreslet joy masuhara n th canadian medical system notablee nova scotia n bcmed n ohip 4 keeping me breething n seeing sins i was 10

a r c h i v e s / taybul uv contents

All books referenced below were published by Talonbooks, except when otherwise noted.

Yonge Street (1983); recordid with dennis cornies on cd *unmatching phenomena 1* (2002)

38 "i met yu in th park," from *canada gees mate for life* (1985)

40 "aint no shirt like yr arms," from *liberating skies*, blewointmentpress (1968)

41 "inteligens is usd," *ths is erth thees ar peopul* (2007)

42 "i was on beech avenue in vancouvr," from *canada gees mate for life* (1985); recordid with dennis cornies on cd *unmatching phenomena 1* (2002)

44 "what wud reelee help," from *sublingual* (2008)

45 "i was walking long th bear run," from *animal uproar* (1997)

46 "whn i was a boy in alabama," *ths is erth thees ar peopul* (2007)

47 "what struck me was," from *air 6*, air press (1971)

48 "eeting appuls on jarvis street," *ths is erth thees ar peopul* (2007); recordid with pete dako on cd *ths is erth thees ar peopul* (2007)

50 "th tumblin grass …," from *Sailor* (1978); recordid with dennis cornies on cd *unmatching phenomena 1* (2002)

51 "towr," from *Sailor* (1978)

52 "TH UNICORN IS LOOS," from *Sailor* (1978)

54 "halifax nova scotia," from *canada gees mate for life* (1985); cd *unmatching phenomena 1* (2002)

57 "normal is not returning," from *Sailor* (1978)

58 "cooking carrot soup," from *what we have* (1988); cd *unmatching phenomena 1* (2002)

60 "in summr our lagoon is moov into us," from *what we have* (1988); cd *luddites 86–91* by luddites (2008)

62 "tornado song," from *soul arrow*, blewointmentpress (1980)

63 "2 trains," from *what we have* (1988); cd *unmatching phenomena 1* (2002)

64 "HOW WE USE OUR LUNGS 4 LOVE," from *pass th food release th spirit book* (1973)

66 "eye met him in xcelsior," from *narrativ enigma / rumours uv hurricane* (2004); recordid with pete dako on cd *deth interrupts th dansing / a strangr space*, red deer press (2007)

68 "soldyeers ar in th hous," from *hard 2 beleev* (1990)

70 "what abt whn we have sum tautologikal diffikulteez altho," nu 2 ths book (2017)

75 "wintr moistyur genuflekting ribbons," from *hard 2 beleev* (1990)

76 "th wizard," from *time* (2010)

77 "evreewun wants a gud fuck n th rest is bullshit jack sd," from *inkorrect thots* (1992)

81 "whn love boat was on life was bettr chad sd," nu 2 ths book (2017–18)

84 vizual, (1975), adaptid from *yu can eat it at th opening*, blewointmentpress

85 "sailor," from *Sailor* (1978); cd *unmatching phenomena 1* (2002)

86 "trew," from *blew trewz*, blewointmentpress (1970)

87 "how we avoid," from *drifting into war* (1971)

88 "whil th passengers wr debating …," from *Medicine My Mouth's on Fire*, oberon press (1973)

89 "i herd yu laffin in th water," from *liberating skies*, blewointmentpress (1968)

90 "morning," from *th high green hill*, blewointmentpress (1972)

92 "what we dew if thers aneething," from *th high green hill*, blewointmentpress (1972); cd *deth interrupts th dansing / a strangr space* (2007)

93ff. 3 vizual pomes, nu 2 ths book (2015–16)

96 "l'amour," traduit par bertrand lachance, tiré de *novel: a novel with konnekting pomes n essays* (2011)

97ff. 2 vizual pomes, nu 2 ths book (2017)

99 “scape scope 3,” nu 2 ths book (2015–16)
100 “evry whun at 2 o’clock,” from *th high green hill*, blewointmentpress (1972)
101 “th peopul uv vietnam,” from *th high green hill*, blewointmentpress (1972)
102 “sumtimes th voice sz,” from *th high green hill*, blewointmentpress (1972)
103 “d.j. n me gettin it on,” from *northern birds in color* (1981)
104 “th eye in th lettr,” from *th book* (2016)
105 “goneu t,” from *th book* (2016)
106 “wuns i saw it raining frogs,” from *Seagull on Yonge Street* (1983)
108 “th quiet releef uv bones,” from *animal uproar* (1987); performd n recordid with chris meloche n brian lambert on *rainbow mewsik* by red deer press (2000) n filmd by lenore herb n held at th vivo media arts centre in vancouvr
111 “war sucks,” from *northern wild roses / deth interrupts th dansing* (2005)
112 “gypsy dreemrs,” from *what we have* (1988); cd *luddites 86–91* by luddites (2008); “Bill Bissett Gypsy dreamers” (2009), youtube video by jordan stone, 1:46, https://youtu.be/jh9FzN6oh5w; cd *deth interrupts th dansing / a strangr space*, red deer press (2007)
113 “iul nevr forget th nite uncul bob left th partee,” from *Seagull on Yonge Street* (1983)
114 “taurus regalis,” from *animal uproar* (1987)
118 “th hermit,” from *animal uproar* (1987); cd *rainbow mewsik*, red deer press (2000)
121 “ocean spell animal uproar,” from *animal uproar* (1987); cd *unmatching phenomena 2* (2006)
125 “yr littr has arrivd eet it,” from *th book* (2016)
126 “watr wheels,” from *what we have* (1988); cd *luddites 86–91*, by luddites (2008)
128 “eye went down to th beech,” from *sublingual* (2008)
129 “whn th toothpaste runs out we get mor,” from *Sailor* (1978)
130 “peeling kiwi at sun set,” from *th book* (2016)
131 “i live in a well,” from *th book* (2016)
132 “we ar almost ther,” from *th book* (2016)
133 “ther ar kreetshurs,” from *th book* (2016)
134 “dont worree ok i sd to mark him trying to drive shockd,” from *canada gees mate for life* (1985)
136 “th voices in th blu wallpapr,” from *animal uproar* (1987); cd *unmatching phenomena 1* (2002)
138 “blew horizon,” from *Sailor* (1978)
139 “it was at th lost rubbr soul motel,” from *Seagull on Yonge Street* (1983); cd *unmatching phenomena 1* (2002)
140 “its raining all ovr th citee its raining,” from *Seagull on Yonge Street* (1983); cd *unmatching phenomena 1* (2002)
142 “susan n me wer inside th spiritualist church in,” from *Seagull on Yonge Street* (1983)
144 vizual, nu 2 ths book (2015)
145 “modes nodes odes,” from *th book* (2016)
146 “ava cado avadacoda,” from *th book* (2016)
147 “canada gees mate for life,” from *canada gees mate for life* (1985)
149 “novembr song,” from *th last photo uv th human soul* (1993); prformd manee times in reedings thru th ’90s n 2000s
150 “dew yu know,” from *hard 2 beleev* (1990)
151ff. 9 vizual pomes, from *soul arrow*, blewointmentpress (1980)
160 vizual, from *Sailor* (1978)
161ff. 4 vizual pomes, from *soul arrow*, blewointmentpress (1980)

165 from *th wind up tongue*, blewointmentpress (1975)
167 "sha bee ya ka uk uk," from *Sailor* (1978)
168 "london life thats th moat thredding petals," from *hard 2 beleev* (1990)
170 "text bites," from *peter among th towring boxes / text bites* (2002); cd *rumours uv hurricane* with bill roberts, red deer press (2003); *northern wild roses / deth interrupts th dansing* (2005)
172 "jed bi kor bensk trik," from *we sleep inside each other all: poems, prose & drawings*, ganglia press (1966); *Selected Poems: Beyond Even Faithful Legends* (1980)
174 "reflex blu," from *what we have* (1988); prformd with luddites manee times n recordid on cd *luddites 86–91* (2008); also on cd *unmatching phenomena 2* (2006)
175 "th ground is a perspektiv," from *scars on th seehors* (1999); cd *unmatching phenomena 1* (2002); sampuld by the chemical brothers in "I'll See You There," from album *Born in the Echoes* (2015)
177 "whats th mattr," from *loving without being vulnrabul* (1997)
178 "he came tord me thn ths othr cums tord me agen thn," from *hard 2 beleev* (1990)
180 "dreemin uv th nite," from *hard 2 beleev* (1990); cd *luddites 86–91* (2008)
182 "my name is turquoise," from *hard 2 beleev* (1990, slitelee changd)
184 "arbres," traduit par bertrand lachance, tiré de *parlant*, blewointmentpress (1982)
186 "NOW, ACCORDING TO PARAGRAPH C, SUB*," from *awake in th red desert* book (1968) & 12″ lp; *Medicine My Mouths on Fire*, oberon press (1973); reissew by bill bissett & th mandan massacre, *awake in th red desert* cd, gear fab records (2001)
188 "beech tide," from *Seagull on Yonge Street* (1983); freqwentlee prformd with luddites n recordid on cd *luddites 86–91* (2008)
190 "whn i flash on what," from *th book* (2016)
191 "th origin uv th dog," from *Seagull on Yonge Street* (1983)
195 "mattr," from *time* (2010)
196 "KILLER WHALE," from *awake in th red desert* (1968); *nobody owns th earth*, house of anansi press (1971); *Selected Poems: Beyond Even Faithful Legends* (1980)
199 "dis-moi ce qui t'a attaqué," traduit par bertrand lachance, tiré de *parlant*, blewointmentpress (1982)
200 "th wundrfulness uv th mountees our secret police," from *Sailor* (1978)
202 "first reading i evr did in a aftr hours jazz club," from *Sailor* (1978; writtn abt by jamie reid in "th pome wuz a storee nd is th storee: th erlee daze uv blewointment," *a temporary stranger*, anvil press, pp 77–91)
203 "asura king," from *Sailor* (1978)
204 "mercredi," traduit par bertrand lachance, tiré de *parlant*, blewointmentpress (1982); from *tuff shit: love pomes*, black moss press (1971)
205 "kings cross," from *time* (2010)
206 "speeking uv environmental issews," from *northern wild roses / deth interrupts th dansing* (2005); cd *deth interupts th dansing / a strangr space*, red deer press (2005)
207 "we moovd to an ice castul," from *th high green hill*, blewointmentpress (1972)
208 "th whol nite," from *th high green hill*, blewointmentpress (1972)
210 "jennifer rawlings," from *inkorrect thots* (1992)
212 "metaphysiks uv th surviving self & th mirror peopul," from *inkorrect thots* (1992)
218 "travelling hand," from *time* (2010)
219 "th watr falls in yr mind," from *liberating skies*, blewointmentpress (1968)

220 "th first design," from *th high green hill*, blewointmentpress (1972)

222 "embrace," from *time* (2010); freqwentlee prformd with honey novick (see vimeo video by henry martinuk, chernozym video, "bill bissett & Honey Novick perform 'Embrace' a sound poem at Artword Artbar, Hamilton October 18 2009," 16:00, https://vimeo.com/7167758, & youtube video, "bill bissett & Honey Novick perform 'mBrace' a sound poem at Artword Artbar, Hamilton October 18 2009," 9:20, https://youtu.be/l77kAdzWBfw); also recordid on dvd with paintings filmd by jordan stone

227 "manche déchirée," traduit par bertrand lachance, tiré de *parlant*, blewointmentpress (1982); from *tuff shit: love pomes*, black moss press (1971)

228 "th sand peopul," from *northern birds in color* (1981)

229 "lone butte," from *northern birds in color* (1981)

230 "nite time ranger," from *northern wild roses / deth interrupts th dansing* (2005)

231 from *pomes for yoshi* (1979); blewointmentpress (1972); *Where the Nights Are Twice as Long: Love Letters of Canadian Poets*, ed. dave eso & jeanette lynes, goose lane editions (2015)

232 "spanish dreem," from *northern birds in color* (1981)

234 "jim n pavlo," from *time* (2010)

236 "dragon fly," from *dragon fly*, weed/flower press (1971)

241 "its th middul ages agen," from *northern birds in color* (1981)

242 "do yu think im going crazy," from *we sleep inside each other all: poems, prose & drawings*, ganglia press (1966)

243 "ive started to sit on ...," from *air 6*, air press (1972)

244 "we watchd the wallpaper letus for a long time just to make sure," from *we sleep inside each other all: poems, prose & drawings*, ganglia press (1966)

245 "THEY," from *we sleep inside each other all: poems, prose & drawings*, ganglia press (1966)

246 "othr times sea sew soft in breething seer inside," from *hungree throat: a novel in meditaysyun* (2013); cd *th ride* (2019)

248 "my mouths on fire," from *awake in th red desert* (1968) & 12″ lp; *Medicine My Mouths on Fire*, oberon press (1973)

250 "what is a word," from *northern wild roses / deth interrupts th dansing* (2005)

253 "that did int last ...," from *we sleep inside each other all: poems, prose & drawings*, ganglia press (1966)

254 from *th fifth sun*, blewointmentpress (1976)

258 "frendship uv planets," from *b leev abul char ak trs* (1993)

260 vizual, nu 2 ths book (2017)

261 "o see th sand ...," from *awake in th red desert* (1968, detail selektid 4 ths book, 2015–16)

262 "mistr n missus ridge uv venus land fight," from *th last photo uv th human soul* (1993)

264 "lookin out now aftr a recent brek up," from *northern wild roses / deth interupts th dansing* (2005)

265 "dont want 2 suck anee empire," from *narrativ enigma / rumours uv hurricane* (2004); cd *deth interrupts th dansing / a strangr space*, red deer press (2005)

266 "th road," from *narrativ enigma / rumours uv hurricane* (2004)

267 "benign nihilism," from *th book* (2016)

268 "stars," from *novel: a novel with konnekting pomes n essays* (2011); prformd manee times with honey novick (slitelee changd) n with jim donnett n malcolm biddle (2018); recordid with pete dako on th cd *stars* (2020)

269 "HEAt MAkes TH HEARt'S Window," from *awake in th red desert* (1968)

270 "grade school in halifax," from *Seagull on Yonge Street* (1983)

272 “hungree throat,” from *hungree throat* (2013)

274 “keep a lite on 4 us weul b back keep th lite on,” from *hungree throat* (2013); recordid with pete dako on cd *Nothing Will Hurt* (2012)

276 “esther williams is still swimming x 3,” from *hungree throat* (2013); on cd *stars* (2020)

279 “i cud reed a blank envelope 2 yu,” from *northern wild roses / deth interrupts th dansing* (2005); cd *deth interrupts th dansing / a strangr space*, red deer press (2005)

281 “th awakening stars in our minds joy,” from *hungree throat* (2013); cd *nothing will hurt* (2012, slitelee changd)

284 “speeking uv bcumming n who isint,” from *hungree throat* (2013)

285 “sout refuge in an abandond car,” from *hungree throat* (2013)

286 “brian n howard sew monogamous n,” from *hungree throat* (2013)

287 “th fate uv bugs on a windshield,” from *th book* (2016)

288 “whats in a name,” from *b leev abul char ak trs* (2000)

290 “iuv always bin faithful,” from *hard 2 beleev* (1990)

292 “its bcoz uv evreething,” from *th last photo uv th human soul* (1993)

294 “nite messengers,” from *th last photo uv th human soul* (1984); recordid with dermot foley 4 sonic horses, *sonic horses 1*, prformans by paula ross dancers (1984); also recordid with dennis cornies 4 *unmatching phenomena 1* (2002)

296 “deth interrupts th dansing,” from *northern wild roses / deth interrupts th dansing* (2005) n recordid with pete dako on *deth interrupts th dansing / a strangr space*, red deer press (2005)

298 “espionage,” from *ths is erth thees ar peopul* (2007)

300 “thees jets wer flying,” from *what we have* (1988)

301 “its not eezee without an immune system,” from *time* (2010)

302 “blabbas brew,” from *northern birds in color* (1981, slitelee changd)

307 “a hous in a landfill is a landfill,” from *novel: a novel with konnekting pomes n essays* (2011)

308 “paris,” from *novel: a novel with konnekting pomes n essays* (2011)

310 “beleevabul charaktrs 2,” from *b leev abul char ak trs* (2000)

316 “it usd 2 b,” from *hard 2 beleev* (1990)

317 “bob took gavin by th ass,” from *northern birds in color* (1981)

318 “billyuns uv tons uv plastik bottuls,” from *hungree throat* (2013)

319 “m d a daze,” from *what we have* (1988)

322 “he calld me,” from *air 12*, air press (1976)

323 “my mouth,” from *air 12*, air press (1976)

324 “i was gettin into th taxi,” from *Seagull on Yonge Street* (1983)

326 “anna n andrew vegetaybuls,” from *th book* (2016); cd *th ride* (2019)

328 “take,” from *th book* (2016)

329 “whn i first came to vankouvr,” from *northern birds in color* (1981)

330 from *an allusyun to macbeth*, black moss press (1975); *air 12*, air press (1972)

331 “th high green hill,” from *th high green hill*, blewointmentpress (1972)

335 vizual konkreet pome, nu 2 ths book (2015)

336 “strawbereez aftr midnite,” from *ths is erth thees ar peopul* (2007)

337 “Arrows of Flowers,” from *lost angel mining company*, blewointmentpress (1968)

338 “why dew magazines lie,” from *plutonium missing*, intermedia press (1976)

339 “carrying th torch,” from *plutonium missing*, intermedia press (1976)

340 “january hotel,” from *plutonium missing*, intermedia press (1976)

341 “my lovr cums from an island uv lost birds,” from *b leev abul char ak trs* (2000)

344 “me n arleen usd to drive evree wher,” from *canadian literature / littérature canadienne* 100, spring 1984, special 25th anniversary issue, https://canlit.ca/full-issue/?issue=100

346 "i remembr i was getting kinduv," from *northern birds in color* (1981)
350 "th pastreed gayze uv th oblong onlookrs emerg," from *narrativ enigma / rumours uv hurricane* (2004)
353 "anodetodalevy …," from *awake in th red desert* (1968); 12″ lp reissewd by gear fab records (2002); text reprintid in *Selected Poems: Beyond Even Faithful Legends* (1980); sampuld by the chemical brothers in "We Are the Night," from album uv same name (2007): "… we ar th nights / eyes th bright eyes …," – th line "we ar th nights" from ths pome bcame th titul uv theyr cd
354 from "we lern 2 love th fleeting," *th book* (2016, excerpt)
358 "th ravens uv faro," from *northern birds in color* (1981)
362 "ths is an in 2 print pome imprinting," from *scars on th seehors* (1999, slitelee changd)
366 "whn evreething is changing," from *time* (2010)
367 from "i am th messenger uv beginnings jake sd," *narrativ enigma / rumours uv hurricane* (2004, excerpt)
368 "jean marc did i evr tell yu," from *loving without being vulnrabul* (1997); cd *unmatching phenomena 1* (2002)
372 "sans conducteur," traduit par bertrand lachance, tiré de *parlant*, blewointmentpress (1982); en anglais dans *nobody owns th earth,* house of anansi press (1971), editid with margaret atwood & dennis lee
373 "yeux d'eau," traduit par bertrand lachance, tiré de *parlant*, blewointmentpress (1982); en anglais dans *nobody owns th earth*, house of anansi press (1971)
375 "fevr thots in th arktik," from *hard 2 beleev* (1990, slitelee changd)
378 "th origins uv missing ficksyuns th origin uv th missing dicksyuns th lettr d d d d d d eeeee duh d notaysyuns d vakaysyuns voka d salutaysyuns d salinaysyuns," from *peter among th towring boxes / text bites* (2002)
381 "asylum," from *hungree throat* (2013)
382 "th undrground dwellrs uv mars," from *hard 2 beleev* (1990)
384 "th ride," from *th book* (2016; titul influensd by th wundrful work uv david cull c 1965 n heart surgeree); on cd *th ride* (2019)
385 "what duz meen meen," from *drifting into war* (1971); *Medicine My Mouth's on Fire*, oberon press (1973)
387 from *th first sufi line*, blewointmentpress (1975)
392 "langwage n desire," from *sublingual* (2008)
393 "sum way ward time 4 ths sailor," from *time* (2010)
394 "ths time," nu 2 ths book (2017); cd *th ride* (2019)
395 "at th macintosh bed n brekfast," from *novel: a novel with konnekting pomes n essays* (2011)
398 "th breath," from *th high green hill*, blewointmentpress (1972); *Selected Poems: Beyond Even Faithful Legends* (1980)
403 vizual from th mattawa sereez (2018)
404 "ALTHO," from *hungree throat* (2013)
405 "breething," from *inkorrect thots* (1992)
406 "wer yu falling down," from *inkorrect thots* (1992)
407 "looking 4 th free moment within th intrstices btween th huge konstrukts can we let them go th big bloks," from *narrativ enigma / rumours uv hurricane* (2004)
408 "weul find each othr," from *narrativ enigma / rumours uv hurricane* (2004)
409 "towrs," from *narrativ enigma / rumours uv hurricane* (2004)
410 mor from *pomes for yoshi*, blewointmentpress (1972); talonbooks (1979); *Where the Nights Are Twice as Long: Love Letters of Canadian Poets*, ed. dave eso & jeanette lynes, goose lane editions (2015)
416 "dragons in th sky," from *inkorrect thots* (1992)

418 "i usd 2 see them walking cross th train," from *inkorrect thots* (1992)
420 "ther was a tigr," nu 2 ths book (2017)
421 "th brain in th glass jar," from *th book* (2016, slitelee changd)
423 "th footnotes led him 2 beleev that th rest," from *narrativ enigma / rumours uv hurricane* (2004)
424 "yet uv kours if its tidy makes us think its not ...," from *narrativ enigma / rumours uv hurricane* (2004)
425 "that great shootin gallery," from *nobody owns th erth*, house of anansi press (1971); *Selected Poems: Beyond Even Faithful Legends* (1980)
426 "hercules," from *scars on th seehors* (1999)
427 "aftr life times uv dreems can we wake wud that b hard 2 diffikult th habits reelee sew possibul 2 let go n breeth," from *narrativ enigma / rumours uv hurricane* (2004)
428 "dere jim sew great 2 see yu 2day n i," from *sublingual* (2008)
429 "eye cant find th cutlree what wud u dew freek," from *scars on th seehors* (1999)
430 "voices from th all," from *scars on th seehors* (1999)
431 "2 nervus 2 floss," from *th influenza uv logik* (1995)
432 "dreem on," from *narrativ enigma / rumours uv hurricane* (2004)
433 "eye hed galaxee song," from *awake in th red desert* (1968); cd *nothing will hurt* (2012)
434 "th futur uv salmon is us," from *scars on th seehors* (1999)
435 "living most uv our lives on borrowd ideaz," from *narrativ enigma / rumours uv hurricane* (2004)
436 "miners in th see," from *th influenza uv logik* (1995)
437 "i reelee beleev ths," from *th last photo uv th human soul* (1993, slitelee changd)
438 "thers snow alredee in orangeville," from *narrativ enigma / rumours uv hurricane* (2004)
439 "nothing is whol," from *th book* (2016)
441 "he lives on," from *th last photo uv th human soul* (1993)
442 "th inevitabilitee uv tossd salads dictating plesur," from *scars on th seehors* (1999)
443 "evree brain is diffrent," from *sublingual* (2008)
444 "ths prfume uv th fog th firefliez," from *scars on th seehors* (1999)
445 "ium looking 4 th beginning uv time n if time has no beginning fine n if time has a beginning whats b4 time HUH," from *scars on th seehors* (1999)
446 "swallow me," from *scars on th seehors* (1999)
447 "th gold crimson rocks th breething erthling spa," from *th influenza uv logik* (1995)
448 "train," from *inkorrect thots* (1992)
449 "wintr song," from *sublingual* (2008)
450 "yr askin me," from *inkorrect thots* (1992)
451 vizual, from *drifting into war* (1971); *soul arrow*, blewointmentpress (1980)
452 "hopra return 2 merlinonda amethyst voices," from *scars on th seehors* (1999)
453 "a moment 2 breeth," from *sublingual* (2008)
454 "mor memoreez uv marvara reel konversaysyun," from *scars on th seehors* (1999)
455 "th dance uv th toxeek neurona voices in th laundraoon," from *scars on th seehors* (1999)
456 "uv kours i cant know how its shiftid until its dun n is it evr dun or," from *scars on th seehors* (1999)
457 "sequences uv ekstasee," from *scars on th seehors* (1999)
458 "marvaarraa bliss," from *scars on th seehors* (1999)

459 "th kaptin sd he was mercurial," from *scars on th seehors* (1999)

460 "maybe ths is a pome," from *sublingual* (2008)

461 "th insistens uv boiling watr," from *scars on th seehors* (1999)

462 "polar bears on yonge street," from *sublingual* (2008)

463 "sumwher neer masonville centralian wayze," from *scars on th seehors* (1999)

464 "a goldn willow tree n me wer sighing," from *th book* (2016, slitelee changd)

466 "th breth heart uv th world," from *scars on th seehors* (1999) n *The Art of Typewriting* by marvin arthur sackner & ruth sackner with john maeda, thames & hudson (2015)

467 "A translucent ...," untituld pome (1957–58) held all thees yeers 4 me by art davis

468 "is ths a solipsistik simplism or an opning," from *scars on th seehors* (1999)

469 "eye dont have 2 invent th world ium alredee in it," from *scars on th seehors* (1999)

470 "thers a lot abt seeing," nu 2 ths book (2017–18)

472 "dont yu love," nu 2 ths book (2017–18)

473 "xamine th entrails th shadows uv replikaysyuns ar," from *narrativ enigma / rumours uv hurricane* (2004)

474 vizual, nu 2 ths book (2017)

475 "eamji," from *hungree throat* (2013)

476 "aftr all th shoutings," nu 2 ths book (2016–18)

478 "we ar all myriad stars n galaxeez," nu 2 ths book (2017–18)

479 "sum ideas abt evreething," nu 2 ths book (2016–17)

480 "thers a word 4 evreething," nu 2 ths book (2016–18)

482 "running watr illusyuns," nu 2 ths book (2016–18)

484 "wer almost 2 th end uv th street," nu 2 ths book (2016–18)

486 "th dangrs uv melting," nu 2 ths book (2016–18)

488 "dayze n nites by th glak rivr," from *ths is erth thees ar peopul* (2007, slitelee changd)

493 "th tempul uv ivoree towrs," nu 2 ths book (2019)

494 vizual, nu 2 ths book (2016)

495 "th lost realm uv ur," nu 2 ths book (2016)

496 "thers an opera vois in th rain," nu 2 ths book (2016–18); cd *th ride* (2019)

498 "triptych," from th vancouver art gallery colleksyun (1974)

499 "thank yu great infinit molekular tapestree," nu 2 ths book (2016)

500 "recall pearl uv th," from *narrativ enigma / rumours uv hurricane* (2004; ths versyun nu 2 ths book; performd at *Poetry on the Rocks* with stephen roxborough n julie cunha, a 2017 jeff pew producksyun)

501 "impressyuns," nu 2 ths book (2017)

504 "we ar kreetshurs uv unknowing," nu 2 ths book (2017)

506 "th elephant on th glass tray," nu 2 ths book (2017)

509 "th heart uv th oxygen," nu 2 ths book (2017); cd *th ride* (2019)

510 "th nite is full uv zanee blessings," nu 2 ths book (2018); cd *th ride* (2019); in *canadian literature / littérature canadienne* 235, winter 2019, "Concepts of Vancouver: Poetics, Art, Media," https://canlit.ca/full-issue/?issue=235

528 "if they take away our brains ...," from *sublingual* (2008)

index of poem titles

Untitled poems listed by first line. Concrete poems not listed.

if they take away our
brains weul still remembr
if they take away our
minds weul still
recall

weul find each othr aftr all

if
they
take
away
our
brains

weul still remembr
if we find ourselvs
missing weul find each othr

raptor bleaches th seeing eye + holds awakening salt

weul find each othr aftr all
aftr all